ICONS

TASCHEN

KÖLN LONDON MADRID NEW YORK PARIS TOKYO

Cover/Back Cover: Eero Aarnio, Ball (or Globe) Chair, 1963–1965

Page 2/3: Charles & Ray Eames, Wire Chairs with Birds, 1952
Eames Office, Venice, CA

Editing: Susanne Husemann, Simone Philippi, Cologne
Cover design: Angelika Taschen, Cologne
German translation: Klaus Binder, Jeremy Gaines,
Frankfurt/Main
French translation: Jacques Bosser, Paris

Printed in Italy
3-8228-5507-3

Chairs

Charlotte & Peter Fiell

"The connections, the connections. It will in the end be these details that give the product its life."[1]
"Eventually everything connects – people, ideas, objects, etc., ... the quality of the connections is the key to quality per se."[2]

Charles Eames, 1961
1. Frederick S. Wright Gallery, University of California, *Connections: The Work of Charles and Ray Eames,* UCLA Arts Council, Los Angeles 1976, p. 48
2. J. & M. Neuhart & R. Eames, *Eames Design: The Work of the Office of Charles and Ray Eames,* Harry N. Abrams, New York 1989, p. 266

The Chair: Design Diversity and the Nature of Connections

The concept of connections is intrinsic to design and nowhere more so than in the design of chairs. No other type of furniture offers the possibilities of making and facilitating connections in the same way or to the same extent. Because of this, more effort and more resources have been invested in the creation of chairs by more people over a longer period of time than any other type of furniture. Indeed, apart from possibly the automobile, the chair is the most designed, studied, written about and celebrated artefact of the modern era.

The success of a particular chair has always depended on the quality and range of the connections it makes while addressing a specific need. At the functional level, a chair makes physical and psychological connections with the individual sitting in it or on it through its form and use of materials. At the same time, it may embody meanings and values which connect with the user at an intellectual, emotional, aesthetic, cultural and even spiritual level. On another level again, fundamental connections are made between the structural components inherent in a chair's design. A chair can also connect visually and/or functionally with the context in which it is to be used, including other objects and styles. More broadly, chair design is connected with different ideologies, approaches to making, and economic theory. Farthest reaching of all, however, are the connections which a chair, its designer and, indeed, its manufacturer make with society at large – through the potential universality of the chair's appeal and the environmental impact of its manufacture, use and eventual disposal.

Over the last 150 years, the evolution of the chair has paralleled developments in architecture and technology and reflected the changing needs and concerns of society to such an extent that it can be seen to encapsulate the history of design. As George Nelson pointed out in 1953, "every truly original idea – every innovation in design, every new

Introduction

application of materials, every technical invention for furniture – seems to find its most important expression in a chair".[3] In our times, this is nowhere more apparent than in the development of better performing, more ergonomically refined chairs. The highly competitive office seating market, in particular, demands continual technical advances, as it is increasingly driven by tougher health and safety legislation and corporate specifiers ever more mindful of the welfare of their workforces.

Achieving a good solution to the problems posed by the chair is a complex and challenging proposition, even though, over its long history, its function as an aid to sitting has remained virtually unchanged. Chairs support people of all different shapes and sizes for different lengths of time and for different purposes, whether it be eating, reading, resting, waiting, writing or office tasking. Furthermore, each sitting position is invested with its own degree of social significance and set of conventions, including orthopaedic constraints. In most cases, the chair must adequately support the weight of the sitter at such a height that the legs hang down and the feet touch the floor. In this conventional sitting position, the weight of the head and torso is carried down to the bones of the pelvis and hip. The timeless problem associated with this physical relationship is that however much a chair seat may be softened, the pressure of the bone will eventually be felt on the flesh of the buttocks as uncomfortable. Ultimately, this results in the user having to change position – something which is done on average every ten to fifteen minutes. Indeed, the more exactly a chair is formed to give "ideal" static support and posture to the average human frame, the more it guarantees discomfort and, thereby, psychological stress for people with non-standard anatomies or those who do not wish to assume that particular posture. It is probably safe to say, therefore, that while the facility for correct lumbar support is important, especially in office seating, it is not as crucial as the chair allowing the user to move their legs freely and to make frequent adjustments of posture. For more healthful sitting, a chair should thus facilitate freedom of movement and encourage a variety of postures while providing flexible continuous support.

Beyond the technical considerations of sitting and how well users can physically and psychologically connect with specific forms according to different functional contexts, chairs are also designed and acquired for reasons to do with symbolic content, aesthetics and fashion. Of all furniture types, chairs especially serve to bolster egos and demon-

3. **George Nelson,** *Chairs,* Whitney Publications Inc., New York 1953, p. 9

Steel tubes, foam springs, and covers have been so developed technically that we can create forms which were unthinkable just a few years ago. Personally, I'd like to design chairs which exhaust all the technical possibilities of the present in which I also live.

Verner Panton, 1985 A. L. Morgan, *Contemporary Designers,* St. James Press, London 1985, p. 471

... the once humble chair has emerged – for the time being, at least – as a thoroughly glamorous object ...

George Nelson, 1953
G. Nelson, *Chairs,* Whitney Publications Inc., New York 1953, p. 7

strate "taste", while revealing their owner's sociopolitical viewpoint and real or would-be social and economic status. To this end comfort, practicality and economy have often been sacrificed in favour of the representation of decorative styles, radical design agendas and/or the self-expressive impulses of designers.

The extraordinary diversity of chairs created since the mid-19th century has largely been due to the fact that, owing to the variety of the intended functions of the chair and the anatomic variability of users, there are no ideal forms. There can be many excellent solutions at any one time to the different contexts of use. While the profusion of designs for a specific function may share numerous similarities, at the outset what fundamentally differentiates one from another is the extent to which the designer has viewed function as either the purpose and goal or the subject of the chair. Whether the preference in approach has been weighted towards utility or aesthetics, the primary object of chair design remains the same – making connections – and over the last 150 years there have been innumerable interpretations of how best to achieve this. More often than not, the creation of a meaningful solution involves a process which not only takes into consideration intended function, appropriate structure (including deployment of materials) and aesthetics, but also method of manufacture, nature of the market, ultimate cost and proposed appeal. Different chairs emphasise different combinations of connections according to the priorities of their designers and the needs and concerns that are being addressed at different times.

A comfortable position, even if it were the most comfortable in the world, would not be so for very long ..., the necessity of changing one's position is an important factor often forgotten in chair design.

Eero Saarinen, 1948
M. Page, *Furniture Designed by Architects,* Whitney Library of Design, New York 1980, p. 208

As the preoccupations of society change, so too do designers' and manufacturers' responses to them. What may be viewed as a rational solution in one period, therefore, may be viewed as exactly the opposite in another. While some designs strive for and achieve an authority which leads to varying degrees of longevity, even those deemed "classic" have a limited functional and aesthetic appeal. Just as tastes change, so too other factors, such as expectations of comfort, vary from period to period and between different cultures. The inherent ephemerality of design, therefore, also accounts for the myriad solutions to the different functional contexts of the chair.

Historically, the design of chairs can be seen as a debate between conflicting opinions about such issues as the role of technology and the industrial process, the needs and concerns of the many versus those of the few, the importance of function and aesthetics in practical objects

Introduction

for use, and whether "less is more" or "less is a bore" or, according to current thinking, "less is more, more or less". Chairs exist as declarations of the attitudes, ideas and values of their creators, and whatever viewpoints may be represented in them, all chairs have a rhetoric and, therefore, some form of persuasiveness.

Although deciphering the rhetoric of chairs from the past can lead to some understanding of their time of origin and the thinking of their designers, our appreciation of the cultural significance and aesthetic value of historic chairs is conditioned by many factors. These include contemporary biases of taste and changing perceptions of technology and historical relevance. For example, in its own time the persuasiveness of Charles and Ray Eames' famous moulded plywood LCW (Lounge Chair Wood) largely hinged on its technological reasoning, whereas today its persuasiveness may have more to do with its character, the mythology surrounding the Eameses, and the fact that it is widely celebrated as a cultural icon. It is therefore difficult to be objective about historic chairs without considering the social, economic, political and technological contexts that gave rise to their appearance.

Our selection for this survey of the chair begins in the early 19th century, when the first attempts were made to shift the chair from the realm of the crafted object to that of the designed product. New technologies and materials processes allowed the chair to be produced in quantity, while systemised methods of manufacture demanded the simplification of form and structure. With this necessary reductivism, the chair began to demonstrate some of the important objectives – such as revealed construction, truth to materials, and a trend towards lightness – that were embraced by later designers and the pioneers of the Modern Movement in particular.

The examples we have selected are virtually all products of the avant-garde. Whether the result of mechanised production or traditional craftsmanship, what they have in common is their powerfully argued rhetoric. Beyond matters of function and structure, the fundamental worth of chairs, past or present, lies in their communication of attitudes, ideas and values. The persuasiveness of a chair depends on the clarity of its rhetoric. The clearer the argument, the more likely it is that connections will be made, either consciously or subconsciously, and it is the quality of these connections, more than anything else, that determines the ultimate success of a chair.

The tubular steel chair is surely rational from technical and constructive points of view; it is light, suitable for mass production, and so on. But steel and chromium surfaces are not satisfactory from the human point of view.

Alvar Aalto, 1940
The Museum of Modern Art, *Alvar Aalto: Furniture and Glass,* The Museum of Modern Art, New York 1984, p. 7

A great chair is like a face ..., you meet thousands but few are memorable.

Ross Lovegrove, 1997

Charles Eames, 1961
1. Frederick S.
Wright Gallery, Uni-
versity of Califor-
nia, Connections:
The Work of
Charles and Ray
Eames, Los Ange-
les: UCLA Arts
Council 1976, S. 48
2. J. & M. Neuhart
& R. Eames, Eames
Design: The Work
of the Office of
Charles and Ray
Eames, New York:
Harry N. Abrams
1989, S. 266

*Stahlrohr, Schaum-
stoffpolster und Be-
züge sind technisch
so weit entwickelt,
daß wir heute For-
men schaffen kön-
nen, die vor einigen
Jahren noch unvor-
stellbar waren. Was
mich angeht, so
möchte ich Stühle
entwerfen, die alle
technischen Möglich-
keiten der Gegen-
wart, der Zeit, in
der ich lebe, aus-
schöpfen.*

Verner Panton, 1985
A. L. Morgan,
Contemporary
Designers, London:
St. James Press
1985, S. 471

**»Die Verbindungen, die Verbindungen. Zuletzt sind es
diese Details, die einem Produkt Leben verleihen.«**[1]
**»Zuletzt verbindet sich alles – Menschen, Ideen, Ob-
jekte, usw., ... die Qualität der Verbindungen ist der
Schlüssel zur Qualität überhaupt.«**[2]

Der Stuhl: Vielfalt des Designs und die Verbindungen

Auf das Konzept der Verbindungen kommt es an. Das gilt nirgends
mehr als für das Design von Stühlen. Kein anderes Möbel bietet derartige und derart viele Möglichkeiten, Verbindungen herzustellen und
zu vereinfachen. Darum haben die Menschen auch in die Herstellung
keines anderen Möbelstücks so viel Anstrengungen und Ressourcen
investiert wie in die von Stühlen, und dies schon über einen sehr langen
Zeitraum hinweg. Tatsächlich ist der Stuhl – abgesehen möglicherweise
vom Auto – das Industrieprodukt der Moderne, das die Designer am
meisten beschäftigt hat; keines wurde genauer untersucht, über keines
wurde mehr geschrieben, keines wurde begeisterter gefeiert.

Stets war der Erfolg eines Stuhlentwurfs abhängig von der Qualität
und dem Charakter der Verbindungen, die dieser bzw. der Designer mit
diesem Stuhl stiften kann, indem er auf ein bestimmtes Bedürfnis ein-
geht. Von seiner Funktion betrachtet, schafft ein Stuhl durch seine Form
und die verwendeten Materialien eine körperliche und eine psychologi-
sche Verbindung zu dem, der auf ihm sitzt. Gleichzeitig vermag ein Stuhl
Inhalte und Werte zu verkörpern, die ihn mit seinem Benutzer in intel-
lektueller, emotionaler, ästhetischer, kultureller und vielleicht sogar
spiritueller Hinsicht verbinden. Auf einer anderen Ebene wiederum
gehen die konstruktiven Elemente des Stuhls und seine spezifische Formgebung grundlegende Verbindungen ein. Ein Stuhl kann sich zudem
visuell und/oder funktional mit seiner Umgebung und den dort vorhande-
nen Objekten und Stilen verbinden. Darüber hinaus ist die Formgebung
von Stühlen verbunden mit verschiedenen Ideen, Herstellungstechniken
und ökonomischen Konzepten. Am weitesten jedoch reichen die Verbindungen, die ein Stuhl, sein Designer und natürlich auch sein Hersteller
mit der gesamten Gesellschaft stiftet – einfach durch seine potentielle
Universalität und durch den Einfluß, den er durch seine Herstellung, seinen Gebrauch und seine schließliche Entsorgung auf die Umwelt ausübt.

Im Verlauf der letzten 150 Jahre vollzog sich die Evolution des Stuhls und seiner Formen im Gleichklang mit den Entwicklungen in Architektur und Technik, und sie spiegelt damit die sich wandelnden Bedürfnisse und Interessen der Gesellschaft so präzise, daß man seine Geschichte als eine Art Designgeschichte im Kleinen betrachten kann. Darauf hat George Nelson 1953 mit der Bemerkung hingewiesen, daß »jede wahrhaft schöpferische Idee – jede Innovation im Design, jede neue Verwendung von Materialien, jede technische Erfindung in der Möbelherstellung – ihren bedeutsamsten Ausdruck in einem Stuhl gefunden hat".3 In unseren Tagen läßt sich dies nirgends klarer ablesen als an der Entwicklung von immer funktionaleren und ergonomisch durchdachteren Stühlen. Insbesondere der von einem scharfen Wettbewerb bestimmte Markt der Bürositzmöbel verlangt permanent technische Neuerungen; eine Tendenz, die noch verstärkt wird durch immer strengere Gesundheits- und Sicherheitsverordnungen, aber auch durch eine Unternehmensführung, die zunehmend bewußter auf das Wohlergehen der Arbeitskräfte achten.

3. George Nelson, Chairs, New York: Whitney Publications Inc. 1953, S. 9

Die Funktion eines Stuhls als Sitzhilfe ist in der langen Geschichte des Stuhldesigns mehr oder weniger gleich geblieben, und trotzdem ist es eine vielschichtige und herausfordernde Aufgabe, überzeugende Lösungen der Probleme zu finden, die mit dem Design eines Stuhls verbunden sind. Stühle müssen in Körperbau und Größe ganz verschiedenen Menschen Stütze und Halt geben, und dies unterschiedlich lange und bei den verschiedensten Tätigkeiten: beim Essen, beim Lesen, beim Warten, beim Schreiben, am Arbeitsplatz im Büro. Darüber hinaus hat jede Sitzposition auch eine bestimmte soziale Bedeutung, ist besetzt mit bestimmten Konventionen und muß orthopädischen Ansprüchen genügen. Gewöhnlich muß ein Stuhl das Gewicht des Sitzenden genau so hoch halten, daß seine Beine herabhängen und die Füße gerade den Boden berühren können. In dieser konventionellen Sitzhaltung ruht das Gewicht von Kopf und Oberkörper auf den Becken- und Hüftknochen. An diesem Problem, das mit unserem Körperbau zusammenhängt, hat sich nicht viel geändert; ganz gleich, wie weich gepolstert ein Sitz sein mag, am Ende wird man den Druck der Knochen in den Hinterbacken als etwas Unbequemes empfinden. Also muß der Sitzende irgendwann seine Position verändern; dies geschieht etwa alle zehn bis fünfzehn Minuten. Und darum wird ein Stuhl, je sorgfältiger er als »ideale« Stütze und Halt für den menschlichen Knochenbau und seine Statik ausge-

... der einstmals so bescheidene Stuhl hat sich – zumindest in unserer Zeit – zu einem durch und durch glanzvollen Gegenstand gemausert ...

George Nelson, 1953
G. Nelson, Chairs, New York: Whitney Publications Inc. 1953, S. 7

Eine bequeme Haltung, und sei es die bequemste der Welt, bleibt nicht lange bequem ... Die Notwendigkeit, die Körperhaltung zu ändern, ist ein entscheidender Faktor, der im Stuhldesign häufig vergessen wird.

Eero Saarinen, 1948
M. Page, Furniture Designed by Architects, New York: Whitney Publications Inc. 1980, S. 208

formt ist, zwangsläufig Unbehagen produzieren, körperliches Unbehagen zunächst und dann auch psychischen Streß für alle die Menschen, deren Körperbau den standardisierten Maßen nicht entspricht oder die sich in einer bestimmten Haltung nicht wohlfühlen. Also läßt sich wohl mit Gewißheit sagen, daß es, bei aller Bedeutung, die insbesondere bei Bürositzmöbeln der korrekten Stütze für die Wirbelsäule zukommt, dennoch wichtiger ist, daß Sitzende ihre Beine frei bewegen und ihre Haltung immer wieder verändern können. Für ein gesundes Sitzen muß ein Stuhl Bewegungsfreiheit gewähren, eine Vielzahl von Sitzhaltungen ermöglichen und dabei kontinuierlich und flexibel Halt bieten.

Aber abgesehen von solchen technischen Überlegungen zum Sitzen und unabhängig von der Frage, wie gut die Benutzer mit den Formen körperlich und psychologisch zurechtkommen, die aus den jeweiligen funktionalen Zusammenhängen erwachsen, werden Stühle auch für Anlässe entworfen und aus Gründen erworben, die von eher symbolischer Bedeutung sind und mit Geschmack und Moden zu tun haben. Unter allen Möbeln ist es wiederum der Stuhl, der am häufigsten dazu benutzt wird, das Ego zu stützen und »Geschmack« zu demonstrieren, womit Stühle immer auch die sozialen und politischen Einstellungen ihrer Besitzer, auch deren gesellschaftlichen und ökonomischen Status demonstrieren: sei es der tatsächliche, sei es der Möchte-Gern-Status. Aus diesem Grund wurde die Bequemlichkeit immer wieder repräsentativen oder dekorativen Zwecken, radikalen Designzielen und/oder dem Selbstverwirklichungsdrang von Designern geopfert.

Daß seit der Mitte des 19. Jahrhunderts Stühle in so außergewöhnlicher Vielfalt geschaffen wurden, hat damit zu tun, daß es – wegen der mannigfaltigen Funktionen eines Stuhls und wegen der anatomischen Vielgestaltigkeit der Benutzer – keine ideale Form für einen Stuhl oder Sessel gibt. Zu jeder Zeit kann es, bezogen auf den jeweiligen Gebrauchskontext, viele gute Lösungen geben. In der Überfülle von Entwürfen für eine spezielle Funktion wird man zahlreiche Ähnlichkeiten feststellen; was sie aber voneinander unterscheidet, ist die Frage, ob der Designer Funktion eher als Zweck betrachtet, der erfüllt werden muß, oder mehr als das, was ein Stuhlentwurf zum Ausdruck bringen soll. Gleichgültig jedoch, ob er in seinem Vorgehen mehr Gewicht auf Nützlichkeit oder auf Ästhetik gelegt hat, am Ende geht es beim Entwerfen eines Stuhls immer um dasselbe: nämlich darum, Verbindungen zu schaffen. In den

Einleitung

letzten 150 Jahren hat es unzählige Antworten auf die Frage gegeben, wie dies am besten zu erreichen sei. Fast immer gehörte zur Entstehung eines richtungsweisenden Prototyps ein Prozeß, bei dem nicht nur die gewünschte Funktion, eine entsprechende Konstruktion (und auch die entsprechenden Materialien) und die Ästhetik eine Rolle spielten, sondern auch Herstellungsverfahren und -kosten, Marktbedingungen, Endpreise und das gewünschte Produktappeal. In ihrer Verschiedenheit zeigen Stühle, auf wie viele Weisen sich derartige Kriterien kombinieren lassen, entsprechend den Zielen der Designer sowie den Bedürfnissen und Interessen, die in jedem einzelnen Fall berücksichtigt wurden.

So wie sich die Vorlieben einer Gesellschaft ändern, so ändern sich auch die Reaktionen von Designern und Herstellern auf gesellschaftliche Anforderungen. Was zu einer bestimmten Zeit als vernünftige Lösung gelten konnte, ist später vielleicht genau entgegengesetzt beurteilt worden. Einige Designer haben nach vorbildlichen und richtungsweisenden Lösungen gesucht und diese auch gefunden, was dann zu mehr oder weniger ausgeprägter Langlebigkeit geführt hat, doch selbst diese als »Klassiker« geschätzten Entwürfe haben nur eine begrenzte Wirkung aufgrund ihrer Funktionalität oder ihrer Ästhetik. So wie sich der Geschmack wandelt, so ändern sich auch andere Faktoren, etwa die Ansprüche an den Komfort, mit jeder Epoche, und sie variieren auch innerhalb der jeweiligen Kulturen. So haftet jedem Entwurf auch etwas Flüchtiges an. Und dies führt wiederum zu den zahllosen Erscheinungsformen, in denen sich dieses Sitzmöbel in verschiedenen Gebrauchszusammenhängen präsentiert.

Historisch läßt sich das Design von Stühlen als Auseinandersetzung zwischen widerstreitenden Standpunkten betrachten. Zur Debatte standen und stehen Themen wie die Bedeutung von Technik und industrieller Fertigung, aber auch Bedürfnisse und Interessen der Mehrheit im Gegensatz zu den Bedürfnissen und Interessen einer Minderheit, die Bedeutung von Funktionalität und Ästhetik in Gebrauchsgegenständen, die Frage, ob »weniger mehr« oder nicht doch »langweilig« ist oder ob, wie man in letzter Zeit glaubt, weniger nur »mehr oder weniger« weniger ist. Stühle leben auch als Ausdruck von Haltungen, Erwartungen und Wertvorstellungen ihrer Schöpfer; und welche Einstellung sie auch immer repräsentieren, alle Stühle besitzen rhetorische Qualitäten und damit jeweils auf ihre Weise Überzeugungskraft.

Wenn man die Rhetorik von Stühlen aus vergangenen Epochen

Der Stahlrohrstuhl ist in technischer und konstruktiver Hinsicht gewiß vernünftig; er ist leicht, für die Massenproduktion geeignet und so weiter. Doch vom menschlichen Standpunkt aus betrachtet sind Oberflächen aus Stahl und Chrom unbefriedigend.

Alvar Aalto, 1940
The Museum of Modern Art, Alvar Aalto. Furniture and Glas, New York: The Museum of Modern Art 1984, S. 7

Mit großen Stühlen
ist es wie mit Gesich-
tern ... man sieht
Tausende, aber erin-
nern kann man sich
nur an wenige ...

Ross Lovegrove,
1997

interpretiert, dann wird man etwas über die Zeit ihrer Entstehung und das Denken ihrer Schöpfer erfahren; allerdings wird unser Verständnis der kulturellen Bedeutung und der ästhetischen Werte historischer Stühle von vielen Faktoren geprägt. Dazu gehören zeitbedingte Geschmacksvorlieben und sich wandelnde Auffassungen von Technik und historischer Relevanz. So beruhte die Überzeugungskraft des berühmten Schichtholzstuhls LCW (Lounge Chair Wood) von Charles und Ray Eames zu seiner Zeit vor allem auf der technischen Rationalität des Entwurfs. Heute sind wohl eher der Charakter des Entwurfs, der Mythos, der die Eames umgibt, und die Tatsache entscheidend, daß der LCW inzwischen als kunsthistorische Ikone gefeiert wird. Deshalb ist es schwierig, historische Stühle objektiv zu beurteilen, ohne dabei die sozialen, ökonomischen, politischen und technischen Zusammenhänge in Betracht zu ziehen, die ihr Entstehen mit ermöglicht haben.

Unsere Auswahl beginnt mit dem frühen 19. Jahrhundert, denn damals, mit der aufkommenden Industrialisierung, wurden die ersten Versuche gemacht, den Stuhl aus dem Bereich des handwerklichen Objekts in den des bewußt gestalteten Industrieprodukts zu holen. Neue Techniken und Methoden der Materialverarbeitung ließen den Stuhl zu einem Möbel werden, das in großen Stückzahlen produziert werden konnte. Gleichzeitig erzwangen systematisierte Fertigungsprozesse eine Vereinfachung der Formen und Konstruktionsweisen. Mit dieser notwendigen Reduzierung wurde der Stuhl zu einem Demonstrationsobjekt für die zentralen Themen, mit denen sich Designer und insbesondere die Pioniere der Moderne von da an beschäftigten: Sichtbarkeit der Konstruktion, Materialtreue und die Tendenz zur Leichtigkeit.

Die ausgewählten Beispiele sind praktisch alle Schöpfungen der Avantgarde. Ob Produkt mechanisierter Fertigung oder traditioneller Handwerkskunst, was ihnen gemeinsam ist und was sie von der großen Menge anderer Stühle unterscheidet, ist ihre kraftvoll vorgetragene Rhetorik. Abgesehen von Funktion und Konstruktionsweise liegt der eigentliche Wert von Stühlen, ob ehemaliger oder zeitgenössischer Produktion, darin, daß sie Einstellungen, Gedanken und Wertvorstellungen vermitteln. Die Überzeugungskraft eines Stuhles hängt ab von der Klarheit seiner Rhetorik. Je klarer die vorgetragene Aussage, desto wahrscheinlicher ist, daß bewußt oder unbewußt Verbindungen entstehen, und schließlich ist es mehr als alles andere die Qualität dieser Verbindungen, die über Erfolg oder Mißerfolg eines Stuhlentwurfs entscheidet.

*« Les connexions, les connexions. C'est finalement ce
type de détail qui donne au produit son existence. »* [1]
*« Tout finit par se connecter – les gens, les idées, les
objets, etc., . . . la qualité des connexions est la clé de
la qualité en soi. »* [2]

Le siège, diversité du design et nature des connexions

Le concept de connexions est inhérent à la notion même de design et
plus encore de design de sièges. Aucun autre type de meuble n'offre
en effet autant de possibilités de créer et de faciliter des connexions du
même genre ou de la même importance. C'est d'ailleurs la raison pour
laquelle beaucoup plus de créateurs ont consacré davantage d'efforts
et de moyens à la création de sièges qu'à n'importe quel autre type de
meuble, et cela pendant une plus longue période de temps. En fait, mis
à part éventuellement l'automobile, le siège est l'artefact le plus étudié
et le plus célébré, l'objet du plus grand nombre d'ouvrages et de créations de notre temps.

Le succès d'un siège a toujours été lié à la qualité et à la variété des
connexions qu'il engendre dans sa réponse à un besoin particulier. Sur
le plan fonctionnel, à travers sa forme et ses matériaux, le siège met en
œuvre diverses relations physiques et psychologiques avec l'individu
qui s'y asseoit. Dans le même temps, il peut représenter des significations et des valeurs qui le relient à son utilisateur à différents niveaux :
intellectuel, émotionnel, esthétique, culturel et même spirituel. À un
autre niveau encore, des connexions fondamentales s'établissent entre
les composants stucturels appartenant à la conception du siège. Ce dernier peut également entrer en relations visuelles et/ou fonctionnelles
avec le contexte dans lequel il est utilisé, y compris avec d'autres objets
et d'autres styles. Plus largement, le design de sièges est connecté à
toutes sortes d'idéologies, de procédés de fabrication et de théories
économiques. Plus globales encore restent toutefois les connexions
qu'un siège, son designer et bien sûr son fabricant établissent avec la
société dans son ensemble, à travers l'universalité potentielle de l'attrait
exercé par le siège, de l'impact de sa fabrication sur l'environnement,
de son usage et de sa destruction éventuelle.

Au cours de ces 150 dernières années, l'évolution du siège a connu

Charles Eames, 1961
1. Frederick S.
Wright Gallery, Uni-
versity of Califor-
nia, Connections :
The Work of
Charles and Ray
Eames, UCLA Arts
Council : Los Ange-
les, 1976, p. 48
2. J. & M. Neuhart
& R. Eames, Eames
Design : The Work
of the Office of
Charles and Ray
Eames, Harry N.
Abrams, New York,
1989, p. 266

*Tubes d'acier, suspen-
sions en mousse et
recouvrements ont
connu une telle évo-
lution technique que
nous pouvons désor-
mais créer des formes
impensables il y a
quelques années en-
core. Personnelle-
ment, j'aimerais
concevoir des sièges
qui épuisent toutes
les possibilités de
l'époque dans la-
quelle je vis.*

Verner Panton, 1985.
A. L. Morgan, Con-
temporary Designers,
St. James Press,
Londres, 1985, p. 471

3. **George Nelson,**
Chairs, Whitney
Publications Inc.,
New York, 1953,
p. 9

... l'humble chaise de jadis se transforme – du moins actuellement – en un objet profondément séduisant ...

George Nelson, 1953
G. Nelson, *Chairs,*
Whitney Publications Inc., New York,
1953, p. 7

des développements parallèles à ceux de l'architecture et de la technologie. Ils reflètent le changement des besoins et des intérêts de la société dans une telle mesure que l'on peut considérer que l'histoire du siège illustre à elle seule toute celle du design. Comme George Nelson le faisait remarquer en 1953 : « Toute idée authentiquement originale – toute innovation en matière de design, toute nouvelle utilisation de matériaux, toute nouvelle invention technique destinée au mobilier – semble trouver son expression la plus forte dans un siège. »[3] À notre époque, cela n'a jamais été plus évident que dans le développement de sièges sans cesse plus performants et de plus en plus ergonomiques. Le marché très concurrentiel du siège de bureau, en particulier, est en permanence à l'affût de progrès techniques, et il est de plus en plus soumis à une réglementation plus stricte concernant la santé et la sécurité, ansi qu'à des acheteurs toujours plus sensibles à la qualité de leurs conditions de travail.

Trouver une solution adéquate aux problèmes posés par le siège est une aventure complexe et une véritable gageure même si la fonction d'aide à la position assise est restée virtuellement inchangée au cours de l'histoire. Les sièges sont destinés à toutes sortes de morphologies, pour des durées variées et des objectifs différents, qu'il s'agisse de manger, de lire, de se reposer, d'attendre, d'écrire ou d'effectuer un travail de bureau. Par ailleurs, chaque position assise possède une signification sociale particulière et se rattache à un ensemble de conventions, y compris des contraintes d'ordre orthopédique. Dans la plupart des cas, le siège doit soutenir correctement le poids de son occupant à une hauteur telle que ses jambes reposent naturellement et ses pieds touchent le sol, le poids de la tête et du torse étant reporté sur les os du bassin et des hanches. L'éternel problème posé par cette relation physique reste que, quel que soit le rembourrage du siège, la pression de l'os finit par se faire sentir sur le fessier et devient inconfortable. Ceci conduit finalement l'utilisateur à changer de position, ce qui se produit en moyenne toutes les dix ou quinze minutes. Plus un siège est conçu pour offrir un soutien statique et une posture « idéale » à une ossature humaine moyenne, plus l'inconfort paraît inévitable qui va imposer un stress psychologique à ceux qui ne possèdent pas cette anatomie standard ou ne souhaitent pas adopter la posture suggérée. Cependant, il est probablement juste de dire que si la présence d'un support lombaire correct est importante, en particulier pour les fauteuils de bureau, elle demeure moins indispensable que la liberté, pour l'utilisateur, de remuer facilement ses jambes ou de changer fréquemment de position. Une bonne assise doit donc permettre la liberté de mouvement et toute une variété de postures, tout en offrant un soutien souple et continu. Au-delà des considérations techniques sur la manière de s'asseoir et sur la façon dont les utilisateurs peuvent physiquement et psychologiquement se connecter à des formes spécifiques en fonction des différents contextes fonctionnels donnés, les sièges sont également conçus et acquis pour des raisons qui tiennent au contenu symbolique, à l'esthétique et à la mode. Parmi tous les types de meubles, le siège est un moyen privilégié de mettre en valeur son ego et d'afficher son « goût », tout en révélant son point de vue sociopolitique ainsi que son statut social et économique, réel ou souhaité. Dans ce dessein, le confort, les aspects pratiques et l'économie ont souvent été sacrifiés à la représentation de styles décoratifs, à des programmes de design radicaux et/ou aux impulsions de designers soucieux de s'exprimer.

L'extraordinaire variété des sièges créés depuis le milieu du XIXe siècle tient largement au fait qu'il n'existe pas de forme idéale, tant est grande la diversité des fonctions attendues et des anatomies des utilisateurs. Pour chaque époque donnée, on peut trouver de nombreuses bonnes solutions à divers contextes d'utilisation. Si la profusion des modèles conçus pour un usage spécifique peut présenter de nombreuses similarités, la différenciation finale et fondamentale se juge à la façon dont le designer a évalué la fonction : est-elle l'objectif ou le sujet du siège ? Que la préférence ait été accordée à l'utilité plutôt qu'à l'esthétique, le but essentiel d'un siège reste le même : créer des connexions. Au cours de ces 150 dernières années, d'innombrables interprétations de la meilleure méthode pour y parvenir ont vu le jour. Le plus souvent, la mise au point d'une solution sensée implique un processus qui non seulement prend en considération la fonction visée, la structure appropriée (y compris la mise en jeu de matériaux) et l'esthétique, mais également la méthode de fabrication, la nature du marché, le coût final et un élément de séduction. Différents sièges peuvent mettre en valeur diverses combinaisons de connexions selon les priorités de leurs designers et les besoins et intérêts exprimés suivant l'époque.

Au fur et à mesure que les préoccupations de la société changent,

Une position confortable, même la plus confortable du monde, ne le reste pas très longtemps... la nécessité de changer de position est un facteur important, souvent négligé par les designers de sièges.

Eero Saarinen, 1948
M. Page, *Furniture Designed by Architects*, Whitney Library of Design, New York, 1980, p. 208

Le siège en tube
d'acier est certaine-
ment rationnel du
point de vue de la
technique et de la
construction; il est
léger, adaptable à la
production en série,
etc. Mais les surfaces
d'acier et de chrome
ne sont pas satisfai-
santes d'un point de
vue humain.

Alvar Aalto, 1940
The Museum of
Modern Art, Alvar
Aalto : Furniture and
Glass. The Museum
of Modern Art, New
York, 1984, p. 7

les réponses des designers et des fabricants évoluent. Ce qui peut être considéré comme une solution rationnelle à une période donnée sera évalué de manière opposée à un autre moment. Tandis que certains modèles parviennent à imposer une autorité qui leur confère une longévité plus ou moins grande, les modèles jugés plus « classiques » possèdent un attrait esthétique ou fonctionnel limité. Si les goûts changent, il en va de même pour d'autres facteurs comme le besoin de confort, qui varie d'une période à l'autre et d'une culture à l'autre. L'aspect intrinsèquement éphémère du design explique ainsi la myriade de réponses apportées aux différents contextes fonctionnels du siège.

Historiquement, le design de sièges peut être perçu comme un débat entre des opinions conflictuelles sur des sujets comme le rôle de la technologie et les processus industriels, les besoins et les intérêts du plus grand nombre contre ceux d'une minorité d'individus où encore comme l'importance de la fonction et de l'esthétique dans les objets pratiques, même si « moins c'est plus » ou « moins c'est l'ennui », ou selon la tendance actuelle, « moins c'est plus, plus ou moins ». Les sièges sont des prises de position intellectuelles et morales de leurs créateurs, et quels que soient les points de vue représentés, ils possèdent tous une certaine rhétorique et de ce fait, une certaine forme de persuasion.

Si le déchiffrement de la rhétorique des sièges du passé peut nous aider à comprendre leur époque et la pensée de ceux qui les ont conçus, notre appréciation de la signification culturelle et de la valeur esthétique des sièges anciens est conditionnée par de nombreux facteurs. Notre appréhension est influencée par notre goût contemporain et par nos perceptions changeantes de la technologie et de la pertinence historique. La séduction du modèle LCW (Lounge Chair Wood) de Charles et Ray Eames à son époque tenait ainsi largement à son raisonnement technologique, alors qu'aujourd'hui elle est davantage liée à son caractère, à la mythologie entourant les Eames et à son statut d'icone culturel. Il est de ce fait difficile d'avoir une attitude objective face aux sièges historiques sans prendre en considération les contextes social, économique, politique et technologique qui ont entouré leur apparition.

Notre sélection d'exemples pour cette étude consacrée aux sièges commence au début du XIXe siècle car c'est de cette époque, avec l'avènement de l'industrialisation, que datent les premières tentatives de tirer le siège du domaine de l'artisanat pour en faire un objet de design.

De nouvelles technologies de traitement de matériaux permirent de produire des modèles en grand nombre tandis que des méthodes de fabrication systématisées entraînèrent la simplification de la forme et de la structure. Avec ce réductionnisme obligé, le siège commence à illustrer quelques-uns des thèmes importants comme la structure apparente, l'honnêteté dans l'utilisation des matériaux et la tendance à la légèreté, qui seront repris par des designers ultérieurs et en particulier par les pionniers du mouvement moderne.

Les modèles que nous avons sélectionnés appartiennent virtuellement tous à l'avant-garde. Que ce soit le résultat d'une mécanisation de la production ou d'une fabrication artisanale, ils ont en commun – et c'est bien ce qui les distingue de l'écrasante majorité des autres sièges – une rhétorique puissamment argumentée. En dehors des critères de fonction et de structure, la valeur fondamentale de ces sièges, passés ou actuels, tient à ce qu'ils communiquent des attitudes, des idées, des valeurs. La séduction d'un siège dépend de la clarté de sa rhétorique. Plus le discours est clair, plus les connexions se produisent, consciemment ou inconsciemment, et c'est bien la qualité de ces connexions, plus que tout autre facteur, qui détermine, au final, le succès d'un siège.

Il en va des sièges comme des visages ... on en rencontre des milliers, mais on ne se souvient que de quelques-uns.

Ross Lovegrove,
1977

▲ **Alvar Aalto**
Armchair, Model No. 37, 1935–1936

ARTEK, HELSINKI, FROM C. 1936 TO PRESENT

▲ **Alvar Aalto**
Armchair, Model No. 44,
1935–1936

ARTEK, HELSINKI, FROM C. 1935 TO PRESENT

Alvar Aalto

Paimio, Model No. 41, 1930–1931

Bent laminated and solid birch frame with lacquered bent plywood seat section | Rahmen aus gebogener, laminierter Birke, Sitzschale aus geformtem Schichtholz, lackiert | Châssis en bouleau contreplaqué cintré, siège en contre-plaqué cintré laqué

HUONEKALU-JA RAKENNU-STYÖTEHDAS, ÅBO, TURKU, 1932–1935 (REISSUED BY ARTEK, FROM 1935 TO PRESENT)

◄▲ **Alvar Aalto**
Bent laminated wood sections for Alvar Aalto's chair designs, Model Nos. 41 & 44

Although not part of the original furnishing scheme at the Paimio Sanatorium, this revolutionary chair is often associated with the project. Where there was a need for great pliancy, such as in the scrolls of the plywood seat and back, Aalto thinned the lamination by removing several layers of veneer.

Auch wenn dieser revolutionäre Stuhl nicht zum ursprünglichen Ausstattungsprogramm des Sanatoriums Paimio gehörte, wird er häufig mit diesem Projekt in Verbindung gebracht. Wo größere Elastizität zum Biegen benötigt wurde, z. B. bei den eingerollten Enden der Sitzschale, machte Aalto das Schichtholz durch Entfernen einiger Furnierschichten dünner.

Bien qu'il ne fasse pas partie du mobilier d'origine du sanatorium de Paimio, ce siège révolutionnaire est souvent associé à ce projet. Lorsqu'il avait besoin d'une grande flexibilité, comme dans l'enroulement du siège et du dossier, Aalto amincissait le contre-plaqué en éliminant quelques couches de placage.

Alvar Aalto

Model No. 60,
1932–1933

Bent laminated birch
construction |
Gebogene, laminierte
Birke | Contre-plaqué
cintré plaqué de
bouleau

HUONEKALU-JA
RAKENNU-
STYÖTEHDAS, ÅBO,
TURKU, 1933–1935
(REISSUED BY ARTEK,
FROM 1935 TO
PRESENT)

▲ **Alvar Aalto**
Model No. 69, c. 1933

HUONEKALU-JA RAKENNUSTYÖTEHDAS, ÅBO,
TURKU, 1933–1935 (REISSUED BY ARTEK,
FROM 1935 TO PRESENT)

▲ Finmar advertisement, c. 1935

Alvar Aalto

Model No. 43, 1936

*Bent laminated wood
and solid birch frame
with textile webbing |
Gestell aus laminier-
tem und gebogenem
Holz und massivem
Birkenholz, Liege-
fläche aus Textil-
geflecht | Bouleau
contre-plaqué cintré,
bouleau massif, textile
tressé*

ARTEK, HELSINKI,
FROM C. 1937 TO
PRESENT

The model No. 60 stool and model No. 69 chair
demonstrate Aalto's interest in basic functional
forms. The later model No. 43 chaise longue and
model No. 406 chair are less utilitarian and more
suited to domestic settings.

*Der Hocker Modell Nr. 60 und der Stuhl Modell
Nr. 69 demonstrieren Aaltos Interesse an funktionalen
Grundformen. Die spätere Liege Modell Nr. 43 und
der Stuhl Modell Nr. 406 wirken weniger funktional,
fügen sich aber besser in Wohnumgebungen ein.*

Le tabouret modèle n° 60 et la chaise modèle n° 69
révèlent l'intérêt d'Aalto pour les formes fonctionnelles
basiques. La chaise longue modèle n° 43 et le fauteuil
modèle n° 406, tous deux ultérieurs, sont moins utili-
taires et mieux adaptés à un usage domestique.

▲ Alvar Aalto
Armchair, Model
No. 406, 1938–1939

ARTEK, HELSINKI,
FROM C. 1939
TO PRESENT

21

Eero Aarnio

Armchair, c. 1967

Fibreglass-reinforced polyester seat shell on painted aluminium base with internal textile-covered foam upholstery and seat cushion | Sitzschale aus geformtem fiberglasverstärktem Polyester, Fuß aus lackiertem Aluminium, Innenpolster und Sitzkissen aus Schaumstoff mit Stoffbezug | Coquille en polyester renforcé de fibre de verre, piètement en aluminium peint, rembourrage interne recouvert de tissu, coussin en mousse

ASKO, LAHTI, FROM
c. 1967

▲ Graphic portrayal of Eero Aarnio's Bubble chair from *Design from Scandinavia*, No. 3

Aarnio's belief that, "Design means constant renewal, realignment and growth", is declared in his iconoclastic furniture. Although he embodied the spirit of the 1960s in the novel forms of his visually exciting designs, he did not embrace Pop culture's ethos of ephemerality and disposability. His furniture is of a high quality and intended for durability.

Aarnios Auffassung, Design sei »ständige Erneuerung, Neuorientierung und Wachstum«, zeigt sich in seinen innovativen Möbeln. Obwohl die avantgardistischen Formen seiner visuell stimulierenden Entwürfe den Geist der 6oer Jahre verkörperten, übernahm er nicht den Kurzlebigkeits- und Wegwerfethos der Popkultur. Seine Möbel sind von hoher Qualität und haltbar.

Eero Aarnio

Ball (or Globe), 1963–1965

Moulded fibreglass-reinforced polyester seating section on painted aluminium base with internal fabric-covered foam upholstery | Sitzschale aus geformtem fiberglasverstärktem Polyester, Fuß aus lackiertem Aluminium, Innenpolster und Sitzkissen aus Schaumstoff mit Stoffbezug | Coquille en polyester renforcé dev fibre de verre, base en aluminium peint, rembourrage intérieur en mousse recouverte de tissu

ASKO, LAHTI
1966–C. 1980
(REISSUED BY ADELTA, FROM 1992 TO PRESENT)

▼ **Eero Aarnio**
Bubble chair, 1968

ASKO, LAHTI, FROM
C. 1968 (REISSUED BY
ADELTA, FROM 1996)

La conviction de Aarnio, pour qui « design signifie renouvellement, réalignement et évolution constants », s'affirme dans ses créations iconoclastes. Si le designer illustra bien l'esprit des années 60 à travers une nouveauté formelle séduisante, il ne se rallia pas pour autant à l'éthique de la culture pop de l'éphémère et du jetable. Son mobilier est de haute qualité et construit pour durer.

Eero Aarnio

Pastille, 1967–1968

*Moulded fibreglass-
reinforced polyester
structure | Schale aus
geformtem fiberglas-
verstärktem Poly-
ester | Polyester moulé
renforcé de fibre de
verre*

ASKO LAHTI,
FINLAND,
1968–c. 1980
(REISSUED BY
ADELTA C/O
FINLAND-CONTACT,
DINSLAKEN, FROM
1991 TO PRESENT)

The "Pastille", sometimes referred to as the "Gyro", is a novel interpretation
of a rocking chair. With its bold organic form, the chair exemplifies the
sophisticated approach of many Scandinavian designers to synthetic materials. Designed for interior or exterior use, it won an A.I.D. award in 1968.
*»Pastille«, manchmal auch »Gyro« genannt, ist die Neuinterpretation eines
Schaukelstuhls. Mit seiner kühnen organischen Form steht der Stuhl stell-
vertretend für den raffinierten Umgang vieler skandinavischer Designer mit
synthetischen Materialien. Für den Innen- und Außenbereich entworfen, erhielt
er 1968 den internationalen Designpreis A.I.D.*
Le « Pastille », parfois appelé « Gyro », est une interprétation entièrement
nouvelle du siège à bascule. De
forme organique, il illustre bien
l'approche raffinée des matériaux
synthétiques de nombreux designers scandinaves. Conçu aussi
bien pour la maison que pour l'extérieur, il remporta en 1968 un prix
international de l' A.I.D.

▶Eero Aarnio's
sitting room in
Helsinki, c. 1970

Franco Albini

Fiorenza, 1952

Wood frame with latex-foam uphol-stered seat, back and armrests | Rahmen aus Holz, Sitzfläche, Rückenlehne und Armlehnen mit Latexschaumstoff-polsterung | Châssis en bois, siège, dossier et accoudoirs rem-bourrés en mousse de latex

ARFLEX, MEDA, MILAN, FROM 1952 TO PRESENT

▼ **Franco Albini**
Rocking chaise, Model No. PS16, 1956

CARLO POGGI, PAVIA, 1956

Albini was the foremost Neo-Rationalist designer. His "Fiorenza" chair, a pared-down reworking of the tradi-tional wing chair, did away with the need for bulky springing through its use of latex-foam upholstery.

Albini war der führende Designer unter den Neo-Rationalisten. Sein Sessel »Fiorenza«, eine aufs notwen-digste reduzierte Version des traditionellen Ohrensessels, machte Schluß mit voluminöser Federung durch den Einsatz einer Polsterung aus Latex-Schaumstoff.

Albini est le principal designer néorationaliste. Son fau-teuil « Fiorenza », une interprétation épurée du tradi-tionnel fauteuil à oreilles, éliminait le problème des en-combrants ressorts par un rembourrage en mousse de latex.

Ron Arad

Rover, 1981

Tubular steel frame supporting a salvaged Rover 2000 car seat | Rahmen aus Stahlrohr, darauf ein recycelter Autositz aus einem Rover 2000 | Châssis en tube d'acier, siège de récupération de Rover 2000

ONE OFF, LONDON, FROM 1981

This "ready-made" design utilises a salvaged car seat and a frame executed from scaffolding – a favourite medium of the High-Tech style. Its rough-and-ready appearance characterises the work of the British avantgarde in the 1980s.

▼ Jean Prouvé
Prototype of adjustable chair, 1924

Design als Ready-made: Ein gebrauchter Autositz in einem Rahmen aus Gerüstteilen – ein beliebter Werkstoff des High-Tech-Stils. Der improvisierte Eindruck ist typisch für die Arbeiten der britischen Avantgarde der 8oer Jahre.

Ce modèle ready-made utilise un siège de voiture récupéré et un châssis fait de morceaux d'échafaudage, l'un des matériaux préférés du style high-tech. Son aspect brut et improvisé caractérise les travaux de l'avant-garde britannique au cours des années 80.

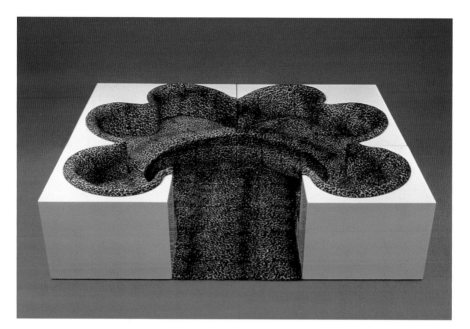

The "Safari" is a modular "livingscape" which, through its use of fake leopard skin and its flower-shaped form, revels in kitsch while mocking the conventional wisdom that "Good Design" equals good taste.

»Safari« bildet eine modulhafte Wohnlandschaft und schwelgt durch die Verwendung von imitiertem Leopardenfell und die Blumenform im Kitsch – ein Spott auf die Binsenweisheit, daß »gutes Design« das gleiche sei wie »guter Geschmack«.

Le « Safari » est un « espace de vie » modulaire qui, avec son faux léopard et sa forme de fleur, prend le parti du kitsch. Il se moque du préjugé selon lequel « Good Design » signifierait « bon goût ».

Archizoom Associati

Safari, 1968

Fibreglass frame
with internal textile-
covered latex foam
upholstery | Rahmen
aus fiberglasver-
stärktem Kunststoff,
integrierte Polsterung
aus Latexschaumstoff
mit Stoffbezug |
Châssis en fibre de
verre, rembourrage
intérieur en mousse
de latex recouverte
de tissu

POLTRONOVA,
MONTALE, PISTOIA,
FROM 1968

◄ Contemporary
photograph showing
Safari, c. 1968

Helmut Bätzner

Bofinger, Model No. BA 1171, 1964–1966

Compression-moulded fibreglass-reinforced polyester resin | Formgepreßtes, fiberglasverstärktes Polyester | Résine de polyester renforcée de fibre de verre et moulée sous pression

MENZOLIT-WERKE, ALBERT SCHMIDT, KRAICHTAL-MENZINGEN FOR WILHELM BOFINGER, ILSFIELD, 1966–1984

The chair No. BA 1171 was the first single-piece plastic chair suitable for mass-production. It was compression-moulded using the "prepreg-process" and a ten-ton double-shell heated press. The production cycle lasted only five minutes.

Der Stuhl Modell Nr. BA 1171 war der erste Plastikstuhl aus einem Stück, der für die Massenproduktion geeignet war. Für das »Prepreg«-Druckpreßverfahren wurde eine zehn Tonnen schwere Doppelmantel-Heißpresse eingesetzt. Ein Produktionszyklus dauerte nur fünf Minuten.

La chaise nᵒ BA 1171 était le premier siège en plastique d'une seule pièce adapté à la production en grande série. Il était moulé sous pression selon le procédé « prepreg » et sur une presse de dix tonnes à double moule. Le cycle de production ne durait que cinq minutes.

Mario Bellini

Cab, Model No. 412,
1976

Enamelled steel frame with zip-fastening saddle-stitched leather covering | Rahmen aus Stahl, einbrennlackiert, Bezug aus sattelvernähtem Kernleder, mit Montagereißverschlüssen | Châssis en acier émaillé recouvert de cuir cousu façon sellier et zippé

CASSINA, MEDA,
MILAN, FROM 1977
TO PRESENT

▼ Mario Bellini
Cab sofa, 1982

CASSINA, MEDA,
MILAN, FROM 1982
TO PRESENT

The leather upholstery of the "Cab" chair zips directly onto the skeletal steel frame and functions as a supporting material. Its high-quality saddle stitching attests to Italy's tradition of producing fine leatherwork.

Der Lederbezug des Stuhls »Cab« wird über das Stahlgestell gezogen und hat, mit Montagereißverschlüssen befestigt, auch tragende Funktion. Die hochwertige Sattelnähung zeugt vom traditionellen Qualitätsstandard italienischer Lederverarbeitung.

Le rembourrage en cuir de la chaise « Cab » se fixe directement sur le châssis métallique par un système de fermeture à glissière et remplit également une fonction de soutien. Sa haute qualité de réalisation façon sellier témoigne de la tradition italienne de la maroquinerie de luxe.

Harry Bertoia

Diamond, Model No. 421LU, 1950–1952

Vinyl-coated or chrome-plated, bent and welded steel rod construction | Konstruktion aus geformtem und verschweißtem Stahldraht, verchromt bzw. vinylbeschichtet | Fil d'acier gainé de vinyle cintré et soudé

KNOLL ASSOCIATES, NEW YORK, FROM C. 1953 TO PRESENT

▼ Herbert Matter
Knoll Associates advertisement showing Diamond chair, Model No. 422LU, c. 1955

Bertoia's designs not only addressed functional requirements but were also studies in form and space. Mechanised production was attempted but it was found that the chairs were easier to produce by hand.

Bertoias Entwürfe sind nicht nur funktional, sondern erkunden auch Form und Raum. Die Sitzmöbel sollten maschinell hergestellt werden, aber es zeigte sich, daß sie leichter von Hand zu produzieren sind.

Non seulement les créations de Bertoia répondaient à des contraintes pratiques mais elles constituaient de remarquables études de forme et de volume. Après quelques essais de production à la machine, on réalisa que ces sièges étaient plus faciles à fabriquer à la main.

Osvaldo Borsani

Model No. P40, 1954

Pressed and tubular steel frame with latex-foam upholstery and rubber-covered steel spring arms | Rahmen aus Stahlrohr und Stahlblech, Latex-schaumstoffpolsterung, Armlehnen aus gummiüberzogenen Stahlfedern | Châssis en tube d'acier et acier estampé, rembourrage en mousse de latex, accoudoirs souples recouverts de caoutchouc

TECNO, MILAN, FROM 1954 TO PRESENT

Based on Borsani's belief that design should be born out of technical research, the P40 and D70 are highly innovative in the flexibility they offer. With all the main elements of its design being adjustable, the remarkably versatile P40 can be manipulated into 486 positions. The D70 functions as a divan-bed with a back that can be adjusted through various angles to 90 degrees. Its seat and back can also fold together vertically for ease of storage.

Borsanis Überzeugung entsprechend, daß Design aus dem Erforschen technischer Möglichkeiten entsteht, sind P40 und D70 mit der Flexibilität, die sie bieten, hoch innovativ. Alle Bestandteile des P40 sind verstellbar, womit dieser bemerkenswert vielseitige Liegesessel in 486 Positionen

▲ **Osvaldo Borsani**
Lounge chair, Model No. P40 & sofa, Model No. D70, 1954

TECNO, MILAN, FROM 1954 TO PRESENT

Osvaldo
Borsani

Model No. D70, 1954

Pressed and tubular steel frame with latex-foam upholstery | Rahmen aus Stahlrohr und Stahlblech, Latexschaumstoffpolsterung | Châssis en tube d'acier et acier estampé, rembourrage en mousse de latex

TECNO, MILAN, FROM 1954 TO PRESENT

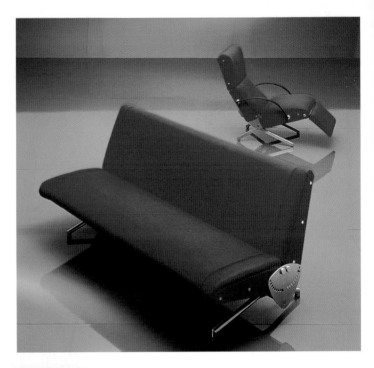

gebracht werden kann. Das Sofa D70 kann durch seine Rückenlehne, die in verschiedenen Winkeln bis zu 90° herablaßbar ist, auch als Schlafgelegenheit benutzt werden. Um das Sofa platzsparend zu verstauen, können Sitzfläche und Rückenlehne vertikal gegeneinander geklappt werden. Fruits de la conviction de Borsani selon laquelle le design doit s'appuyer sur une recherche technique, le P40 et le D70 innovent radicalement par leur souplesse d'utilisation. Ses principaux éléments étant tous réglables, la P40, remarquablement polyvalente, peut prendre jusqu'à 486 positions. La D70 servait de divan-lit avec un dossier pouvant s'abaisser à 90°. Le siège et le dossier peuvent également se replier verticalement pour faciliter son rangement.

Marcel Breuer

*Wassily, Model
No. B3, 1925–1927*

Bent, nickelled
tubular steel frame
(later chrome-plated)
with canvas, fabric or
leather seat and back
sections | Rahmen
aus gebogenem
Stahlrohr, vernickelt
(später verchromt),
Sitzfläche, Rücken-
und Armlehnen mit
Leinen-, Textil- oder
Lederbespannung |
Châssis en tube
d'acier cintré et
nickelé (ultérieure-
ment chromé), siège
et dossier en toile,
tissu ou cuir

STANDARD-MÖBEL,
BERLIN & GEBRÜDER
THONET, FRANKEN-
BERG, FROM C. 1928
(REISSUED BY KNOLL
INTERNATIONAL,
FROM 1968 TO
PRESENT)

Designed for Wassily Kandinsky's quarters at the
Dessau Bauhaus, the No. B3 utterly transformed the
language of chair design. It was particularly revolutionary in its use of tubular steel and its method of manufacture.

*Nr. B3, ursprünglich ein Entwurf für die Wohnung von
Wassily Kandinsky am Bauhaus in Dessau, stellt eine
völlige Erneuerung des traditionellen Sitzmöbels dar.
Revolutionär waren insbesondere die Verwendung von
Stahlrohr und das Herstellungsverfahren.*

Créé pour l'appartement de Kandinsky au Bauhaus de
Dessau, le n° B3 modifia profondément la conception
du siège moderne. Il était particulièrement révolutionnaire par son utilisation du tube d'acier et son processus de fabrication.

▲ Marcel Breuer
Model No. B4, 1926–1927

STANDARD-MÖBEL, BERLIN
(REISSUED BY TECTA FROM 1981 AS D4)

Marcel Breuer

Model No. B33,
1927–1928

Chrome-plated
tubular steel frame
with "Eisengarn"
or leather seat and
back | Rahmen aus
gebogenem Stahlrohr,
verchromt, Sitzfläche
und Rückenlehne
mit Bespannung aus
Eisengarngewebe oder
Leder | Châssis en
tube d'acier chromé,
siège et dossier en
cuir tendu ou en toile
« Eisengarn »

GEBRÜDER THONET,
FRANKENBERG,
FROM C. 1929 TO
PRESENT

▼ **Marcel Breuer**
Cantilever stool,
1927

▶▼ **Walter Gropius**
Reading room of an
apartment house,
"Bauausstellung",
Berlin, 1931

Unlike Stam's S33, on which their designs were based, Breuer's B33 and slightly later B64 utilise non-reinforced tubular steel. This gives their constructions greater resilience and, thereby, more comfort. These designs, like other cantilevered chairs, eliminate the visual division between the base and seat sections through the use of a continuous supporting frame.

Für seinen Stuhl B33 und den wenig später entwickelten B64 nutzt Breuer, anders als Stam für den zuvor entworfenen S33, unverstärktes Stahlrohr. Das verleiht dem B33 größere Elastizität und damit mehr Sitzkomfort. Diese Entwürfe heben, wie andere Freischwinger-Typen auch, die optische Trennung zwischen Unterbau und Sitz auf, indem sie einen durchgängigen tragenden Rahmen verwenden.

À la différence du S33 de Stam, le B33 de Breuer et le B64 légèrement ultérieur font appel à des tubes non renforcés, ce qui donne au siège plus d'élasticité et donc plus de confort. Ces modèles, comme d'autres en porte à faux, suppriment la différenciation visuelle entre le piètement et le siège lui-même grâce à une structure de soutien continue.

Marcel Breuer

Model No. B32 and Model No. B64, 1928

Chrome-plated tubular steel frames with stained bentwood and woven cane seats and backs | Rahmen aus gebogenem Stahlrohr, Sitzfläche und Rückenlehne aus Rohrgeflecht in geformtem Holzrahmen, schwarz gebeizt | Châssis en tube d'acier chromé, sièges et dossiers en bois cintré teinté, cannage

GEBRÜDER THONET, FRANKENBERG, FROM C. 1929 TO PRESENT (REISSUED BY KNOLL INTERNATIONAL, FROM 1968 TO PRESENT)

Marcel Breuer

Model No. 301,
1932–1934

Bent aluminium
frame with painted
moulded and
laminated seat
and backrest |
Rahmen aus gebo-
genem Aluminium-
profil, Sitzfläche und
Rückenlehne aus
geformtem Schicht-
holz, lackiert | Châssis
en aluminium cintré,
siège et dosseret en
contre-plaqué moulé,
peints

EMBRU, RÜTI,
ZURICH, FROM 1934

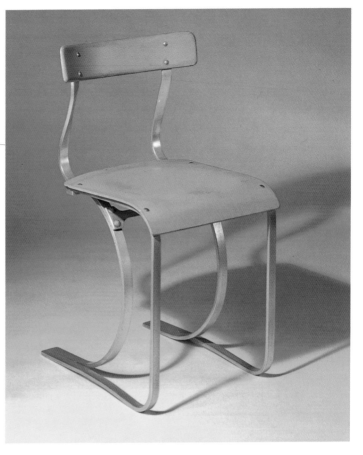

▼ Marcel Breuer
Armchair, Model
No. 301 & armchair,
Model No. 336,
1932–1934

EMBRU, RÜTI,
ZURICH, FROM 1934

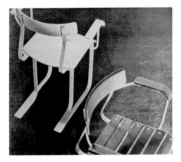

In the early 1930s, Breuer experimented with flat aluminium in his designs for seating. Although not as
resilient or strong as tubular metal, this medium was
considerably cheaper. Intended for the mass-market, his
flat steel designs were retailed through the Wohnbedarf
stores in Switzerland. The concave back legs are a
hybrid of the cantilever principle and were a structural
necessity.

In den frühen 30er Jahren experimentierte Breuer in seinen
Entwürfen für Sitzmöbel mit Aluminiumprofilen. Auch
wenn dieses Material weniger elastisch und stark ist als
Stahlrohr, so ist es doch erheblich preiswerter. Für den
Massenmarkt konzipiert, wurden diese Aluminiummodell

durch die Läden der Schweizer Firma Wohnbedarf vertrieben. Die konkav geschwungenen, zusätzlichen hinteren Beine, eine unechte Freischwinger-Lösung,
waren aus statischen Gründen notwendig.

Au début des années 30, Breuer expérimente la réalisation de sièges en aluminium. Moins élastique ou résistant que le métal tubulaire, il était toutefois bien moins cher. Conçus pour le marché grand public, ces modèles en
acier plat furent commercialisés en Suisse par les magasins Wohnbedarf.
Les pieds arrière concaves sont une solution hybride de porte-à-faux et répondaient à une nécessité structurelle.

Marcel Breuer

Model No. 313,
1932–1934

*Bent aluminium
frame with
aluminium slats and
beech armrests |
Rahmen aus geboge-
nem Aluminiumprofil
und Aluminium-
streben, Armlehnen
aus Buche | Châssis
en aluminium cintré,
traverses en alu-
minium et accoudoirs
en bois de hêtre*

EMBRU, RÜTI,
ZURICH, FROM 1934

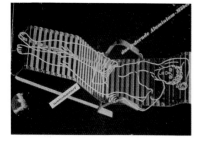

◄ **Herbert Bayer**
Cover of Wohn-
bedarf catalogue,
*Das federnde
Aluminium-Möbel,*
1934

Marcel Breuer

Chaise longue,
1935–1936

Bent laminated birch
frame with bent
plywood seat section |
Rahmen aus geboge-
ner und laminierter
Birke, Liegefläche aus
geformtem Schicht-
holz | Châssis en
bouleau contre-
plaqué cintré, siège en
contre-plaqué cintré

ISOKON FURNITURE
COMPANY, LONDON,
FROM 1936

Breuer's plywood and laminated wood chaise longue and lounge chair were part of a group of furniture designed for Jack Pritchard's Isokon Furniture Company. Reflecting the popularity of Aalto's designs, which had been exhibited in London in 1933, Breuer's designs are all-wood translations of his earlier metal designs. These later designs were structurally flawed, for the tenon joins which attached the seat section to the frame loosened over time.

Breuers Liege und Sessel aus Schicht- und Formholz gehören zu einer Möbel-serie, die für Jack Pritchards Isokon Möbelwerke geschaffen wurde. Als Ganzholz-versionen seiner früheren Entwürfe belegen sie den Einfluß Alvar Aaltos, dessen Möbel ab 1933 in London zu sehen waren. Breuers Konstruktion litt darunter, daß sich die Verzapfungen zwischen Sitz und Rahmen nach einiger Zeit lösten.

▶ **Marcel Breuer**
Working drawing,
1936

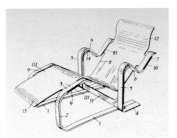

Marcel Breuer

Armchair, 1936

Bent laminated birch frame with bent plywood seat section | Rahmen aus gebogener und laminierter Birke, Liegefläche aus geformtem Schichtholz | Châssis en bouleau contreplaqué cintré, siège en contre-plaqué cintré

ISOKON FURNITURE COMPANY, LONDON, FROM 1936

Les fauteuils et les chaises longues en contre-plaqué faisaient partie d'un groupe de meubles dessinés pour la firme de meubles Isokon de Jack Pritchard. Rappelant les modèles d'Aalto, qui avaient été exposés à Londres en 1933, les créations de Breuer sont des adaptations tout en bois de ses œuvres antérieures en métal. Avec le temps, apparaît une faiblesse structurelle au niveau du tenon qui joint la partie du siège au cadre.

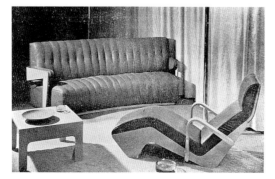

◄ **Marcel Breuer**
Group of furniture designed for Heal's, c. 1936

attributed to
Ford Madox
Brown

Sussex, c. 1864–1865

*Ebonised, turned
wood construction
with woven rush seat |
Gestell aus gedrech-
seltem, schwarz
gebeiztem Holz,
Sitzfläche aus
Binsengeflecht |
Chêne noirci, siège
en jonc tressé*

MORRIS & CO.,
LONDON,
c. 1864–1940

▼ Morris & Co.
catalogue, c. 1910

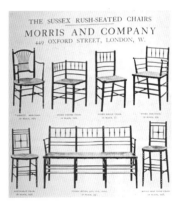

The "Sussex" chair is generally credited to the painter Ford Madox Brown, who discovered its antique arche-type in a shop in Sussex. It has, however, also been attributed to William Morris.

Der »Sussex«-Stuhl wird allgemein dem Maler Ford Madox Brown zugeschrieben, der den altertümlichen Archetyp die-ses Entwurfs in einem Geschäft in Sussex aufstöberte. Der Stuhl ist aber auch schon William Morris zugeschrieben worden.

Ce fauteuil «Sussex» est généralement attribué au peintre Ford Madox Brown, qui s'inspira d'un modèle ancien trouvé dans une boutique du Sussex. Il a égale-ment été attribué à William Morris.

By the 1900s, Bugatti's style had become more inspired by Orientalism. With their tassels and intricate inlay, his designs from this period appear to have been smuggled from some exotic harem.

Nach 1900 wurde der Stil Bugattis immer stärker durch orientalisierende Formen beeinflußt. Mit ihren Quasten und komplexen Intarsien wirken seine Entwürfe aus jener Zeit, als seien sie aus einem exotischen Harem herausgeschmuggelt worden.

À partir de 1900, le style de Bugati s'inspire de plus en plus de l'orientalisme. Avec leurs franges et leur décor complexe, les modèles de cette période semblent tout droit sortis d'un harem.

Carlo Bugatti

Bench, c. 1900

Part-stained wood construction inlaid with vellum, brass and pewter and adorned with tassels | Rahmen aus Holz, teilweise gebeizt, Intarsien und Verzierungen aus Pergament, Messing und Zinn, mit Quasten geschmückt | Bois teinté, incrustations en vélin, cuivre, étain et franges

CARLO BUGATTI,
MILAN

▶ **Carlo Bugatti**
Chair, c. 1902

CARLO BUGATTI,
MILAN

◀ **Carlo Bugatti**
Chair, c. 1895

CARLO BUGATTI,
MILAN

Achille &
Pier Giacomo
Castiglioni

Mezzadro, 1957

Lacquered tractor seat on chromed flat steel stem with wing-nut and solid beech footrest | Traktorsitz, lackiert, verchromte Stahlfeder mit Flügel-mutter, Fußstütze aus Buche | Siège de tracteur laqué, pied en acier plat chromé, repose-pied en hêtre massif, fixation par vis à papillon

ZANOTTA, MILAN,
FROM 1983 TO
PRESENT

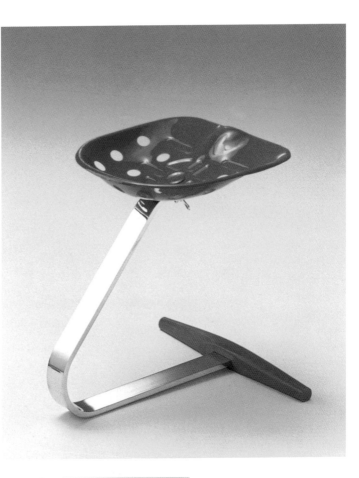

▼ **Benjamin Baldwin**
Tractor seat chair,
c. 1953

BALDWIN-MACHADO,
NEW YORK

▲ Canadian tractor seat, 19th century

▲ **Mies van der Rohe**
Sketch of tractor seat, c. 1940

Exploiting Duchamp's concept of the ready-made in furniture design, the "Mezzadro" and "Sella" stools were deemed too radical to be put into production until 1983. Interestingly, earlier precedents for tractor-seat stools exist including Benjamin Baldwin's design of c. 1953.

Der »Mezzadro«- und der »Sella«-Hocker, die von Duchamps Konzept des Ready-made im Möbeldesign Gebrauch machen, galten als zu radikal und gingen erst 1983 in Produktion. Interessanterweise gibt es für den Traktorsitz-Hocker Vorläufer, so etwa den um 1953 entstandenen Entwurf von Benjamin Baldwin.

Exploitant le concept des ready-made de Marcel Duchamp dans la création de mobilier, les modèles « Mezzadro » et le « Sella » furent jugés trop radicaux pour êtres mis en production avant 1983. D'autres exemples d'utilisation détournée de sièges de tracteurs avaient été publiés par le passé, dont celui de Benjamin Baldwin, vers 1953.

Achille &
Pier Giacomo
Castiglioni

Sella, 1957

Racing bicycle saddle on lacquered tubular steel column with cast-iron base | Fahrrad-Rennsattel auf einer lackierten Stahlstange, Fuß aus Gußeisen | Selle de vélo de course, pied-colonne en tube d'acier peint, base en fonte de fer

ZANOTTA, MILAN, FROM 1983 TO PRESENT

Wendell Castle

Molar chair, 1969

Moulded fibreglass-
reinforced polyester |
Geformtes, fiberglas-
verstärktes Polyester |
Polyester moulé
renforcé de fibre de
verre

BEYLERIAN, NEW
YORK, 1970–C. 1975

▼ Wendell Castle
Castle armchair,
1969

BEYLERIAN, NEW
YORK, 1970–C. 1975

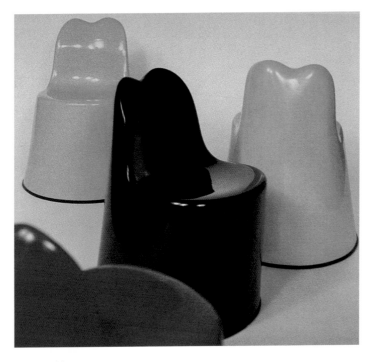

Best known for his superbly crafted wooden furniture,
Castle translated his highly organic forms into plastic.
The surrealistic "Molar" love-seat and matching
"Molar" chairs were based on the shape of back teeth.
Not intended for high-volume production, the "Molar"
group and similar "Castle" series of chairs were exclus-
ively distributed by Stendig, New York.

*Castle, der sich vor allem mit seinen qualitativ hoch-
wertigen Holzmöbeln einen Namen machte, übertrug
deren extrem organische Formen auf das Medium Kunststoff. Das surrealistische Sofa »Molar« und die dazu pas-
senden Stühle basieren auf der Form von Backenzähnen.
Die Sitzgruppe »Molar« war nicht für die Serienproduktion gedacht und wurde, wie die Sitzgruppe »Castle«,
ausschließlich durch Stendig, New York, vertrieben.*

Surtout connu pour ses meubles en bois superbement réalisés, Castle adapta ses formes extrêmement organiques à la production en plastique. Le siège surréaliste « Molar» et les fauteuils assortis « Molar» sont inspirés de la forme d'une molaire. Conçue pour une production limitée, la série « Molar» et les autres créations de Castle étaient distribuées en exclusivité par Stendig, New York.

Wendell Castle

Molar sofa, 1969

Moulded fibreglass-reinforced polyester | Geformtes, fiberglas-verstärktes Polyester | Polyester moulé renforcé de fibre de verre

BEYLERIAN, NEW YORK, 1970–C. 1975

Donald Chadwick & William Stumpf

Aeron, 1992

*Recycled aluminium
and fibreglass-
reinforced polyester
frame and base with
polyester mesh seat
and back, on castors |
Rahmen aus recycel-
tem Aluminium und
fiberglasverstärktem
Polyester auf Rollen,
Sitzfläche und
Rückenlehne aus
Polyestergeflecht |
Châssis et piètement
en aluminium recyclé
et polyester renforcé
de fibre de verre, siège
et dossier en toile
polyester, roulettes*

HERMAN MILLER
FURNITURE CO.,
ZEELAND,
MICHIGAN, FROM
1994 TO PRESENT

▼ Herman Miller's
developments in
office seating:
Ergon (1970–1976),
Equa (1984),
Aeron (1992)

The "Aeron" radically fulfils ergonomic, functional, anthropometric and environmental considerations and represents state-of-the-art office seating. The low-cost "SoHo" was developed for the small office/home-office market.
Der »Aeron« erfüllt ergonomische, funktionale, anthropometrische und ökologische Anforderungen und steht so für die fortgeschrittensten Standards in der Büromöbelherstellung. Der preiswerte »SoHo« wurde für das kleine Büro oder private Arbeitszimmer entwickelt.
Prenant en compte des considérations ergonomiques, fonctionnelles, anthropométriques et écologiques, le modèle « Aeron » représente le dernier cri en matière de siège de bureau. Moins coûteux, « SoHo » fut mis au point pour le marché des petits bureaux ou du travail à domicile.

Luigi Colani

Zocker (Sitzgerät Colani), 1971–1972

Rotationally moulded polyethylene | Polyethylen, Rotationssinterverfahren | Polyéthylène mis en forme par rotation

TOP SYSTEM
BURKHARD LÜBKE,
GÜTERSLOH,
1973–1982

▼ Luigi Colani
testing the Sitzgerät
Colani, c. 1972

Initially, Colani designed a child's version of this "sitting tool" with its integrated seat and desk. This multifunctional, ergonomically inspired design could either be straddled or used in a conventional sitting position.

Zunächst hatte Colani eine Kinderversion dieses »Sitzwerkzeugs« mit integriertem Sitz und Pult entworfen. Auf diesem auf Multifunktionalität und Ergonomie ausgelegten Modell kann man entweder in konventioneller Haltung oder rittlings wie in einem Sattel sitzen.

Colani produisit d'abord une version pour enfants de ce tabouret à siège et plan de travail intégrés. Modèle ergonomique multifonctionnel, il permettait de s'asseoir à califourchon ou de manière plus conventionnelle.

Joe Colombo

Elda, 1963–1965

Moulded fibreglass frame on metal swivelling mechanism with internal fabric or leather-covered foam upholstery and cushions attached with metal hooks | Sitzschale aus geformtem fiberglasverstärktem Kunststoff, auf einer Drehvorrichtung aus Metall, Innenpolsterung aus Schaumstoff mit Leder- bzw. Stoffbezug, Kissen mit Metallhaken befestigt | Châssis en fibre de verre moulée, système pivotant, rembourrage en mousse recouverte de cuir, coussins fixés par des crochets métalliques

COMFORT, MILAN, FROM C. 1965 TO PRESENT

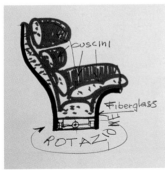

▲ Joe Colombo
Working drawing of Elda armchair, c. 1963

The "Elda" was the first large armchair to utilise a self-supporting fibreglass frame. Its seven sausage-like cushions, rotating base and generous proportions provide a great deal of comfort.

»Elda« war der erste große Sessel mit einem freitragenden Rahmen aus fiberglasverstärktem Kunststoff. Seine sieben wurstähnlichen Polsterkissen, sein Drehfuß und seine großzügigen Proportionen bieten hohen Komfort.

Le modèle « Elda » est le premier grand fauteuil à faire appel à un châssis autoporteur en fibre de verre. Ses sept coussins en forme de boudins, sa base pivotante et ses proportions généreuses assurent un très grand confort.

Joe Colombo

**Model No. 4801,
1963–1964**

*Lacquered moulded
plywood three-part
construction with
rubber stoppers |
Dreiteilige Konstruk-
tion aus geformtem
Schichtholz, lackiert,
Gummipuffer |
Construction en trois
éléments, contre-
plaqué moulé laqué,
pièces de blocage en
caoutchouc*

KARTELL, NOVIGLIO,
MILAN, 1964–1975
(LIMITED EDITION)

▼ Joe Colombo
Model No. 4801,
1963–1964, with nat-
ural finish

KARTELL, NOVIGLIO,
MILAN

Colombo strived for material and structural unity in his
work. The armchair No. 4801 is constructed of only
three interlocking moulded plywood elements that curve
and flow into one another. The fluidity of this chair's
form anticipates Colombo's later designs in plastic.
*Colombo strebte in seinen Arbeiten stets nach der Einheit
von Material und Konstruktion. Der Sessel Nr. 4801 besteht
lediglich aus drei ineinandergreifenden Schichtholzteilen,
die gebogen sind und einander durchdringen. Das Fließende
dieser Sesselform findet sich in Colombos späteren Kunst-
stoffentwürfen erneut.*
Colombo était très attaché à l'unité de structure et de
matériaux. Le fauteuil n° 4801 est constitué de trois éléments entrelacés en contre-plaqué moulé. La fluidité de
la forme de ce siège annonce les futures créations en
plastique du designer.

49

Joe Colombo

*Universale, Model
No. 4860, 1965–1967*

*Injection-moulded
"Cycolac" ABS plastic
(1974 to 1975 PAG
nylon & from 1975
to present polypropy-
lene) | Spritzgußge-
formter »Cycolac«
ABS-Kunststoff,
1974–1975 aus PAG-
Nylon, seit 1975
aus Polypropylen |
Plastique ABS
« Cycolac » moulé
par injection (de 1974
à 1975 nylon PAG,
depuis, polypropylène)*

KARTELL, NOVIGLIO,
MILAN, FROM 1967
TO PRESENT
(RENAMED AS
MODEL NO. 4867
IN 1974)

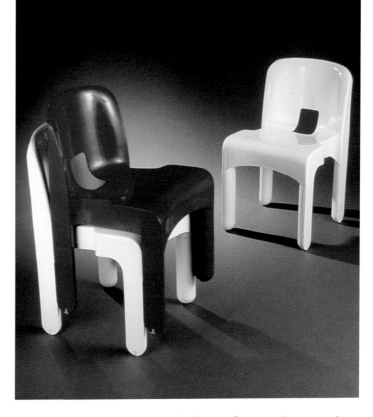

▼ **Joe Colombo**
Working drawing for
Universale chair,
c. 1965

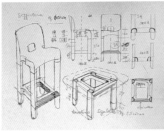

Intended originally for manufacture in aluminium, the
"Universale" stacking chair was produced in ABS from
1967 as the first adult-sized injection-moulded chair. Its
detachable legs were available in two heights.

*Der ab 1967 in ABS-Kunststoff produzierte stapelbare Stuhl
»Universale«, der ursprünglich aus Aluminium hergestellt
werden sollte, war der erste spritzgußgeformte Stuhl für
Erwachsene. Die Beine ließen sich abmontieren und waren
in zwei Höhen lieferbar.*

Conçu au départ pour être fabriqué en aluminium, le modèle empilable
« Universale » fut réalisé en ABS à partir de 1967. C'est la première chaise
pour adultes à avoir été moulée par injection. Ses pieds démontables exis-
taient en deux tailles.

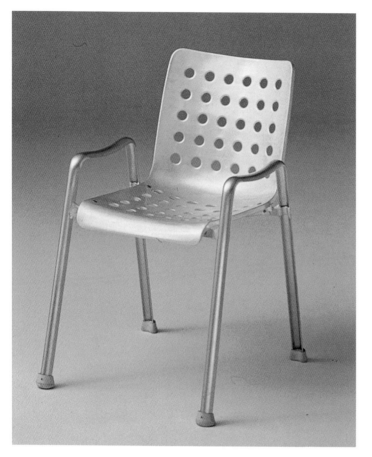

Hans Coray

Landi, 1938

*Bent and pressed
aluminium
construction |
Konstruktion aus
gestanztem und
geformtem
Aluminium |
Aluminium cintré
et estampé*

P. & W. BLATTMANN
METALLWAREN-
FABRIK, WÄDENSWIL,
FROM C. 1939
(REISSUED BY
ZANOTTA, FROM 1971
AS 2070 SPARTANA)

▼ Attributed to Josef
Hoffmann & Oswald
Haerdtl
Armchair, 1929

PROBABLY THONET-
MUNDUS, VIENNA

The "Landi" chair was designed for the grounds of the
1939 "Landesausstellung" exhibition, Zurich. Its perforations reduced weight and allowed water drainage for
outdoor use.

*Der »Landi«-Stuhl wurde für die Züricher Landesausstel-
lung von 1939 entworfen. Die Perforation der Sitzschale hat
zwei Vorteile: Sie reduziert das Gewicht, und das Regen-
wasser kann ablaufen, wenn der Stuhl im Freien benutzt
wird.*

Le fauteuil « Landi » avait été conçu pour les installa-
tions de la « Landesausstellung » de Zurich (1939). Ses
perforations l'allégeaient et permettaient l'écoulement
de l'eau en utilisation extérieure.

▲ **Robin Day**
Polyprop,
c. 1962–1963

S. HILLE & CO.,
LONDON, (LATER TO
BECOME HILLE
INTERNATIONAL),
FROM 1963 TO
PRESENT

▲ **Robin Day**
Upholstered
Polyprop, c. 1963

S. HILLE & CO.,
LONDON, (LATER TO
BECOME HILLE
INTERNATIONAL),
FROM 1963 TO
PRESENT

▲ **Robin Day**
Polo chair,
1975

S. HILLE & CO.,
LONDON, (LATER TO
BECOME HILLE
INTERNATIONAL),
FROM 1975 TO
PRESENT

Inspired by the Eameses' "Plastic Shell" chairs, Day developed the "Polyprop" chair as an even lower cost seating solution. Its single-form seat shell was the first to be injection-moulded in polypropylene – a recently developed inexpensive, durable and lightweight thermoplastic. A single injection moulding tool can produce 4,000 seat shells a week. From 1963 to the present, over 14 million chairs from the "Polyprop" programme have been sold.

Angeregt durch die »Plastic Shell«-Stühle von Charles und Ray Eames, entwickelte Day mit dem »Polyprop«-Stuhl ein noch preiswerteres Sitzmöbel. Die einteilige Sitzschale war die erste aus Polypropylen – einem kurz zuvor entwickelten preiswerten, dauerhaften und leichten Thermoplast – im Spritzgußverfahren hergestellt wurde. Mit einer einzigen Spritzgußmaschine können pro Woche 4000 Sitzschalen gefertigt werden. Seit 1963 wurden mehr als 14 Millionen Stühle dieser Serie verkauft.

Robin Day

Polyprop,
1962–1963

Injection-moulded polypropylene seat shell on enamelled bent tubular steel base | Im Spritzgußverfahren hergestellte Sitzschale aus Polypropylen, Stuhlbeine aus gebogenem Stahlrohr, einbrennlackiert | Coquille en polypropylène moulé par injection, piètement en tube d'acier émaillé cintré

S. HILLE & CO.,
LONDON (LATER
TO BECOME HILLE
INTERNATIONAL),
FROM 1963 TO
PRESENT

▲ **Robin Day**
Series E educational
seating, 1972

S. HILLE & CO.,
LONDON (LATER TO
BECOME HILLE
INTERNATIONAL),
FROM 1972 TO
PRESENT

Inspiré par les sièges à coquille plastique des Eames, Day mit au point ce modèle « Polyprop » encore meilleur marché. La coquille d'une pièce est la première à avoir été réalisée en polypropylène moulé par injection, un plastique bon marché, résistant, léger et récemment découvert. Un seul moule pouvait produire 4 000 coquilles de siège par semaine. Depuis 1963, plus de 14 millions de ces chaises ont été vendues.

Michele De Lucchi

First, 1983

Tubular steel frame with painted wood seat, back and armrests | Gestell aus lackiertem Stahlrohr, Armlehnen, Sitz und Rückenlehne aus lackiertem Holz | Châssis en tube d'acier, siège, dossier et accoudoirs en bois

MEMPHIS, MILAN, FROM 1983 TO PRESENT

▼ Memphis graphics for the First chair, c. 1983

The playful formal vocabulary of the "First" chair symbolises the electronic age and embodies the Post-Modern belief that the communication of meanings and values is the paramount concern of design.

Die spielerische Formensprache des Stuhls »First« spiegelt das Elektronikzeitalter wider und demonstriert die postmoderne Überzeugung, daß die eigentliche Aufgabe von Design in der Kommunikation von Bedeutungen und Werten liegt.

Le vocabulaire formel ludique de la chaise « First » symbolise l'âge de l'électronique et incarne la conviction postmoderne selon laquelle la communication des significations et des valeurs est l'objet essentiel du design.

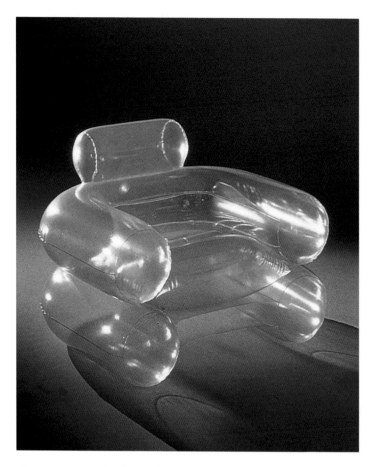

Gionatan De
Pas, Donato
D'Urbino,
Paolo Lomazzi
& Carla Scolari

Blow, 1967

*Radio-frequency
welded PVC
(polyvinylchloride) |
Hochfrequenz-
verschweißtes PVC
(Polyvinylchlorid) |
PVC soudé électro-
niquement (chlorure
de polyvinyle)*

ZANOTTA, MILAN,
1968–1969 &
1988–1992

▼ Working drawing
of Blow chair,
c. 1967

The first mass-produced inflatable chair in Italy, the
"Blow" chair is an icon of 1960s' popular culture.
Its inherent expendability dismissed the traditional
associations of furniture with high cost and permanence.

*»Blow«, der erste aufblasbare Sessel aus Italien, der in
Serie produziert wurde, ist eine Ikone der Popkultur der
6oer Jahre. Dieses Sitzmöbel, auf schnellen Verschleiß
angelegt, verabschiedet sich von der traditionellen
Vorstellung, daß Möbel teuer und haltbar sein müssen.*

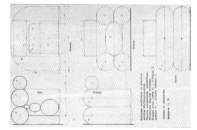

Premier siège gonflable produit en Italie, le fauteuil « Blow » est un icone de
la culture populaire des années 60. Il balayait d'un coup l'idée traditionnelle
selon laquelle un meuble devait être cher et durable.

Gionatan De Pas, Donato D'Urbino & Paolo Lomazzi

Joe, 1970

Leather or stretch fabric-covered moulded polyurethane foam | Geformter Polyurethanschaumstoff, mit Leder oder Stretchgewebe bezogen | Mousse de polyuréthane moulée recouverte de cuir ou de tissu stretch

POLTRONOVA, MONTALE, PISTOIA, FROM 1971 TO PRESENT

Named after the baseball legend Joe DiMaggio, this gigantic glove was inspired by the oversized and out-of-context sculptures of Claes Oldenburg. The form of the "Joe" chair can also be seen as an ironic comment on the proliferation of reissued Bauhaus furniture covered with high-priced glove leather.

Dieser riesenhafte Handschuh, nach dem legendären Baseballspieler Joe DiMaggio benannt, wurde inspiriert durch die überdimensionalen und verfremdeten Skulpturen von Claes Oldenburg. Die Gestaltung des »Joe«-Sessels kann auch als ein ironischer Kommentar zur neuerlichen Konjunktur reedierter Bauhaus-Möbel verstanden werden, die mit teurem Handschuhleder bezogen wurden.

Nommé d'après le joueur de base-ball légendaire Joe DiMaggio, cet énorme gant s'inspire des sculptures géantes hors contexte de Claes Oldenburg. La forme du fauteuil « Joe » peut également être analysée comme un commentaire ironique de la prolifération des rééditions de meubles du Bauhaus, qui étaient recouverts de cuir fin.

Erich Dieckmann

Armchair, c. 1926

*Stained beech frame
with upholstered seat
and back | Rahmen
aus Buche, gebeizt,
Sitzfläche und
Rückenlehne
gepolstert | Châssis en
hêtre teinté, siège et
dossier rembourrés*

FURNITURE WORK-
SHOP, STAATLICHE
BAUHOCHSCHULE,
WEIMAR

While training at the Bauhaus in Weimar, Dieckmann designed his cherry and cane chair synthesising craft and functionalism. Later, he headed the furniture and interior design department at the Staatliche Bauhochschule.

Während seiner Ausbildung am Weimarer Bauhaus entwarf Dieckmann seinen Armlehnstuhl aus Kirschholz und Rohrgeflecht, der Handwerk und Funktionalismus in Einklang bringt. Er wurde später zum Leiter des Fachbereichs Möbel und Innenarchitektur an der Staatlichen Bauhochschule berufen.

C'est pendant ses études au Bauhaus de Weimar que Dieckmann conçoit ses sièges en cerisier et cannage qui associent artisanat et fonctionnalisme. Plus tard, il dirigera le département de mobilier et d'architecture intérieure de la Staatliche Bauhochschule.

▼ **Erich Dieckmann**
Armchair, 1930–1931

FURNITURE WORK-
SHOP, KUNST-
GEWERBESCHULE
BURG GIEBICHEN-
STEIN, HALLE

Charles & Ray Eames

LCW (Lounge Chair Wood), 1945

Bent birch-faced plywood frame attached to moulded birch-faced plywood seat and back with rubber shock-mounts | Rahmen, Sitzfläche und Rückenlehne aus geformtem Schichtholz mit Birkenfurnier, Gummipuffer zwischen Rahmen und Sitzfläche| Châssis en contreplaqué cintré, placage de bouleau, siège et dossier plaqués bouleau, amortisseurs de suspension en caoutchouc

EVANS PRODUCTS
COMPANY, VENICE,
CALIFORNIA,
1946–1949 AND
HERMAN MILLER
FURNITURE CO.,
ZEELAND,
MICHIGAN,
1949–1958

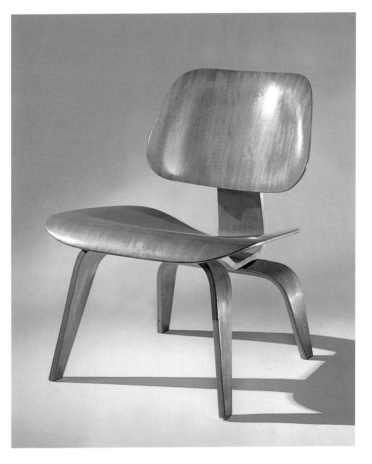

◄◄ Charles &
Ray Eames
Child's chair, 1945

EVANS PRODUCTS
COMPANY, VENICE,
CALIFORNIA

◄ Charles &
Ray Eames
Prototype lounge
chair, 1946

Charles &
Ray Eames

*LCM (Lounge Chair
Metal), 1945–1946*

*Chrome-plated
tubular steel frame
attached to "Slunk-
skin" (animal hide) –
covered moulded ply-
wood seat and back
with rubber shock-
mounts | Rahmen aus
gebogenem Stahlrohr,
verchromt, Sitzfläche
und Rückenlehne aus
geformtem Schicht-
holz mit Pelzbespan-
nung, Gummipuffer
zwischen Rahmen
und Sitzfläche |
Châssis en tube
d'acier chromé, siège
et dossier en contre-
plaqué moulé
recouvert de peau,
amortisseurs en
caoutchouc*

EVANS PRODUCTS
COMPANY, VENICE,
CALIFORNIA
1946–1949 AND
HERMAN MILLER
FURNITURE CO., ZEE-
LAND, MICHIGAN,
FROM 1949 (THIS
VERSION PRODUCED
TO 1953)

The Eameses' landmark plywood chairs were mainly the result of their
wartime research into the development of an inexpensive and efficient
method of moulding plywood into compound forms.

*Die Schichtholzstühle von Ray und Charles Eames, Meilensteine im modernen
Möbelbau, sind das Ergebnis eines Forschungsprogramms, an dem die beiden
während des Krieges arbeiteten. Es ging darum, eine preiswerte und effektive
Methode zu entwickeln, mit der sich Schichtholz in dreidimensionale Formen
pressen ließ.*

Cette célèbre chaise en contre-plaqué réalisée par les Eames est principalement issue des recherches qu'ils menèrent pendant la guerre pour mettre
au point une méthode efficace et économique de moulage du contre-plaqué.

**Charles &
Ray Eames**

La Chaise, 1948

Fibreglass seat shell
on a wood and steel
rod base | Sitzschale
aus Fiberglas, Unter-
gestell aus Stahl-
stäben auf Holz-
sockel | Coquille de
siège en fibre de verre,
piètement en acier et
en bois

VITRA, BASLE, FROM
1990 TO PRESENT

Submitted by the Eameses for the Museum of Modern Art's "International
Competition for Low-Cost Furniture Design" in 1948, this highly abstract
organic design proved too expensive to manufacture.

*Dieser auf das notwendigste reduzierte organische Stuhlentwurf wurde 1948 von
den Eames zu dem »International Competition for Low-Cost Furniture Design«
des Museum of Modern Art eingereicht. Als »La Chaise« dann in Produktion
gehen sollte, erwies sich diese zunächst als zu teuer.*

Proposé par les Eames au concours « International Competition for Low-
Cost Furniture Design », organisé par le Museum of Modern Art en 1948,
ce modèle organique abstrait se révéla trop coûteux à fabriquer.

▶ **Charles & Ray Eames**
Stacking chairs, 1955

HERMAN MILLER FURNITURE CO., ZEELAND,
MICHIGAN, FROM 1955 TO PRESENT

Charles &
Ray Eames

*DAR (Dining
Armchair Rod),
1948–1950*

Moulded fibreglass-
reinforced polyester
seat shell connected
to an "Eiffel Tower"
metal rod base with
rubber shock mounts |
Sitzschale aus ge-
formtem, fiberglasver-
stärktem Polyester,
Untergestell »Eiffel
Turm« aus Stahl-
stäben, Gummi-
puffer | Coquille en
poly-ester moulé
renforcé de fibre de
verre, piètement en
tiges de métal « Tour
Eiffel », montage sur
amortisseurs en
caoutchouc

ZENITH PLASTICS,
GARDENA, CALIFOR-
NIA, 1950–C. 1953
AND HERMAN
MILLER FURNITURE
CO., ZEELAND,
MICHIGAN
C. 1953–C. 1972

The culmination of earlier experiments in moulded
plywood, the revolutionary Plastic Shell Group of chairs
was amongst the very first unlined plastic seat furniture
to be truly mass-produced.

*Der Höhepunkt früherer Experimente mit geformtem
Schichtholz waren die Schalensitze der revolutionären
»Plastic Shell Group«, die zu den allerersten unge-
polsterten Sitzmöbeln gehörten, die tatsächlich in
Serienproduktion gingen.*

Aboutissement d'expériences antérieures dans le moulage du contre-plaqué, cette série révolutionnaire de fauteuils à coque plastique figure parmi les premiers sièges
en plastique non armé réellement fabriqués en série.

Charles & Ray Eames

DKW-2 (Dining Bikini Wood), 1951

Bent and welded steel rod seat shell with leather "Harlequin" upholstery on birch and metal rod base | Sitzschale aus ver-schweißtem Draht-geflecht, Lederpolste-rung »Harlekin«, Stuhlbeine aus Birke mit Verstrebungen aus Stahlstäben | Coquille en tige de métal cintrée et sou-dée, rembourrage « Harlequin » en cuir, piètement en bouleau et tiges de métal

BANNER METALS, COMPTON, FOR HER-MAN MILLER FURNI-TURE CO., ZEELAND, MICHIGAN, 1951–1967

▼ PKW, DKW, DKR, LKX, RKR & LKR versions, Herman Miller catalogue, 1952

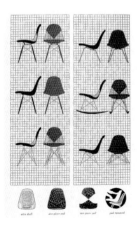

The Eameses first considered a series of wire-mesh chairs when they were working on their "Plastic Shell Group". Utilising the same bases, the wire-mesh seat sections echoed the form of the plastic shells.
Während ihrer Arbeit an der »Plastic Shell Group« kam den Eames die Idee, die Sitzschalen dieser Stuhlserie aus Drahtgeflecht herzustellen. Die Formgebung der Sitz-schalen blieb dabei gleich.
Les Eames commencèrent à s'intéresser à une série de sièges en fil de fer alors qu'ils travaillaient sur leur projet « Plastic Shell Group ». Sur les mêmes bases, leurs sièges en fil de fer rappelaient la forme des co-quilles de plastique.

Based on a prototype exhibited at the Museum of Modern Art's "Organic Design in Home Furnishings" competition in 1940, the No. 670 was the Eameses' most constructionally complex chair and their first design for the luxury end of the market.

Der Sessel Nr. 670 basiert auf einem Prototyp, der 1940 für den vom Museum of Modern Art ausgeschriebenen Wettbewerb »Organic Design in Home Furnishings« entworfen wurde. Konstruktionstechnisch ist dieser Sessel der aufwendigste Entwurf der Eames' und außerdem ihr erster für das obere Marktsegment.

Issu d'un prototype présenté au concours « Organic Design in Home Furnishings » au Museum of Modern Art en 1940, le n° 670 est le siège le plus complexe jamais réalisé par les Eames et leur premier projet pour le marché haut de gamme.

Charles & Ray Eames

Model No. 670 &
Model No. 671, 1956

Rosewood-faced moulded plywood seat shells with leather-covered cushions, cast aluminium base | Sitzschalen aus geformtem Schichtholz, Palisanderfurnier, lederbezogene Kissen, Fuß aus Aluminiumformguß | Coquilles en contre-plaqué moulé, placage de bois de rose, coussins en cuir, piètement en aluminium

HERMAN MILLER FURNITURE CO., ZEELAND, MICHIGAN, FROM 1956 TO PRESENT

Charles &
Ray Eames

Aluminium Group,
Model No. EA 105,
1958

Aluminium frame
with leather- or vinyl-
upholstered sling
seat | Rahmen und
Untergestell aus
Aluminium,
gepolsterte Sitz-
bespannung mit
Leder- bzw. Vinyl-
bezug | Châssis en
aluminium, siège
tendu de cuir ou de
vinyle rembourré

HERMAN MILLER
FURNITURE CO.,
ZEELAND, MICHIGAN
& VITRA AG, BASLE,
FROM 1958 TO
PRESENT

▼ Charles &
Ray Eames
Aluminium Group
lounge chair with
ottoman, 1958

HERMAN MILLER
FURNITURE CO., ZEE-
LAND, MICHIGAN,
FROM 1958 TO

The "Aluminium Group" was originally designed for indoor and outdoor domestic use, and during its development was often referred to as the "Leisure Group".
Ironically, it is now used almost exclusively in offices.
Die Sitzmöbel der »Aluminium Group« wurden ursprüng-
lich für die private Nutzung im Innen- und Außenbereich
entworfen und daher auch »Leisure Group« (Freizeit) ge-
nannt. Heute werden diese Möbel meist in Büros verwendet.
L' « Aluminium Group » fut conçu à l'origine aussi bien
pour l'intérieur que l'extérieur de la maison. Au
cours de sa mise au point, il portait le nom de « Leisure
Group» (série Loisirs). Il est aujourd'hui surtout utilisé
dans les bureaux.

Model No. SE18 ,
1952

*Beech frame with
beech-faced moulded
plywood seat and
back with metal
fittings | Rahmen aus
Buche, Sitzfläche und
Rückenlehne aus
formgebogenem
Schichtholz, mit
Birkenfurnier, Metall-
beschläge | Châssis en
hêtre, siège et dossier
en contre-plaqué
moulé, placage de
hêtre, garnitures en
métal*

WILDE & SPIETH,
ESSLINGEN, FROM
C. 1952

▼ **Egon Eiermann**
Model No. SE42,
1949
WILDE & SPIETH,
ESSLINGEN,
1950–1955

Known primarily as an architect, Eiermann was also a
skilled furniture designer. The SE18 is an inexpensive
and highly functional folding design which was exhibited at the Milan X Triennale in 1954.
*Eiermann hat sich vor allem als Architekt einen Namen ge-
macht, doch er war ein ebenso erfahrener Möbeldesigner.
Der SE18 ist ein preiswerter und sehr funktionaler Klappstuhl, der 1954 auf der X. Mailänder Triennale gezeigt wurde.*
Essentiellement connu pour ses réalisations en architecture, Eiermann était également un bon designer de mobilier. Le SE18 est un modèle pliant bon marché et très
fonctionnel qui fut exposé à la Xᵉ Triennale de Milan en
1954.

Jorge Ferrari-Hardoy, Juan Kurchan & Antonio Bonet

Butterfly, Model No. 198, 1938

Enamelled tubular steel frame with leather sling seat | Gestell aus Stahlrohr, lackiert, Sitzbespannung aus Leder | Châssis en tube d'acier peint, siège en cuir

KNOLL ASSOCIATES, NEW YORK, C. 1947–C. 1975 (REISSUED BY STÖHR IMPORT-EXPORT)

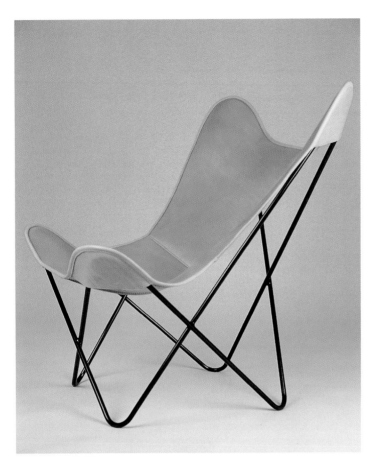

▼ Unlicensed copy of the Butterfly chair, 1950s

Originally manufactured by Artek-Pascoe, production was taken over by Knoll after 1945. Later, Knoll lost a copyright infringement lawsuit which allowed the Butterfly to be copied by a plethora of firms.

Dieser Stuhl wurde zunächst von Artek-Pascoe, nach 1945 dann von Knoll produziert. Später verlor Knoll einen Rechtsstreit um das Urheberrecht, so daß der Butterfly schließlich von sehr vielen Firmen hergestellt und vertrieben werden konnte.

Réalisée à l'origine par Artek-Pascoe, la production de ce siège fut reprise par Knoll après 1945. Plus tard, Knoll perdit un procès sur ses droits de reproduction, ce qui permit à d'innombrables fabricants de copier ce modèle.

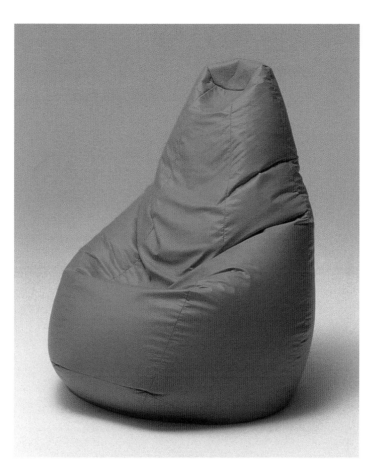

Piero Gatti,
Cesare Paolini
& Franco
Teodoro

Sacco, 1968

*Vinyl bag containing
semi-expanded
polystyrene pellets |
Sack aus Kunstleder,
Füllung aus Poly-
styrol-Kugeln | Sac
de vinyle rempli de
billes de polystyrène
semi-expansé*

ZANOTTA, MILAN,
FROM 1968 TO
PRESENT

▼ Working drawing
of Sacco's cover,
c. 1968

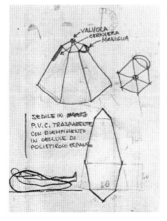

The "Sacco" beanbag seat adapts to whatever position
the user assumes. The designers initially proposed a
fluid-filled envelope, but excessive weight eventually led
to the inspired choice of polystyrene beads.

*Das Sackmöbel »Sacco« paßt seine Form der Position des
Nutzers an. Die Designer hatten ursprünglich eine Füllung
mit Flüssigkeit vorgeschlagen; das aber hätte zu übermäßi-
gem Gewicht geführt, und so kam man schließlich auf den
genialen Einfall, den Sitzsack mit Polystyrol-Kugeln zu füllen.*

Le fauteuil-sac « Sacco » s'adapte à toutes les positions
de l'utilisateur. Les designers avaient pensé initialement
le remplir de liquide mais le poids excessif de cette solution lui fit préférer les billes de polystyrène.

Antonio Gaudí y Cornet

Armchair for the Casa Calvet,
c. 1898–1900

Carved oak construction | Rahmen aus Eiche, geschnitzt | Chêne sculpté

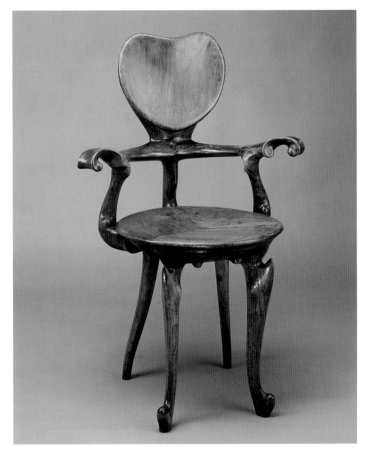

▼ **Antonio Gaudí y Cornet**
Chair for the Casa Calvet, c. 1898–1900

▲ **Antonio Gaudí y Cornet**
Casa Battló, Barcelona, 1906

Designed for a specific site, this chair was part of a greater decorative scheme. Gaudí's interpretation of Art Nouveau was more robust and stylistically abstract than that of his French and Belgian counterparts.
Gaudí entwarf diesen Stuhl für ein bestimmtes Interieur als Element eines umfassenden dekorativen Programms. Gaudís Interpretation des Jugendstils war schnörkelloser und strenger als die der Franzosen und Belgier.
Conçu pour un intérieur précis, ce siège faisait partie d'un projet décoratif global et ambitieux. L'interprétation gaudienne du style Art nouveau est plus vigoureuse et stylistiquement plus abstraite que celle de ses confrères français et belges.

Frank O. Gehry

Wiggle, 1972

*Laminated cardboard
construction |
Konstruktion aus
verleimtem
Wellkarton | Carton
contrecollé*

JACK BROGAN, USA
1972–1973
(REISSUED BY VITRA,
FROM 1992 AS
WIGGLE SIDE CHAIR)

The "Easy Edges" series comprised fourteen pieces of cardboard furniture.
Initially conceived as low-cost furniture, these designs were so immediately
successful, that Gehry withdrew them from production after only three
months, fearing that his ascendancy as a popular furniture designer would
distract him from realising his potential as an architect.

*Zur Serie »Easy Edges« gehörten vierzehn Möbel aus Wellkarton. Konzipiert als
Billigmöbel, waren sie sofort so erfolgreich, daß Gehry sie nach nur drei Monaten
aus der Produktion zurückzog. Er fürchtete, daß seine Karriere als populärer
Möbeldesigner ihn daran hindern würde, sich als Architekt zu verwirklichen.*

La série « Easy Edges » comprenait quatorze éléments en carton. Conçus
au départ comme des meubles bon marché, leur succès immédiat poussa
Gehry à arrêter leur production au bout de trois mois, tant il craignait que
cette réussite ne l'empêche de poursuivre son œuvre d'architecte.

Edward William Godwin

Chair, c. 1883

Birch construction with woven cane seat | Rahmen aus Birke, Sitz aus Rohrgeflecht | Bouleau, siège canné

PROBABLY WILLIAM WATT, ARTISTIC FURNITURE WAREHOUSE, LONDON

▼ Art furniture designed by E. W. Godwin, illustrated in William Watt's catalogue, 1877

The most abstract of all Godwin's designs, the form of this chair makes reference to Egyptian furniture. Its simplified, graceful lines lend it a remarkable modernity.
Dieser wohl radikalste Stuhlentwurf Godwins spielt auf ägyptische Möbel an. Die einfachen und anmutigen Konturen geben dem Stuhl ein erstaunlich modernes Flair.
Cette chaise, la plus abstraite de toutes les créations de Godwin, évoque le mobilier égyptien. Ses lignes épurées et gracieuses témoignent d'une remarquable modernité.

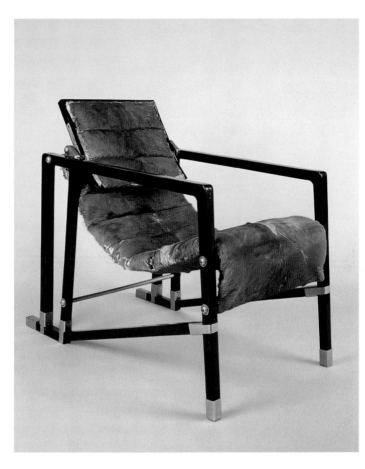

Eileen Gray

Transat, 1925–1926

*Lacquered wood
frame, upholstered
sling seat and
chromed metal
fittings | Rahmen aus
Holz, eingehängtes
Sitzpolster aus Leder,
Metallbeschläge,
verchromt| Châssis en
bois laqué noir, siège
suspendu rembourré ,
garnitures en metal
chromé*

JEAN DÉSERT, PARIS,
FROM C. 1926
(REISSUED BY ECART,
FROM 1978)

▼ **Eileen Gray**
Drawing for Transat,
c. 1925

Gray's designs rejected historicism and conveyed a strong
sense of modernity. They can be seen as concrete expres-
sions of her belief that the challenges of the machine age
necessitated new ways of thinking.

*Grays Entwürfe stehen für Modernität. Historische Formen
lehnte sie ab. Man kann diese Entwürfe als konkrete Um-
setzung ihrer Überzeugung betrachten, daß den Heraus-
forderungen des Maschinenzeitalters nur mit neuen Denk-
weisen zu begegnen war.*

Les modèles de Gray rejettent l'historicisme au profit
d'un sens appuyé de la modernité. Ils expriment sa
conviction selon laquelle l'âge de la machine posait de
nouveaux défis aux modes de pensée.

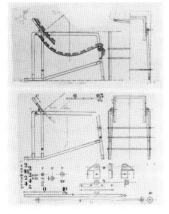

Gruppo Strum

Pratone, 1966–1970

*Self-skinning moulded
polyurethane foam |
Geformter Polyurethan-
Integralschaumstoff |
Mousse de poly-
uréthane moulée*

GUFRAM,
BALANGERO, TURIN,
FROM 1971 TO
PRESENT

▼ **Paolo Ruffi**
La Cova (The Nest),
1973

POLTRONOVA,
MONTALE, PISTOIA,
FROM 1973

In 1963, Gruppo Strum was founded in Turin and its
radical ambition was the creation of "instrumental
architecture", hence its title. "Pratone" is a contesting
design that invites different modes of interaction.
*Gruppo Strum wurde 1963 in Turin gegründet; das mit
radikalem Ehrgeiz verfolgte Ziel der Gruppe war die
Schaffung einer »instrumentellen Architektur«, daher der
Name. »Pratone« ist ein provozierender Entwurf, der zu
ganz verschiedenen Möglichkeiten der Benutzung einlädt.*
En 1963, se crée à Turin le Gruppo Strum dont l'ambition était la création « d'une architecture instrumen-
tale ». « Pratone » est un projet contestataire qui invite
à différents modes d'échanges.

Hector
Guimard

Chair, c. 1900

*Carved pear frame
with tooled leather-
upholstered seat
and back | Rahmen
aus Birnenholz,
geschnitzt, mit
geprägtem Leder
bezogenes Sitzpolster |
Poirier sculpté, siège
et dossier en cuir
repoussé*

▼ **Hector Guimard**
Chair for the "Salle
Humbert de
Romans", c. 1901

The popularity of Guimard's Art Nouveau designs was
such that the term "Style Guimard" was coined. His
swirling organicism was perhaps best expressed in his
cast iron designs for the entrances to the Paris Métro.
*Guimards Jugendstilformen wurden so populär, daß
man direkt von einem »Stil Guimard« sprach. Seine
verschlungene organische Formgebung kam in den gußeisernen Eingängen der Pariser Metro am besten zur
Geltung.*
La popularité des modèles Art nouveau de Guimard fut
telle que naquit l'expression « style Guimard ». Son caractère organique s'exprime avec un bonheur particulier
dans les entrées du métro parisien.

René Herbst

Sandows chair,
1928–1929

Chromed tubular
steel frame with
elasticated straps |
Rahmen aus
Stahlrohr, verchromt,
Gummi-Spanngurte |
Châssis en tube
d'acier chromé,
sandows

ÉTABLISSEMENTS
RENÉ HERBST, PARIS,
FROM C. 1930
(REISSUED BY
FORMES NOUVELLES)

▼ **René Herbst**
Chairs, c. 1930

ÉTABLISSEMENTS
RENÉ HERBST, PARIS

These designs form part of a series of chairs that were executed between 1928 and 1929. Herbst's use of elasticated straps, or "sandows", is a very early example of incorporating "objets trouvés" into the design of chairs. The structural simplicity and transparency of form give these designs a skeletal minimalism.

Diese Entwürfe gehören zu einer Serie von Sitzmöbeln, die zwischen 1928 und 1929 entstanden sind. Herbst hat Gummi-Spanngurte (»sandows«) benutzt – ein sehr frühes Beispiel für den Einsatz von »objets trouvés« im Stuhldesign. Die konstruktive Einfachheit und Transparenz verleihen diesen Stühlen eine minimalistische Aura.

René Herbst

Fauteuil de repos,
1928–1929

Enamelled tubular
steel frame with
elasticated straps |
Rahmen aus
Stahlrohr, schwarz
lackiert, Gummi-
Spanngurte | Châssis
en tube d'acier
émaillé, sandows

ÉTABLISSEMENTS
RENÉ HERBST, PARIS,
FROM C. 1930
(REISSUED BY
FORMES NOUVELLES)

▼ René Herbst
Interior, c. 1932

Ces modèles font partie d'une série de sièges exécutés entre 1928 et 1929. L'utilisation de sandows est un des premiers exemples d'incorporation d'objets trouvés dans la conception de sièges. La simplicité structurelle et la transparence de la forme confèrent à ces modèles un minimalisme extrême.

Josef Hoffmann

Armchair, Model No. 728/F, 1905–1906

Stained, bent solid beech frame with moulded laminated wood seat and turned beech elements | Rahmen aus gebogener Buche, Sitzfläche aus geformtem Schichtholz, gedrechselte Verbindungselemente | Châssis en hêtre massif cintré teinté, siège en bois contre-plaqué cintré et éléments en hêtre tourné

JACOB & JOSEF
KOHN, VIENNA

▼ Jacob & Josef Kohn, sales catalogue, 1916, Suite Model No. 728

▶ **Josef Hoffmann**
Bar room of the Cabaret Fledermaus, Vienna, 1907

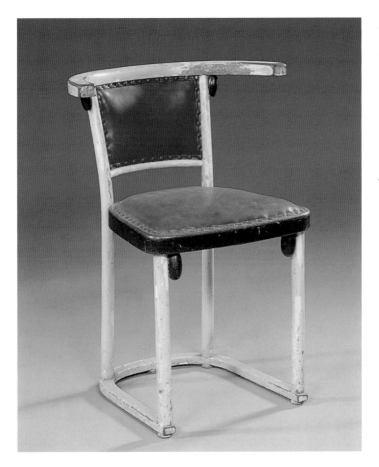

Josef Hoffmann

*Variation of the
Cabaret Fledermaus
chair, 1905–1906*

Stained, bent solid
beech frame with
moulded laminated
wood seat and turned
beech elements | *Rahmen aus geboge-
ner Buche, schwarz-
weiß lackiert, Sitz-
fläche und Rücken-
lehne gepolstert | Châssis en hêtre
massif cintré, siège
en bois contre-plaqué
moulé et éléments
en hêtre tourné*

GEBRÜDER THONET,
VIENNA

"It [the Cabaret Fledermaus] is wonderful – the proportions, the light atmos-
phere, cheerful flowing lines, elegant light fixtures, comfortable chairs of
new shape and, finally, the whole tasteful ensemble. Genuine Hoffmann."
Ludwig Hevesi, 1907 (L. Hevesi, "Kabarett Fledermaus" in: *Altkunst-
Neukunst, Vienna, 1894–1908*, p. 243)
»*Es [das Kabarett Fledermaus] ist wunderbar – die Proportionen, die helle Atmo-
sphäre, die fröhlich fließenden Linien, die eleganten Leuchten, die bequemen
Stühle mit ihren neuen Formen und, schließlich, das ganze geschmackvolle
Ensemble. Echter Hoffmann.*« Ludwig Hevesi, 1907
« Il [le modèle Cabaret Fledermaus] est superbe : les proportions, le senti-
ment de légèreté, les lignes allègrement fluides, les détails légers et élé-
gants, l'ensemble plein de goût. Du pur Hoffmann. » Ludwig Hevesi, 1907

Josef Hoffmann

Chair for the dining room of the Purkersdorf Sanatorium, Model No. 322, c. 1904

Stained, bent solid wood and laminated wood frame with leather-upholstered seat | Rahmen aus massiver und laminierter Buche, gebeizt, Sitzfläche mit Lederpolster | Châssis en bois massif et en contre-plaqué cintrés teintés, siège en cuir rembourré

JACOB & JOSEF KOHN, VIENNA, FROM C. 1904

▶ **Josef Hoffmann**
Chair, Model No. 371, c. 1906

JACOB & JOSEF KOHN, VIENNA

▶▶ **Josef Hoffmann**
Dining room of the Purkersdorf Sanatorium, c. 1906

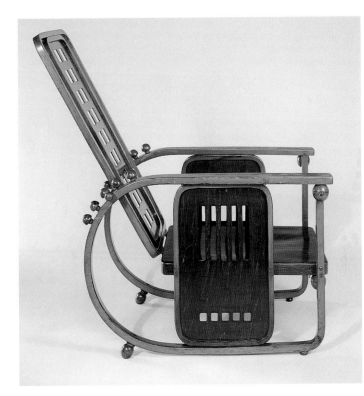

Josef Hoffmann

Sitzmaschine, Model No. 670, c. 1908

Stained, laminated wood, bent solid beech and turned wood frame with brass fittings | Rahmen aus Buche und Schichtholz, teilweise gedrechselt, gebeizt, Messingbeschläge | Châssis en bois contre-plaqué teinté, hêtre massif cintré, éléments tournés et garnitures en laiton

JACOB & JOSEF KOHN, VIENNA

▼ Josef Hoffmann
Hall interior of a small country house, Jacob & Josef Kohn display at the "Wiener Kunstschau", Vienna, 1908

Although originally sold with seat and back cushions, the "Sitzmaschine" can be regarded as having predicted later Rietveld designs because of its strict geometric vocabulary of form.

Die »Sitzmaschine« wurde ursprünglich mit Sitz- und Rückenkissen vertrieben, aber selbst gepolstert nimmt sie mit ihrer streng geometrischen Formensprache spätere Schöpfungen Rietvelds vorweg.

Vendue à l'origine avec des coussins pour le siège et le dossier, cette « Sitzmaschine » aux formes strictement géométriques peut être considérée comme l'anticipation de certaines réalisations de Rietveld.

Arne Jacobsen

Ant, Model No. 3100, 1951–1952

*Teak-faced plywood seat connected to tubular steel base, rubber cap feet |
Sitzschale aus geformtem Schichtholz mit Teakfurnier, Stuhlbeine aus Stahlrohr, Gummikappen |
Siège en contre-plaqué, placage de teck, piètement en tube d'acier, patins en caoutchouc*

FRITZ HANSEN, ALLERØD, FROM 1952 TO PRESENT

▼ Fritz Hansen photograph of Ant chairs

None of his earlier moulded plywood chairs were as visually resolved nor as strong in character as Jacobsen's highly successful "Ant" chair.

Keiner seiner schon früher produzierten Stühle aus geformtem Schichtholz wirkt optisch so gelungen wie Jacobsens äußerst erfolgreicher »Ant«(Ameisen)-Stuhl.

Bien que d'autres chaises aient déjà été réalisées auparavant en contre-plaqué, aucune n'était aussi réussie et de caractère aussi affirmé que le modèle « Ant » (Fourmi) de Jacobsen qui allait connaître un très grand succès.

Arne Jacobsen

Series 7, Model No. 3107, 1955

Teak-faced moulded plywood seat connected to chromed bent tubular steel base with rubber cap feet | Sitzschale aus geformtem Schichtholz mit Teakholzfurnier, Stuhlbeine aus Stahlrohr, verchromt, mit Gummikappen | Siège en contre-plaqué moulé, placage de teck, piètement en tube cintré chromé, patins en caoutchouc

FRITZ HANSEN, ALLERØD, FROM C. 1955 TO PRESENT

◀Fritz Hansen promotional photograph of series 7 chairs

Arne Jacobsen

**Egg, Model No. 3316,
1957–1958**

*Fabric-covered, foam-
upholstered moulded
fibreglass seat shell
on a swivelling cast
aluminium base with
loose seat cushion |
Sitzschale aus ge-
formtem, fiberglasver-
stärktem Kunststoff
mit Schaumstoff-
polsterung und Stoff-
bezug, loses Sitz-
kissen, drehbares
Untergestell aus
Aluminiumguß |
Coquille en fibre de
verre moulée rem-
bourrée de mousse
et recouverte de tissu,
piètement pivotant,
en fonte d'alu-
minium, coussin
de siège amovible*

FRITZ HANSEN,
ALLERØD, FROM 1958
TO PRESENT

▼ Egg chairs in Fritz
Hansen showroom,
c. 1960

Designed originally for the Royal SAS Hotel in Copen-
hagen, these highly sculptural chairs were the result of
Jacobsen's search for lightweight, fluid seating forms
which required a minimum of padding for comfort.
*Diese betont skulpturalen Sessel, ursprünglich für das
Royal SAS Hotel in Kopenhagen entworfen, sind das
Resultat von Jacobsens Suche nach leichten, fließenden
Formen für Sitzmöbel, die auch mit einem Minimum
an Polsterung Bequemlichkeit bieten.*
Conçus à l'origine pour le Royal SAS Hotel de Copenhague, ces fauteuils
sculpturaux résultaient des recherches de Jacobsen dans le domaine des
formes fluides et légères qui ne nécessitaient qu'un minimum de rembour-
rage pour être très confortables.

Arne Jacobsen

Swan, Model No. 3320, 1957–1958

Fabric-covered, foam-upholstered moulded fibreglass seat shell on a swivelling cast aluminium base | Sitz-schale aus geform-tem, fiberglasverstärk-tem Kunststoff mit Schaumstoffpolste-rung und Stoffbezug, loses Sitzkissen, dreh-bares Untergestell aus Aluminiumguß, mit Kippvorrichtung | Coquille en fibre de verre moulée rem-bourrée de mousse et recouverte de tissu, piètement pivotant en fonte d'alu-minium, coussin de siège amovible

FRITZ HANSEN,
ALLERØD, FROM 1958
TO PRESENT

▲ Fritz Hansen photograph showing interior with Swan chairs, c. 1960

▲ **Arne Jacobsen**
Swan sofa, 1957–1958

FRITZ HANSEN, ALLERØD

Finn Juhl

Chieftain, 1949

Rosewood frame with leather-covered upholstered seat and back | Rahmen aus Palisander, Sitzfläche und Rückenlehne mit Lederpolsterung | Châssis en bois de rose massif, siège et dossier en cuir rembourré

NIELS VODDER,
COPENHAGEN,
FROM 1949
(REISSUED BY NIELS
ROTH ANDERSEN)

Most of the 78 "Chieftain" chairs originally produced by the master crafts-man Niels Vodder were purchased for Danish embassies. A very masculine chair, its title, which alludes to King Frederik, was coined by Juhl at a Furniture Guild exhibition which was opened by the monarch. The NV-45 is, perhaps, his most representative design with its graceful curves and crisp lines.
Die meisten der 78 »Chieftain«-Sessel, ursprünglich vom Schreinermeister Niels Vodder produziert, wurden für dänische Botschaften aufgekauft. Der Name des sehr maskulin wirkenden Stuhls spielt auf den dänischen König Frederik IX. an, der die Ausstellung der Möbelinnung eröffnete, auf der der Stuhl präsentiert wurde. Mit dem NV-45 schuf Juhls seinen vielleicht repräsentativsten Entwurf, der durch seine eleganten Schwünge und klare Linienführung überzeugt.

Finn Juhl

Model No. NV-45, 1945

Mahogony frame with textile-covered upholstered seating section | Rahmen aus Mahagoni, Sitzfläche und Rückenlehne gepolstert und mit Stoffbezug | Châssis en bois d'acajou, siège en tissu rembourré

NIELS VODDER, COPENHAGEN, FROM 1945 (REISSUED BY NIELS ROTH ANDERSEN)

▼ Finn Juhl
Model No. NV-48, 1948

NIELS VODDER, COPENHAGEN (REISSUED BY NIELS ROTH ANDERSEN)

La plupart de ces fauteuils « Chieftain », réalisés à l'origine par le maître-artisan Niels Vodder, furent acquis pour des ambassades danoises. Le nom de ce fauteuil très masculin, qui fait allusion au roi Frédéric IX, fut trouvé par Juhl lors d'une exposition de la Guilde du meuble inaugurée par le monarque. Le modèle NV-45, avec ses courbes gracieuses et ses lignes tendues, est l'œuvre la plus caractéristique du style de ce designer.

Toshiyuki Kita

Wink, 1976–1980

Steel frame, textile-
covered polyurethane
foam | Rahmen aus
Stahl, Polsterung aus
Polyurethanschaum-
stoff | Châssis en
acier, mousse de
polyuréthane

CASSINA, MEDA,
MILAN, FROM 1980
TO PRESENT

The articulated frame of the "Wink" took four years to develop and allows
the design to be configured in a variety of comfortable positions. It was
launched at the 1981 Milan Furniture Fair to great acclaim.
*Die Entwicklung des verstellbaren Rahmens des »Wink«-Sessels nahm vier Jahre
in Anspruch, doch nun läßt sich das Modell in eine Vielzahl bequemer Positionen
bringen. Zur Mailänder Möbelmesse von 1981 wurde »Wink« unter großem
Beifall auf den Markt gebracht.*
Le châssis articulé du « Wink » a nécessité quatre années de recherches. Il
permet une multiplicité de positions confortables. Son lancement à la Foire
du meuble de Milan en 1981 fut largement salué.

Both the "Deck" chair and "Safari" chair are reinterpretations of existing types. Klint's belief in the "rightness" of forms that have evolved over a period of time was in complete opposition to the Modern Movement's distaste of historicism. The idea of evolution rather than revolution in design is a more humanist approach and is often demonstrated in Scandinavian design.

Sowohl der »Deck«- als auch der »Safari«-Stuhl stellen Neuinterpretationen bereits existenter Stuhltypen dar. Klint war überzeugt von der »Angemessenheit« solcher Formen, die sich über längere Zeit entwickelt haben, und stand damit in direkter Opposition zur Bewegung der Moderne und ihrer Abneigung gegen jeglichen Historismus.
Daß evolutionäre Entwicklungen in der Formgebung humaner sind als revo- lutionäre Brüche, wird vom skandinavischen Design immer wieder vorgeführt.

Kaare Klint

Deck, 1933

Solid teak construction with retractable footrest | Rahmen aus mas- sivem Teakholz, mit ausziehbarer Fußstütze | Teck massif, repose-pied rétractable

RUD RASMUSSENS SNEDKERIER, COPENHAGEN, FROM C. 1933 TO PRESENT

◀ **Knud Friis & Elmar Moltke Nielsen**
Interior of a house in Denmark, 1958

Kaare Klint

Safari, 1933

*Collapsible ash frame
with leather straps,
canvas seat and back
coverings | Rahmen
aus Esche, zerlegbar,
Sitzfläche und
Rückenlehne aus
Segeltuch, Armlehnen
und Verspannung aus
Lederriemen | Châssis
démontable en frêne,
sangles de cuir, siège
et dossier en toile*

RUD RASMUSSENS
SNEDKERIER,
COPENHAGEN, FROM
C. 1933 TO PRESENT

Cette chaise longue « Deck » et le modèle « Safari » sont des réinterpréta-
tions de modèles existants. Klint croyait beaucoup en la « justesse » des
formes qui ont évolué avec le temps, ce qui était en complète opposition
avec le mépris des modernistes à égard de l'historicisme. L'idée d'une évolution des formes plutôt que d'une révolution est une approche plus huma-
niste, souvent illustrée par le design scandinave.

Yrjö Kukkapuro

Karuselli, 1964–1965

Foam-upholstered
reinforced fibreglass
seat shell with
chromed steel cradle
on steel-reinforced
moulded fibreglass
base | Sitzschale und
Fuß aus geformtem
Fiberglas mit
Schaumstoffpolste-
rung, Aufhängung aus
Stahl, verchromt |
Coquille en fibre de
verre, rembourrage
mousse, berceau en
acier chromé, base
en fibre de verre
renforcée d'acier

HAIMI, HELSINKI,
FROM 1965
(REISSUED BY
AVARTE, HELSINKI)

The ergonomic form of the "Karuselli's" seat shell was
inspired, according to Terence Conran, by the imprint
of the designer's body in snow.
Die ergonomische Form der »Karuselli«-Sitzschale wurde,
wenn man Terence Conran glauben darf, vom Abdruck
des Designers im Schnee inspiriert.
La forme ergonomique de la coquille du « Karuselli »
aurait été inspirée, si l'on en croit Terence Conran,
par l'empreinte du corps du designer dans la neige.

Shiro Kuramata

*How High the
Moon, 1986*

*Nickel-plated wire-
mesh construction |
Konstruktion aus
vernickeltem Streck-
metall | Treillis en
métal nickelé*

KUROSAKI, TOKYO,
FROM 1986
(REISSUED BY VITRA,
BASLE, FROM 1987
TO PRESENT)

▼ **Shiro Kuramata**
Begin the Beguine,
Homage to
Hoffmann, 1985

Through his intriguing choice of materials and graceful
use of proportions, Kuramata was able to express a
highly refined sense of space and lightness in his poetic
designs.

*Durch die faszinierende Materialauswahl und anmutig ge-
stalteten Proportionen zeigen diese poetischen Entwürfe
Kuramatas einen ausgeprägten Sinn für Raum und
Leichtigkeit.*

Par un choix étonnant de matériaux et une utilisation
élégante des proportions, Kuramata réussissait à exprimer un sens hautement raffiné de l'espace et de la
légèreté dans des créations poétiques.

Shiro Kuramata

Miss Blanche, 1989

Paper flowers cast in acrylic resin with tubular aluminium legs | Stuhlbeine aus Aluminiumrohr, Sitzschale aus Acryl mit eingegossenen Papierblumen | Pieds en aluminium, siège, dossier et accoudoirs en résine acrylique avec inclusion de fleurs en papier

KOKUYO, TOKYO, FROM 1989

Erwine & Estelle Laverne

Champagne, 1957

Moulded perspex seat shell on aluminium base with loose fabric-covered foam-filled cushion | Sitzschale aus formgebogenem Plexiglas, Untergestell aus Aluminium, lose Sitzkissen mit Schaumstoffüllung und mit Stoff bezogen | Coquille en Perspex moulé, piètement en aluminium, coussin amovible en tissu rembourré de mousse

LAVERNE
INTERNATIONAL,
NEW YORK,
1957–C. 1972

▼ **Erwine & Estelle Laverne**
Daffodil & Jonquil chairs from the Invisible Group, 1957

LAVERNE INTERNA-
TIONAL, NEW YORK,
1957–C. 1972

Inspired by Saarinen's earlier "Tulip" chair, the "Champagne" chair – a masterpiece of visual lightness and timeless sophistication – forms part of the Lavernes' "Invisible Group".

Von Saarinens früherem »Tulip«-Stuhl inspiriert, gehört der »Champagne«-Stuhl – ein Meisterwerk optischer Leichtigkeit und zeitloser Raffinesse – zu den »Invisible Group«-Stühlen, die von den Lavernes entworfen wurden.

Inspiré de la chaise tulipe de Saarinen, le fauteuil « Champagne » appartient à l' « Invisible Group » des Laverne. Le mince piètement et la coquille transparente confèrent à ce modèle une légèreté visuelle et une sophistication intemporelle.

Le Corbusier, Pierre Jeanneret & Charlotte Perriand

Grand Confort, Model No. LC2, 1928

Chromed bent tubular steel frame with leather-upholstered cushions | Rahmen aus verchromtem Stahlrohr, Polsterkissen mit Lederbezug | Châssis en tube d'acier cintré chromé, coussins en cuir

THONET FRÈRES, PARIS, FROM C. 1929 (REISSUED BY CASSINA)

▼ **Le Corbusier, Pierre Jeanneret & Charlotte Perriand**
Grand Confort, Model No. LC3, 1928

THONET FRÈRES, PARIS (REISSUED BY CASSINA)

With its external frame and sumptuous cushions, the "Grand Confort" projects luxury and epitomises the International Style.

Mit seinem nach außen sichtbaren Rahmen und den üppigen Polstern vermittelt der »Grand Confort« Luxus und verkörpert zugleich den Internationalen Stil.

Avec son cadre apparent et ses somptueux coussins, le «Grand Confort» affiche son luxe et incarne le style international.

Le Corbusier, Pierre Jeanneret & Charlotte Perriand

Basculant, Model No. B301, c. 1928

Chromed bent tubular steel frame, calfskin seat and back with slung leather arms | Rahmen aus Stahlrohr, verchromt, Metallbeschläge, Sitzfläche und Rückenlehne mit Kalbfellbespannung, Armlehnen aus Ledergurten | Châssis en tube d'acier cintré chromé, siège et dossier en vachette, accoudoirs en cuir tendu

THONET FRÈRES, PARIS, FROM 1929 (REISSUED BY CASSINA)

▲ Le Corbusier, Pierre Jeanneret & Charlotte Perriand
Model No. B306 (early version used as rocking chair)

▲ Le Corbusier, Pierre Jeanneret & Charlotte Perriand
Apartment interior, "Salon d'Automne", Paris, 1929

The first systemised tubular steel designs by Le Corbusier's studio appeared in 1928 and were described as "équipement de l'habitation". The best known of this furniture group is the B306 which has an ergonomically resolved form.

Das erste Programm von Stahlrohrmöbeln aus Le Corbusiers Atelier wurde 1928 als »équipement de l'habitation« vorgestellt. Das bekannteste Stück aus dieser Gruppe ist die Liege B306, ein betont ergonomischer Entwurf.

Les premiers modèles en tube d'acier du studio de Le Corbusier apparaissent en 1928. Ils sont alors décrits comme des « équipements de l'habitation ». Le modèle le plus connu de cette série est le B306, à la forme ergonomique.

Le Corbusier, Pierre Jeanneret & Charlotte Perriand

Model No. B306, 1928

Painted bent tubular metal frame with canvas covering painted sheet steel base | Rahmen aus gebogenem Stahlrohr, lackiert, Leinenbespannung, Gestell aus verschweißtem Stahlblech | Châssis en tube métallique peint, recouvrage de toile, base en tôle métallique peinte

THONET FRÈRES, PARIS, FROM C. 1929 & EMBRU, RÜTI (REISSUED BY CASSINA)

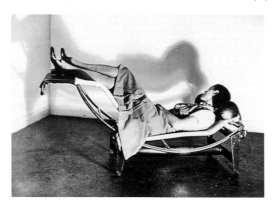

◀ Charlotte Perriand sitting in the chaise longue at the "Salon d'Automne", Paris, 1929

Ross Lovegrove

Crop, 1996

Cherry-faced moulded plywood seat, chromed tubular steel base, polyurethane connectors | Sitzfläche aus geformtem Schichtholz mit Kirschholzfurnier, Stuhlbeine aus Stahlrohr, verchromt, Verbindungselemente aus Thermoplast | Siège en contreplaqué moulé, placage de cerisier, piètement en tube d'acier, fixations en thermoplastique

FASEM, VICOPISANO, PISA, FROM 1996 TO PRESENT

▼ Ross Lovegrove
Crop armchair, 1996

FASEM, VICOPISANO, PISA, FROM 1996 TO PRESENT

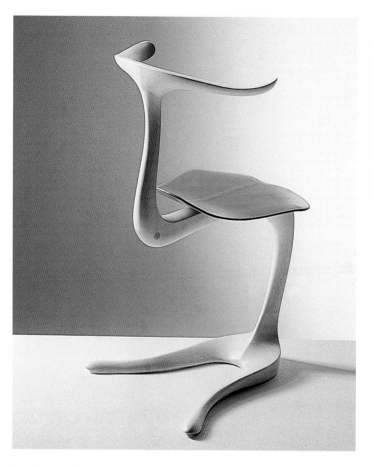

Ross Lovegrove

Bone, 1996

Carved maple frame
with stitched leather
saddle seat | Rahmen
aus Ahorn, Sitzfläche
aus vernähtem
Sattelleder | Châssis
en érable sculpté,
siège en cuir de selle
piqué

CECCOTTI, CASCINA,
PISA, FROM 1996 TO
PRESENT

The rhetoric of Lovegrove's "Crop" and "Bone" chairs is emotionally persuasive because it is expressed through a highly refined and seductive organic vocabulary. His "Crop" armchair is remarkable for its single-form seat shell with integral armrests.

Die Rhetorik von Lovegroves Stühlen »Crop« und »Bone« ist emotional überzeugend, weil sie sich in einem raffinierten und verführerisch-organischen Vokabular ausdrückt. Bemerkenswert ist die aus einem Stück geformte Sitzschale mit integrierten Armlehnen des Armlehnstuhls »Crop«.

La rhétorique de ces deux créations de Lovegrove convainc parce qu'elle s'exprime dans un vocabulaire organique à la fois raffiné et séduisant. La chaise « Crop » est remarquable pour son siège d'une seule pièce et ses accoudoirs intégrés.

Charles Rennie Mackintosh

High-backed chair for the luncheon room of the Argyle Street Tea Rooms, 1897

Stained oak frame with horsehair upholstered seat | Rahmen aus Eiche, gebeizt, Sitzfläche mit Roßhaarpolsterung | Châssis en chêne teinté, siège rembourré de crin de cheval

(REISSUED BY CASSINA)

▶ Charles Rennie Mackintosh
Design for high-backed chairs for the luncheon room of the Argyle Street Tea Rooms, Glasgow, 1897

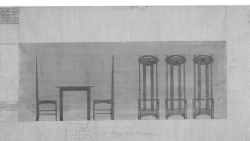

Mackintosh created a highly individual and symbolic vocabulary of form through a combination of Celtic and Japanese influences. This is powerfully demonstrated by the chairs he designed for the Argyle Street Tea Rooms, which achieve a startling modernity while remaining rooted in a strong cultural tradition.

Von keltischen und japanischen Formen beeinflußt, entwickelte Mackintosh eine äußerst individuelle und hochsymbolische Formensprache. Ein gutes Beispiel dafür sind die Stühle, die er für den Teesalon in der Argyle Street entwarf. Sie wirken erstaunlich modern und sind zugleich doch in einer starken kulturellen Tradition verwurzelt.

Mackintosh a créé un langage de formes symbolique et très personnel, en combinant influences celtes et japonaises. Ces sièges, qu'il créa pour le salon de thé d'Argyle Street, en sont une parfaite démonstration : ils atteignent à une modernité frappante tout en restant enracinés dans une forte tradition culturelle.

Charles Rennie Mackintosh

Pair of armchairs for the smoking room of the Argyle Street Tea Rooms, 1897

Stained oak construction | Rahmen aus Eiche, gebeizt | Chêne teinté

◄ **Charles Rennie Mackintosh**
Smoking room, Argyle Street Tea Rooms, Glasgow, c. 1898

Vico Magistretti

Selene, 1969

Compression-
moulded "Reglar"
fibreglass reinforced
polyester structure |
Konstruktion aus
formgepreßtem,
fiberglasverstärktem
»Reglar«-Polyester |
Polyester « Reglar »
renforcé de fibre de
verre, moulé sous
pression

ARTEMIDE, MILAN,
FROM 1969 TO
PRESENT

Aiming to create a single-piece chair in compression-moulded plastic with a traditional four-legged form, Magistretti resolved the technical difficulties associated with the strength of the legs by configuring them in an S shape.

Magistretti wollte einen aus einem Stück geformten Kunststoffstuhl in traditionell vierbeiniger Form schaffen und löste die technischen Probleme, die sich dabei ergaben, indem er den Stuhlbeinen eine stabilisierende S-Form gab.

Pour cette chaise traditionnelle d'une seule pièce en plastique moulé sous pression, Magistretti résolut le délicat problème de la résistance des pieds en les dotant d'une forme en S.

Although bearing a strong similarity to designs by Aalto, Mathsson's "Eva" chair and "Pernilla" chaise longue, lounge chair and ottoman exude a greater sense of luxury. The seat frames of these designs, to which the hemp webbing was attached, were not actually made of laminated wood like the supporting frames, but were executed from solid wood that had been carved into curved sections and then jointed.

Bruno Mathsson

Eva, 1934

Bent plywood and solid birch frame with hemp webbing | Rahmen aus gebogener, laminierter und massiver Birke, Bespannung aus Hanfgeflecht | Châssis en contre-plaqué cintré et bouleau massif, sangles de chanvre

KARL MATHSSON, VÄRNAMO, FROM 1935 (REISSUED BY DUX)

Mathssons Stuhl »Eva«, die Liege »Pernilla«, der Sessel und die Ottomane haben eine starke Ähnlichkeit mit Aaltos Entwürfen, dennoch zeigen sie ein etwas luxuriöseres Flair. Die Rahmen, an denen das Hanfgewebe befestigt ist, bestehen nicht wie die tragenden Teile aus laminiertem Formholz, sondern aus massivem Holz, das in Einzelteilen in geschwungene Formen geschnitten und dann verbunden wurde.

Bien que très similaires aux modèles d'Aalto, le fauteuil « Eva », la chaise longue « Pernilla », la chaise de salon et l'ottomane de Mathsson, sont beaucoup plus luxueux. Le cadre de la partie siège de ces modèles n'était pas en contre-plaqué mais en bois massif sculpté et assemblé.

Alessandro
Mendini

Proust's armchair,
1978

*Existing chair with
hand-painted
decoration* | *Alter
Sesseltyp mit hand-
gemaltem Dekor* |
*Fauteuil existant,
décor peint à la main*

STUDIO ALCHIMIA,
MILAN, FROM 1978
(REISSUED BY
CAPPELLINI, AROSIO)

Redesign or Banal Design highlighted the intellectual and cultural void
which was perceived to exist in the furnishings of industrial society. The
banality of existing objects was emphasised by applying bright colours
and quirky decoration, as in "Proust's" armchair and the "Kandissi" sofa.
*Redesign bzw. das Banal-Design betonte die intellektuelle und kulturelle Leere,
die man im Massendesign der Industriegesellschaft zu finden glaubte. Die
Banalität vorhandener Objekte wurde mit hellen Farben und schrillen Dekors
unterstrichen, so etwa beim »Proust«-Sessel oder dem »Kandissi«-Sofa.*
Le redesign ou le design banal tentèrent de combler le vide intellectuel et
culturel que l'on pouvait percevoir dans le design de masse conçu pour la
société industrialisée. La banalité des objets existants était soulignée par
des couleurs vives ou d'étranges décors appliqués, comme pour ce fauteuil
« Proust » ou ce canapé « Kandissi ».

Ludwig Mies van der Rohe

Model No. MR20, 1927

Nickel-plated bent tubular steel frame and steel stretcher with woven cane seat and back | Rahmen aus gebogenem Stahlrohr, vernickelt, Querstreben aus Stahl, Sitzfläche und Rückenlehne aus Rohrgeflecht | Châssis en tube d'acier nickelé et traverse d'acier, siège et dossier cannés

BERLINER METALL-
GEWERBE JOSEF
MÜLLER, BERLIN,
1927–1930
(REISSUED BY
THONET & KNOLL
INTERNATIONAL)

◄ **Ludwig Mies van der Rohe**
Interior, "Bauausstellung" Berlin, 1939

► **Ludwig Mies van der Rohe**
Model No. MR20, 1927

BERLINER METALL-
GEWERBE JOSEF
MÜLLER, BERLIN
(REISSUED BY
THONET & KNOLL
INTERNATIONAL)

◄ **Ludwig Mies van der Rohe**
Model No. MR10, 1927

BERLINER METALLGEWERBE JOSEF MÜLLER,
BERLIN (REISSUED BY THONET & KNOLL INTER-
NATIONAL)

Ludwig Mies van der Rohe

Model No. MR10, 1927

Chrom-plated bent tubular steel frame and steel stretcher with "Eisengarn" textile seat and back | Rahmen aus gebogenem Stahlrohr, verchromt, Querstrebe aus Stahl, Sitzfläche und Rückenlehne mit Eisengarngewebe bespannt | Châssis en tube d'acier nickelé et traverse d'acier, siège et dossier en tissu « Eisengarn »

BERLINER METALL-GEWERBE JOSEF MÜLLER, BERLIN, 1927–1930 (REISSUED BY THONET & KNOLL INTERNATIONAL)

The MR10 and MR20 are more aesthetically refined but more awkward in use than most other cantilevered designs, because of their arced frames.

Die Freischwinger MR10 und MR20 sind ästhetisch raffinierter, doch wegen ihrer geschwungenen Rahmen nicht so sicher im Gebrauch wie die meisten anderen freischwingenden Konstruktionen.

Les modèles MR10 et MR20 sont esthétiquement plus raffinés, mais leurs courbes amples les rendent moins pratiques à utiliser que la plupart des sièges en porte à faux.

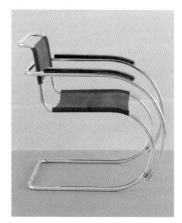

Ludwig Mies van der Rohe

Barcelona, Model No. MR90, 1929

Bent chromed flat steel frame with leather straps and buttoned leather-upholstered cushions | Rahmen aus gebogenem Flachstahl, verchromt, Lederriemen, darauf durchgeknöpfte lederbezogene Polsterkissen | Châssis en acier plat chromé, sangles de cuir et coussins de cuir capitonnés

BERLINER METALL-GEWERBE JOSEF MÜLLER, BERLIN, FROM C. 1929 (REISSUED BY KNOLL ASSOCIATES INTERNATIONAL, FROM 1948)

▼ Ludwig Mies van der Rohe
Barcelona Pavilion for the 1929 Barcelona International Exhibition

The MR90 was designed by Mies van der Rohe for use in the German Pavilion at the 1929 International Exhibition Barcelona. Opulent, yet imparting a Modern appearance, the chair's form was based on the *sella curulis*, a Roman magistrate's stool.

Der MR90 wurde von Mies van der Rohe für den Deutschen Pavillon auf der Weltausstellung 1929 in Barcelona entworfen. Luxuriös, aber dennoch von moderner Erscheinung, basiert die Formgebung dieses Sessels auf dem »sella curulis«, einem römischen Magistratsstuhl.

Le MR90 fut conçu par Mies van der Rohe pour le pavillon allemand de l'Exposition internationale de Barcelone (1929). Opulente, mais d'apparence résolument moderne, cette chauffeuse tire sa forme de la chaise curule pliante romaine.

Carlo Mollino

Armchair, 1952

Bent laminated wood
frame with uphol-
stered seat and back
section with brass
fittings | Rahmen aus
gebogenem, laminier-
tem Holz, Sitzfläche
und Rückenlehne
gepolstert, Messing-
beschläge | Châssis
en bois lamellé-collé,
siège et dossier
rembourrés, garniture
en laiton

PROBABLY APELLI &
VARESIO, TURIN

▼ Carlo Mollino
Chair for the Casa
Catlaneo, Agra, 1953

APELLI & VARESIO,
TURIN

Unlike his American counterparts, who progressed the
utilitarian potential of plywood, Mollino exploited its expressive qualities. This chair relates to an earlier reclining chair designed for the Casa del Sole in Cervinia.
*Die Amerikaner entwickelten das funktionelle Potential des
Schichtholzes weiter, Mollino hingegen dessen expressive
Qualitäten. Mit diesem Modell bezieht er sich auf seinen
frühen Ruhesessel für die Casa del Sole in Cervinia.*
À la différence de ses pairs américains, qui s'intéres-
sèrent surtout aux possibilités techniques du contre-
plaqué, Mollino sut exploiter ses qualités expressives.
Ce fauteuil se rapproche d'une chaise longue antérieure
conçue pour la Casa del Sole à Cervinia.

Jasper Morrison

Thinking Man's Chair, 1987

Painted tubular steel
and flat steel bar
construction |
Rahmen aus Stahl-
rohr und Flachstahl,
lackiert | Tube d'acier
et lattes en acier plat
peints

CAPPELLINI, AROSIO,
COMO, FROM
1987 TO PRESENT

The "Thinking Man's Chair" was designed for both indoor and outdoor use. Constructed from a combination of welded tubular and flat steel, it was conceived for limited production. The circular discs on its arms act as supports for drinking glasses.

Der »Thinking Man's Chair« ist sowohl für den Gebrauch in Innenräumen als auch für den Außenbereich entworfen worden. Seine Konstruktion aus geschweißtem Flachstahl und Stahlrohr war für eine limitierte Produktion konzipiert. Die kreisförmigen Platten am Ende der Armlehnen bieten Abstellplatz für Trinkgläser.

Ce fauteuil bas est destiné à un usage intérieur ou extérieur. Combinant le tube et l'acier plat, il a été conçu pour une production limitée. Les disques en bout d'accoudoirs servent de plateaux pour les verres.

Koloman Moser

Armchair for the main hall of the Purkersdorf Sanatorium, 1902

Painted beech frame with wickerwork seat | Rahmen aus Buche, weiß lackiert, Sitzfläche aus Korbgeflecht | Châssis en hêtre teinté, siège en vannerie

PRAG-RUDNIKER
KORBWAREN,
VIENNA
(REISSUED BY
WITTMANN)

Used in the entrance hall of the Sanatorium designed by Hoffmann, this chair's cubic form and restricted use of colour typify the Secessionist style and anticipate the geometric abstraction of the Modern Movement.

In der Eingangshalle des von Hoffmann entworfenen Sanatoriums aufgestellt, verkörpert dieser Stuhl durch seine kubische Gestalt und den sparsamen Einsatz von Farbe den Stil der Secessionisten und nimmt die geometrische Abstraktion der Moderne vorweg.

Utilisé dans l'entrée du sanatorium dessiné par Hoffmann ce fauteuil illustre par sa forme cubique et son économie chromatique le style sécessionniste, et annonce l'abstraction géométrique du mouvement moderne.

Olivier Mourgue

Djinn chaise longue,
1965

Stretch fabric-covered,
polyurethane foam-
upholstered, bent
tubular steel frame |
Rahmen aus gebogenem Stahlrohr, Polsterung aus Polyurethanschaumstoff, mit
Stretchgewebebezug |
Châssis en tube
d'acier cintré, rembourrage en mousse
de polyuréthane
recouverte de stretch

Used in Stanley Kubrick's film, *2001: A Space Odyssey*, the "Djinn" series'
title was derived from a spirit in Islamic mythology that can assume human
or animal form and control men with its supernatural powers. During the
1960s, the emerging popular interest in Eastern mysticism influenced the
decorative arts in Europe and America. The low height of this seating mirrors the informal lifestyle of the period.

Die »Djinn«-Sitzmöbelserie war in Stanley Kubricks Film »2001: Odyssee
im Weltraum« zu sehen; ihren Namen verdankt sie einem Geist aus der
Islamischen Mythologie, der abwechselnd Menschen- und Tiergestalt annehmen
kann und die Menschen mit seiner übernatürlichen Macht beherrscht. Während
der 6oer Jahre hat das damals aufkommende und sich verbreitende Interesse an
orientalischem und fernöstlichem Mystizismus die dekorativen Künste in Europa
und Amerika beeinflußt. In der niedrigen Sitzhöhe dieser Möbel spiegelt sich der
informelle Lebensstil dieser Jahre.

◄ Scene from the
film *2001: A Space*
Odyssey by Stanley
Kubrick, 1968

Utilisée dans le film de Stanley Kubrick *2001, l'odyssée de l'espace*, la série
« Djinn » doit son nom à ces génies des pays islamiques qui peuvent
prendre des formes humaines ou animales pour exercer leur pouvoir sur-
naturel sur les hommes. Au cours des années 60, un regain d'intérêt pour
le mysticisme oriental influença les arts décoratifs en Europe comme en
Amérique. La faible hauteur de ces sièges rappelle le style de vie décontracté
de cette époque.

Olivier Mourgue

Djinn series, 1965

*Fabric-covered poly-
urethane foam-uphol-
stered, bent tubular
steel frames | Geboge-
nes Stahlrohr, Poly-
urethanschaumstoff,
Stoffbezug | Châssis
en tube d'acier cintré,
rembourrage en
mousse de polyuré-
thane recouverte de
tissu*

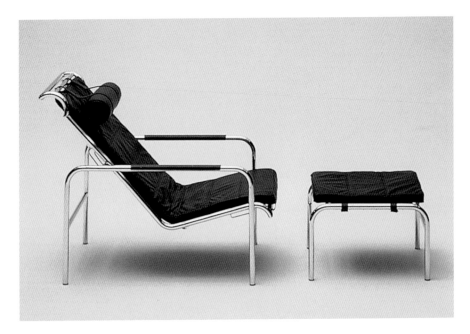

Gabriele Mucchi

Genni, 1935

Chromed tubular steel frame with steel springs and leather armrests, leather-upholstered seat cushion and headrest | Rahmen aus gebogenem Stahlrohr, verchromt, Stahlfeder, Sitzfläche, Rückenlehne und Nackenstütze mit Lederpolsterung | Châssis en tube d'acier chromé, ressorts en acier, accoudoirs en cuir, coussin de siège et repose-tête en cuir rembourré

CRESPI, EMILIO PINA, MILAN, FROM C. 1935 (REISSUED BY ZANOTTA, FROM 1982)

Active in the anti-Fascist group "Corrente", Mucchi was part of the Rationalist movement in design and architecture. Ironically, Rationalism is frequently identified with the Italian Fascist movement.

Mucchi, ein Aktivist in der antifaschistischen Gruppe »Corrente«, gehörte zur Bewegung der Rationalisten in Design und Architektur. Ironischerweise wird der Rationalismus häufig mit dem italienischen Faschismus in Verbindung gebracht.

Participant actif au groupe antifasciste « Corrente », Mucchi faisait partie du mouvement rationaliste de design et d'architecture. Ironiquement, le rationalisme est fréquemment identifié au fascisme italien.

◄ Prototype of the Genni lounge chair, c. 1935

Peter Murdoch

Spotty, 1963

*Polyethylene-coated,
laminated paper-
board construction |
Laminierter Karton,
mit Polyethylen-
beschichtung | Papier
cartonné enduit de
polyéthylène*

INTERNATIONAL
PAPER, 1964–1965

Murdoch's polka-dot child's chair "Spotty" is an icon of the Pop era. Its low production costs and inherent disposability were ideally suited to the demands of the mass consumer market.

Murdochs Kinderstuhl »Spotty« wurde mit seinem Punktmuster zu einer Ikone der Pop-Ära. Niedrige Produktionskosten und seine universelle Verwendbarkeit machten ihn zum idealen Produkt für den Massenkonsum.

Ce siège d'enfant à pois, dessiné par Murdoch, est un symbole de la période Pop. Son faible coût de fabrication et le fait qu'il était jetable répondaient idéalement aux attentes du marché de la grande consommation.

George Nelson

Coconut, 1955

Fabric-covered, foam-upholstered steel shell on chromed tubular metal and metal rod legs | Sitzschale aus Stahl, Schaumstoffpolsterung mit Stoffbezug, Beine aus Aluminiumröhren und -stäben | Coquille en acier rembourrée de mousse et recouverte de tissu, piètement en tube d'acier chromé et cintré

HERMAN MILLER
FURNITURE CO.,
ZEELAND,
MICHIGAN,
1955–1978
(REISSUED BY VITRA,
BASLE, FROM 1988)

▼ Herman Miller advertising photograph of Coconut chairs

Although visually light, the "Coconut" chair is in fact extremely heavy owing to its steel seat shell. As its name suggests, the chair's form was inspired by a cracked section of coconut.

Obwohl der »Coconut«-Sessel optisch sehr leicht wirkt, weist er durch seine Sitzschale aus Stahl ein sehr hohes Gewicht auf. Wie der Name andeutet, wurde die Stuhlform von einem Fragment einer aufgeschlagenen Kokosnußschale inspiriert.

Malgré son apparence légère, le siège « Coconut » est en fait extrêmement lourd à cause de sa coquille en métal. Comme son nom le suggère, sa forme était inspirée d'un morceau de noix de coco.

George Nelson

Marshmallow, 1956

Painted tubular steel frame with vinyl-covered latex foam-filled circular pads backed with steel discs | Rahmen aus Stahlrohr, lackiert, Polsterung aus runden Latexkissen mit Schaumstoffpolsterung und Vinylbezug auf Stahlscheiben | Châssis en tube d'acier peint, « pastilles » réalisées à partir d'un disque d'acier rembourré de mousse de latex et recouvert de vinyle

HERMAN MILLER FURNITURE CO., ZEELAND, MICHIGAN, 1956–1965

▼ George Nelson
Sketch for the Marshmallow sofa, c. 1956

Like his clock designs, the form of Nelson's "Marshmallow" sofa has been exploded into separate parts. The bold colour scheme, which emphasised this separateness, and the geometry of the sofa predicted Pop design.

Wie bei Nelsons Uhrenentwürfen ist auch die Form des »Marshmallow«-Sofas in ihre Einzelteile zerlegt. Die kühne Farbkombination, mit der die Wirkung der Einzelformen noch unterstrichen wird, und die Geometrie des Sofas nehmen die Formensprache späterer Entwürfe des Pop-Designs vorweg.

La forme du canapé « Marshmallow » de Nelson est explosée en multiples pastilles. Ses couleurs vives, qui renforçaient l'autonomie de chaque élément et la géométrie de l'ensemble, annonçaient le Pop design.

Marc Newson

Felt, 1994

Fibreglass-reinforced polyester and anodised aluminium frame with textile upholstery | Konstruktion aus fiberglasverstärktem Polyester und eloxiertem Aluminium, Stoffpolsterung | Châssis en aluminium anodisé et polyester renforcé de fibre de verre, rembourrage textile

CAPPELLINI, AROSIO, COMO, FROM 1994 TO PRESENT

Marc Newson's designs are characterised by strong sculptural forms with an innate biomorphism. The form of his "Orgone" chaise is reminiscent of a surfboard – a testament to Newson's Australian origins – while his "Felt" chair has a powerful anthropomorphism. Sacrificing comfort to aesthetics, the "Lockheed Lounge" was influenced by the riveted structure of aircraft and stylistically reflects 1930s' streamlining. It is very expensive due to its laborious and time-consuming method of manufacture.

Typisch für Marc Newsons Entwürfe sind skulpturale, biomorphe Formen. Die Liege »Orgone« erinnert an die Form eines Surfbretts – ein Verweis auf Newsons Herkunft aus Australien. »Felt« dagegen hat etwas stark Anthropomorphes.

▶ **Marc Newson**
Orgone, 1991

CAPPELLINI, AROSIO, COMO, FROM 1991 TO PRESENT

»Lockheed Lounge«, von der genieteten Oberfläche eines Flugzeugs und der Stromlinienbegeisterung der 30er Jahre beeinflußt, opfert den Sitzkomfort der Ästhetik. Die Liege ist wegen der arbeitsintensiven und aufwendigen Herstellung sehr teuer.

Les créations de Marc Newson se caractérisent par des formes sculpturales affirmées qui intégrent des aspects biomorphiques. La forme de sa chaise longue « Orgone » rappelle une planche de surf – évocation des origines australiennes du designer – alors que son fauteuil « Felt » est presque anthropomorphique. Sacrifiant le confort à l'esthétique, la méridienne « Lockheed Lounge » s'inspire des constructions rivetées des avions et renvoie au style épuré des années 30. Les méthodes artisanales et le temps de fabrication qu'elle requièrt en font un meuble très coûteux.

Marc Newson

**MN-01 LC1,
Lockheed Lounge,
1985–1986**

*Fibreglass-reinforced
polyester core covered
in riveted sheet
aluminium skin |
Kern aus fiberglas-
verstärktem Polyester,
überzogen mit einer
Haut aus genietetem
Aluminiumblech |
Âme en polyester
renforcé de fibre de
verre et recouverte
d'une peau de feuille
d'aluminium riveté*

IDÉE, TOKYO, FROM
1986 TO PRESENT

Isamu Noguchi

*Sofa, Model
No. IN 70 &
ottoman, Model
No. IN 71, 1946*

Fabric-covered
upholstered seat and
back section on
tapering birch legs |
*Sitzfläche und
Rückenlehne gepol-
stert und mit Stoff-
bezug, Füße aus
Birke* | *Siège et dossier
rembourrés, recou-
verts de tissu, pieds
fuselés en bouleau*

HERMAN MILLER
FURNITURE CO.,
ZEELAND,
MICHIGAN,
FROM 1946

Through his work as a sculptor and designer, Noguchi
considered himself "an interpreter of the East to the
West". Informed by nature, his highly abstract and
sculptural furniture designs were often intended to express the essence of natural landscape.

*Der Designer und Bildhauer Noguchi betrachtete sich als
»Dolmetscher des Ostens für den Westen«. Von der Natur
inspiriert, sollten seine sehr reduzierten und skulpturalen
Möbelentwürfe das Wesen natürlicher Landschaften wider-
spiegeln.*

Par son œuvre de sculpteur et de designer, Noguchi
se considérait comme « un interprète de l'Orient en
Occident ». Inspirés de l'observation de la nature, ses
modèles de meubles abstraits et sculpturaux se pro-
posaient souvent d'exprimer l'essence d'un paysage.

Isamu Noguchi

Rocking stool, 1954

*Painted wood seat
and base-connected
with chromed steel
rod structure |
Sitzfläche und Sockel-
platte aus farbigem
Holz, Verbindungs-
gestell aus verchrom-
ten Stahlstäben |
Siège et base en bois
peint, réunis par une
structure en tige de
métal chromé*

KNOLL ASSOCIATES,
NEW YORK, FROM
1954

▼ Isamu Noguchi
Prototype woven
bamboo lounge
chair, 1951

Noguchi's rocking stool and prototype bamboo chair
reveal his fascination with the formal qualities of structure. The stool in particular is imbued with a balanced
tension.

*Noguchis Schaukelhocker und sein Prototyp eines Bambus-
stuhls zeigen, wie sehr ihn die formalen Qualitäten einer
Konstruktion faszinierten. Insbesondere der Hocker ist von
ausgewogener Spannung.*

Ce tabouret de Noguchi et son prototype de fauteuil en
bambou révèlent la fascination de l'artiste pour les qualités formelles des structures. Le tabouret en particulier
fait preuve d'une tension pleine d'équilibre.

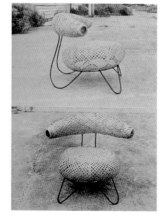

Verner Panton

Cone, 1958

Fabric-covered foam-upholstered bent sheet metal construction, metal base | Gebogenes Stahlblech, Schaumstoffpolsterung mit Stoffbezug, Kreuzfuß | Structure en tôle cintrée, rembourrage de mousse recouverte de tissu, piètement métallique

PLUS-LINJE, COPENHAGEN (REDESIGNED AND REISSUED IN 1994 BY POLYTHEMA)

The futuristic "Cone" chair and slightly later "Heart" chair were the result of a conscious decision by Panton to divorce himself from any preconceived notions of what a chair should look like.

Der futuristische »Cone«-Stuhl und der etwas später entstandene »Heart«-Stuhl waren das Resultat von Pantons entschiedenem Bestreben, sich von allen vorgefaßten Vorstellungen, was ein Stuhl sein soll, zu lösen.

Ce fauteuil « Cone » futuriste, ainsi que la chauffeuse légèrement ultérieure « Heart », résultant de la volonté de Panton de se débarrasser de tous les préjugés existants sur la forme d'un fauteuil.

Verner Panton

Panton, 1959–1960

1968–1970: Moulded "Baydur" (PU-hard-foam) construction, 1970 onwards: Injection-moulded "Luran-S" (thermoplastic) construction | Konstruktion aus Spritzguß, 1968–1970: Polyurethan-Hartschaum »Baydur«, ab 1970: Thermoplast-Spritzguß »Luran-S« | 1968–1970: « Baydur » moulé (mousse solide PU). Depuis 1970 : « Luran S » (thermoplastique) moulé par injection

VITRA, BASLE, FOR
HERMAN MILLER
FURNITURE CO.,
ZEELAND, MICHI-
GAN, FROM 1968
(REISSUED BY VITRA,
BASLE, FROM 1990
TO PRESENT)

Unlike Colombo's No. 4860 and Zanuso and Sapper's child's chair, Panton's stacking chair was wholly unified. It was the first single-material, single-form injection-moulded chair.

Anders als Colombos Nr. 4860 und Zanusos und Sappers Kinderstuhl bestand Pantons Stapelstuhl aus einem Stück. Damit war er der erste spritzgußgeformte Stuhl, der mit nur einem Werkstoff und einer Form hergestellt wurde.

À la différence du modèle n° 4860 de Colombo et de la chaise pour enfants de Zanuso et Sapper, la chaise de Panton était réalisée en un seul bloc. C'est le premier siège moulé par injection en un seul matériau et une pièce.

Verner Panton

Pantower,
1968–1969

Textile-covered poly-
urethane foam-uphol-
stered frame | Poly-
urethanschaumstoff,
Stoffbezug | Mousse
de polyuréthane
recouverte de tissu

The "Pantower" and Panton's related room design for the 1970 "Visiona II" exhibition held by Bayer AG demonstrate the contemporary interest in micro-environments. Seating came to be seen in some quarters in the late 1960s not so much as "equipment for living" but as apparatus for interactive play.

Der »Pantower« und Pantons verwandte Raumgestaltung für die »Visiona II«-Ausstellung, die 1970 von der Bayer AG veranstaltet wurde, demonstrieren das zeitgenössische Interesse an Wohnlandschaften. Sitze galten während der 6oer

Jahre in bestimmten Kreisen nicht als »Wohnmöbel«, sondern zunehmend als Geräte für interaktive Spiele.

Le modèle « Pantower » est la contribution de Panton à l'exposition « Visiona » organisée en 1970 par Bayer AG. Elle témoigne de l'intérêt de l'époque pour les micro-environnements. Un siège était considéré dans certains cercles de la fin des années 60, non pas tant comme un « équipement pour la maison », mais comme un support de relations interactives.

Pierre Paulin

Tongue, Model No. 577, 1967

Fabric-covered foam-upholstered tubular steel frame | Rahmen aus Stahlrohr, Schaumstoffpolsterung, mit Stoffbezug | Châssis en tube d'acier, rembourrage en mousse recouverte de tissu

ARTIFORT, MAASTRICHT, FROM 1967 TO PRESENT

▼ Artifort advertising photograph, c. 1967

The model No. 577, sometimes referred to as the "Tongue" because of its lingual form, rests directly on the floor allowing the user to assume a relaxed and informal posture.

Die Schale des Modells Nr. 577, das wegen seiner Form manchmal auch »Tongue« (Zunge) genannt wird, steht direkt auf dem Boden und erlaubt den Sitzenden eine bequeme, entspannte Haltung.

Le modèle n° 577, parfois appelé « Tongue » (langue) à cause de sa forme, repose directement sur le sol afin de permettre à son utilisateur de prendre une position totalement détendue.

Jorge Pensi

Toledo, 1986–1988

Cast-aluminium
frame | Rahmen aus
Gußaluminium |
Fonte d'aluminium

AMAT, MARTORELL,
BARCELONA, FROM
1989 TO PRESENT

The "Toledo" is a reworking of earlier designs used in
Spanish open-air cafés. Its perforated ribs allude to antique armour, while its title refers to the city renowned
for the sharpness of its steel sword blades.

*»Toledo« ist eine Überarbeitung älterer Modelle, die in spa-
nischen Straßencafés verwendet wurden. Seine perforierten
Rippen erinnern an alte Rüstungen, der Name ist eine
Anspielung auf die Stadt, die für die Schärfe ihrer Schwert-
klingen berühmt war.*

Le « Toledo » est une interprétation de modèles anté-
rieurs de chaises de cafés espagnols. Ses côtes perfo-
rées rappellent une armure ancienne. Son nom évoque
la ville célèbre pour la finesse des lames de ses épées.

Gaetano Pesce

Donna, Model Nos. Up 5 & Up 6, 1969

Stretch fabric-covered moulded polyurethane foam | Geformter Polyurethanschaumstoff mit Stretchgewebebezug | Mousse de polyuréthane moulée recouverte de tissu stretch

C & B ITALIA, NOVEDRATE, COMO, 1969–1973 (LATER TO BECOME B & B ITALIA)

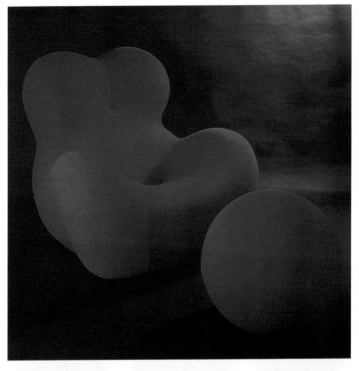

▶ C & B Italia series of photographs showing Up 5 being unwrapped

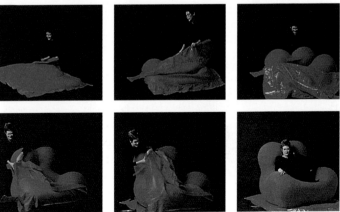

Compressed and vacuum-packed in PVC wrappers, the "Up Series" literally bounced into life when unwrapped. Described by Pesce as "transformation" furniture, these iconoclastic designs turned the act of purchasing a chair into a "happening".

Zusammengepreßt und in PVC-Folie vakuumverpackt, sprangen die Möbel der

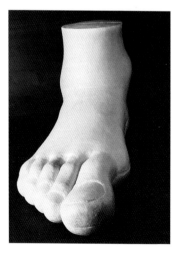

»Up Series« buchstäblich ins Leben, wenn sie ausgepackt wurden. Pesce hat sie auch als Transformations-Möbel bezeichnet; dieses ikonoklastische Design machte den Akt des Stuhleinkaufs zu einem »Happening«. Comprimés et livrés dans un emballage sous vide, les sièges de la série « Up » prenaient littéralement vie au déballage. Désignés par Pesce comme mobilier « à transformation », ces modèles iconoclastes faisaient du simple acte d'achat d'un siège une sorte de happening.

Gaetano Pesce

Up Series, 1969

Stretch fabric-covered moulded polyurethane foam | Geformter Polyurethanschaumstoff, mit Stretchgewebebezug | Mousse de polyuréthane moulée recouverte de tissu stretch

C & B ITALIA,
NOVEDRATE, COMO
(LATER TO BECOME
B & B ITALIA),
1970–1973

◀ Gaetano Pesce
Up 7, 1969

C & B ITALIA,
NOVEDRATE, COMO,
1970–1973

Giancarlo
Piretti

Plia, 1969

*Chromed steel frame
with moulded perspex
seat and back |
Rahmen aus Stahl-
rohr, verchromt, Sitz-
fläche und Rücken-
lehne aus geformtem
Plexiglas | Châssis en
acier chromé, siège et
dosseret en Perspex
moulé*

CASTELLI, OZZANO
DELL'EMILIA,
BOLOGNA, FROM
1969 TO PRESENT

The "Plia" is an efficient modern reworking of the traditional wooden folding chair. When collapsed, it is only an inch in depth, excluding the central hub. The chair won several awards, including the federal German award "Gute Form" in 1973.

Der Klappstuhl »Plia« ist eine strapazierfähige und moderne Weiterentwicklung der älteren Modelle aus Holz. Zusammengeklappt ist der Stuhl nur 2,5 cm tief, nur die Klappnabe in der Mitte ist etwas breiter. Der Stuhl gewann mehrere Preise, darunter auch den Bundespreis »Gute Form« von 1973.

La chaise « Plia » est une adaptation moderne de la traditionnelle chaise pliante en bois. Repliée, elle ne mesure que 2,5 cm d'épaisseur environ, en dehors du moyeu central. Elle a remporté plusieurs récompenses, dont le prix fédéral allemand « Gute Form » en 1973.

Warren Platner said, "As a designer, I felt there was room for the kind of decorative, gentle, graceful kind of design that appeared in a period style like Louis XV. But it could have a more rational base instead of being applied decoration ... A classic is something that every time you look at it, you accept it as it is and you see no way of improving it."

Warren Platner: »Als Designer war mir klar, daß es Raum gab für ein dekoratives, liebenswürdiges, anmutiges Design, so wie zur Zeit des Louis Quinze. Aber es sollte auf rationalerer Basis stehen, es geht nicht um appliziertes Dekor ... Ein Klassiker ist etwas, das dir jedesmal, wenn du es anschaust, gefällt und von dem du nicht weißt, wie man es verbessern könnte.«

Warren Platner: « En tant que designer, je sentais qu'il y avait une place pour le type de meubles décoratifs, agréables et pleins de grâce apparus dans une période comme celle du style Louis XV. Mais ce mobilier pourrait s'appuyer sur une base beaucoup plus rationnelle, au lieu de se contenter d'un décor appliqué ... Un classique est quelque chose qui plaît chaque fois qu'on le regarde, et que l'on ne saurait améliorer. »

Warren Platner

Model No. 1725 A, 1966

Nickel-plated steel construction with fabric-covered, foam-rubber upholstery | Rahmen aus Stahl, vernickelt, Schaumstoffpolsterung mit Stoffbezug | Construction en acier nickelé, rembourrage en mousse de caoutchouc recouverte de tissu

KNOLL INTERNATIONAL, NEW YORK, FROM 1966 TO PRESENT

Gio Ponti

Superleggera, Model No. 699, 1951–1957

Ash frame with woven rush seat | Rahmen aus Esche, Sitzfläche aus Binsengeflecht | Châssis en frêne, siège en jonc tressé

CASSINA, MEDA, MILAN, FROM 1957 TO PRESENT

▼ Cassina photograph demonstrating the lightness of the Superleggera of 1957

The remarkably light "Superleggera" was based on a traditional Italian chair design. Ponti created interiors and objects of a timeless classicism and this chair has been described as "the consummate chair".

Der bemerkenswert leichte »Superleggera«-Stuhl basiert auf einem traditionellen italienischen Stuhltyp. Ponti schuf zeitlos klassische Interieurs und Objekte, und dieser Stuhl wurde als »Stuhl an sich« bezeichnet.

Cette remarquable « Superleggera » s'inspire d'une chaise traditionnelle italienne. Ponti créa des intérieurs et des objets d'un classicisme sans âge et sa chaise fut qualifiée de « chaise par excellence ».

Jean Prouvé

Chaise standard demontable, 1930

Painted bent tubular steel and steel frame with lacquered moulded plywood seat and back, rubber feet | Rahmen aus Stahlrohr und Stahlblech, lackiert, Sitzfläche und Rückenlehne aus geformtem Schichtholz, Gummifüße | Châssis en tube d'acier cintré et peint, tôle peinte, siège et dossier en bois contreplaqué moulé et peint, pieds en caoutchouc

JEAN PROUVÉ, NANCY (REISSUED BY TECTA, 1980)

▼ Jean Prouvé
Office swivelling chair, 1920s

JEAN PROUVÉ, NANCY

This standardised stacking chair and the earlier prototype office swivelling chair illustrate Prouvé's early interest in providing solutions for the institutional and contract markets.

Dieser standardisierte Stapelstuhl und der ältere Prototyp eines Bürodrehstuhls zeigen Prouvés frühes Interesse an Lösungen für Großkunden und Auftragsarbeiten.

Cette chaise empilable standardisée et le prototype plus ancien de chaise de bureau pivotante illustrent l'intérêt précoce de Prouvé pour le mobilier de bureau.

Ernest Race

Antelope chair, 1950

Painted bent steel rod
frame with moulded
plywood seat |
Rahmen aus geboge-
nen Stahlstäben,
Sitzfläche aus geform-
tem Schichtholz |
Châssis en tige d'acier
cintré peint, siège en
contre-plaqué moulé

ERNEST RACE,
LONDON (LATER TO
BECOME RACE
FURNITURE), FROM
1951 TO PRESENT

Constrained by national rationing, Race designed the "Antelope" and "Springbok" chairs for use on the Royal Festival Hall's outdoor terraces during the 1951 Festival of Britain. The chairs' spindly legs terminating on ball feet echoed popular interest in the imagery of molecular chemistry and nuclear physics.

Beschränkt durch die kriegsbedingte Materialrationierung in England, hat Race den »Antelope«- und den »Springbok«-Stuhl 1951 aus Anlaß des Festival of Britain für die Außenterrassen der Royal Festival Hall entworfen. Die dünnen Stuhlbeine, die auf Kugelfüßen stehen, spiegeln das damals weit verbreitete Interesse an der Metaphorik von Molekularchemie und Kernphysik wider.

Soumis au rationnement de l'après-guerre, Race conçoit les fauteuils « Antelope » et « Springbok » pour les terrasses extérieures du Royal Festival Hall, à l'occasion du Festival of Britain de 1951. Les pieds maigrelets se terminant par de petites boules rappelaient l'intérêt de l'époque pour la chimie moléculaire et la physique nucléaire.

Chair for a music room, 1898–1899

Solid oak frame with upholstered leather seat | Rahmen aus massiver Eiche, Sitzfläche mit Lederpolster | Châssis en chêne massif, siège en cuir rembourré

VEREINIGTE WERK-
STÄTTEN FÜR KUNST
IM HANDWERK,
MUNICH, FROM C.
1898 (ALSO LIBERTY
& CO., LONDON,
AFTER 1899)

▼ Richard
Riemerschmid
Room of an art
lover, 1900 Paris
Exhibition

First shown at the 1899 Dresden Art Exhibition, this chair was originally designed for use by musicians. Its armless form allows the freedom of movement necessary when playing musical instruments.

Dieser Stuhl, zuerst 1899 auf der Dresdner Kunstausstellung präsentiert, wurde ursprünglich für Musiker entworfen. Seine Formgebung ist auf die zum Musizieren notwendige Bewegungsfreiheit abgestimmt.

Présenté pour la première fois à l'Exposition d'art de Dresde de 1899, ce siège fut conçu à l'origine pour des musiciens. L'absence d'accoudoirs permet la liberté de mouvements nécessaire.

▼ Gerrit Rietveld
(seated) with G. A.
van der Groenekan
(behind chair),
Utrecht, c. 1918

▲ **Gerrit Rietveld**
White version of the
Red/Blue chair, 1921

GERRIT RIETVELD,
UTRECHT

Originally designed in 1917–1918 with a natural wood finish, Rietveld painted this revolutionary chair in 1921 as a result of his association with the De Stijl movement. With its simplified construction, the design speculated on going into standardised production.

Ursprünglich zwischen 1917 und 1918 ohne Lackierung entworfen, bemalte Rietveld 1921 diesen revolutionären Stuhl, nachdem er in engen Kontakt zu der De Stijl-Bewegung gekommen war. Die einfache Bauweise des Stuhls zielte auf eine spätere Serienproduktion.

Conçu à l'origine avec une finition en bois naturel (1917–1918), ce siège révolutionnaire fut peint par Rietveld en 1921 au moment où il se rapprocha du groupe De Stijl. De conception simplifiée à l'extrême, ce modèle était prévu pour une production en série.

Gerrit Rietveld

Zig-Zag chair,
c. 1932–1934

Oak construction with
brass fittings | Eiche,
Messingbeschläge |
Chêne, garnitures en
cuivre

METZ & CO.,
AMSTERDAM,
1935–C. 1955
(REISSUED BY
CASSINA)

▶ ▼ **Gerrit Rietveld**
Working drawing of
Zig-Zag chair,
1932–1934

▼ **Gerrit Rietveld**
Interior in Stoop
Family House, 1950

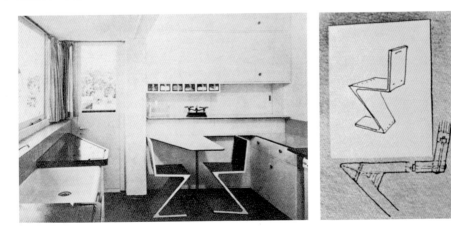

Aluminium chair,
1942

Pressed and stamped
aluminium construc-
tion | Konstruktion
aus gestanztem und
geformtem Alumi-
nium | Aluminium
moulé et estampé

GERARD VAN DE
GROENEKAN & WIM
RIETVELD, UTRECHT,
FROM 1942

▼ Gabriele Mucchi
Aluminium chairs
shown at the VII
Milan Triennale,
1940

This chair was probably inspired by military aircraft
seats. Constructed from a bent, single sheet of stamped
aluminium, the design pushed the material's technical
and aesthetic limits further than ever before.
Dieser Sessel hat sein Vorbild vermutlich in den Sitzen von
Militärflugzeugen. Aus einem einzigen gestanzten und
geformten Stück Aluminiumblech hergestellt, hat dieser
Entwurf technische und ästhetische Maßstäbe für die
Verwendung von Aluminium gesetzt.
Ce fauteuil a probablement été inspiré par les sièges
des avions militaires. Réalisé à partir d'une seule feuille
d'aluminium estampée et cintrée, il a repoussé les
limites techniques et esthétiques de son matériau.

Eero Saarinen

Womb chair, Model No. 70, 1947–1948

Bent tubular steel frame with fabric-covered upholstered moulded fibreglass seat shell and latex foam cushions, nylon glides | Rahmen aus glasfaserverstärktem Polyester, Latex-schaumstoffpolsterung mit Stoffbezug, Gleitfüße aus Nylon | Châssis en tube d'acier cintré, coquille de siège en fibre de verre moulée et tissu rembourré, coussins en mousse de latex, patins en nylon

KNOLL ASSOCIATES, NEW YORK, 1948–1993

▼ **Eero Saarinen**
The Womb collection, 1947–1948

KNOLL ASSOCIATES, NEW YORK, 1948–1993

The No. 70 incorporated a moulded fibreglass seat shell. With its generous proportions and organic form, it invited the user to curl up in it. Because of this it eventually became known as the "Womb" chair.

Die Sitzschale des Nr. 70 besteht aus glasfaserverstärktem Polyester. Großzügig bemessen und organisch in der Form lädt der Sessel zum Zusammenrollen ein. Er wurde darum auch »Womb chair« (Mutterschoß) genannt.

Ce n° 70 faisait appel à une coquille de siège en fibre de verre moulée. De proportions généreuses, il incitait à se blottir dans sa forme organique. C'est une des raisons pour lesquelles il fut appelé le « Womb chair » (la matrice).

Eero Saarinen

Tulip, Model No. 150, 1955–1956

Plastic-coated cast aluminium base supporting moulded fibreglass seat shell with loose upholstered latex foam cushion | Fuß aus Gußaluminium, lackiert, Sitzschale aus geformtem, fiberglasverstärktem Polyester, lackiert, loses Sitzkissen mit Schaumstoffüllung | Piètement en fonte d'aluminium gainée de plastique soutenant une coquille en fibre de verre moulée, coussin amovible en mousse de latex

KNOLL ASSOCIATES, NEW YORK, FROM 1956 TO PRESENT

▼ **Eero Saarinen**
Tulip, Model No. 151, 1955–1956

KNOLL ASSOCIATES, NEW YORK, FROM 1956 TO PRESENT

Plastics technology precluded Saarinen from achieving a single-material, single-form chair. The "Pedestal Group" did, however, fulfil his objective of cleaning up the "slum of legs" in domestic interiors.

Die damalige Kunststofftechnologie machte es Saarinen unmöglich, einen Stuhl aus einem Material und einem Guß zu schaffen. Mit der »Pedestal Group« konnte er aber eines seiner Ziele erreichen: mit dem »elenden Wirrwarr aus Beinen« in Häusern und Wohnungen aufzuräumen.

Saarinen aurait voulu fabriquer des sièges en un seul matériau et un seul élément. Avec le « Pedestal Group », il atteignit un de ses objectifs : débarrasser la maison de tout ce « misérable fouillis de pieds ».

Karl Friedrich Schinkel

Armchair,
c. 1820–1825

Painted, cast-iron
construction with
wrought iron rods |
Gußeisen und
schmiedeeiserne
Stäbe, lackiert |
Fonte peinte et
barreaux en fer forgé

KÖNIGLICHE EISEN-
GIESSEREI SAYNER-
HÜTTE, NEAR
NEUWIED
(REISSUED BY TECTA)

▼ Karl Friedrich
Schinkel
Bench, c. 1820–1825

KÖNIGLICHE EISEN-
GIESSEREI SAYNER-
HÜTTE, NEAR
NEUWIED
(REISSUED BY TECTA)

Cast-iron chairs were produced in significant quantities from the mid-18th century, but it was not until Schinkel's contribution to this field that such economy of form and efficiency of production was achieved.
Seit Mitte des 18. Jahrhunderts wurden Gußeisenstühle in großen Stückzahlen produziert. Erst durch Schinkel erhielten diese Stühle schlichtere Formen, die effizienter zu produzieren waren.
Des chaises en fonte sont produites en quantités importantes dès le milieu du XVIIIe siècle, mais il faudra attendre Schinkel pour arriver à un tel degré de perfection dans l'économie des formes et l'efficacité du processus industriel.

Mart Stam

Model No. S33, 1926

*Lacquered, cast
tubular steel frame,
internally reinforced
with metal rods,
fabric seat and back |
Rahmen aus Guß-
stahlrohr, lackiert, im
Innern durch Metall-
stäbe verstärkt,
Sitzfläche und
Rückenlehne mit
Stoffbespannung |
Châssis en tube
d'acier laqué renforcé
par des tiges de métal
internes, siège et
dossier en tissu*

L. & C. ARNOLD,
SCHORNDORF
(REISSUED BY
GEBRÜDER THONET,
FRANKENBERG)

▼ **Mart Stam**
Living room,
Weißenhof-Siedlung,
Stuttgart, 1927

In 1926 Stam constructed a prototype of his revolutionary cantilever chair from welded gas pipes. He showed
drawings of the prototype to Mies van der Rohe who,
inspired by the concept, designed his own versions.
*1926 konstruierte Stam den ersten Prototyp eines Frei-
schwingers aus verschweißten Gasrohren. Er zeigte Mies
van der Rohe Zeichnungen des Prototyps, der nun seiner-
seits, von Stams Konzept inspiriert, eigene Versionen schuf.*
En 1926, Stam construisit un prototype de sa chaise en
porte à faux révolutionnaire à partir de tuyaux de gaz
soudés. Il montra des dessins de ce prototype à Mies
van der Rohe qui s'inspira de ce concept pour créer ses
propres versions.

Philippe Starck

Costes, 1982

Enamelled tubular steel frame with bent mahogany-faced plywood back and leather-covered foam-upholstered seat | Rahmen aus Stahlrohr, emailliert, Rückenlehne aus geformtem Schichtholz mit Mahagonifurnier, Sitzfläche aus Schaumstoff, gepolstert, mit Lederbezug | Châssis en tube d'acier émaillé, dossier en contre-plaqué cintré, placage d'acajou, siège rembourré en mousse recouverte de cuir

DRIADE, FOSSADELLO DI CAORSO, PIACENZA, FROM 1985 TO PRESENT

One of Starck's best-known designs, the "Costes" was originally designed for the Café Costes in Paris. It was designed with three legs so that waiters at the café would trip up only half as many times as usual.

»Costes«, einer von Starcks bekanntesten Entwürfen, wurde ursprünglich für das gleichnamige Café in Paris entworfen. Der Stuhl wurde mit nur drei Beinen konzipiert, damit die Kellner im Café nur halb so oft stolperten wie gewöhnlich.

▶ **Philippe Starck**
Pratfall, 1982

DRIADE, FOSSADELLO DI CAORSO, PIACENZA, FROM 1985 TO PRESENT

L'une des créations les plus célèbres de Starck, le « Costes » fut à l'origine conçu pour le Café Costes, à Paris. Grâce à ses trois pieds au lieu de quatre, les serveurs avaient deux fois moins de chances de le bousculer.

Philippe Starck

Dr. Glob, 1988

*Tubular steel frame
with polypropylene
seat/front leg section |
Rahmen aus Stahl-
rohr, Sitzfläche und
vordere Stuhlbeine
aus Polypropylen |
Châssis en tube
métallique, siège
et pieds avant en
polypropylène*

KARTELL, NOVIGLIO,
MILAN, FROM
1988 TO PRESENT

◄ **Philippe Starck**
Super Glob chairs,
1990

KARTELL, NOVIGLIO,
MILAN, FROM
1990 TO PRESENT

◄◄ **Philippe Starck**
Hi Glob stools, 1990

KARTELL, NOVIGLIO,
MILAN, FROM
1990 TO PRESENT

Philippe Starck

Lord Yo, 1994

Injection-moulded polypropylene seat shell on tubular aluminium legs | Sitzschale aus spritzgußgeformtem Polypropylen, Stuhlbeine aus Aluminiumrohr | Coquille en polypropylène moulé par injection, pieds en tube d'aluminium

DRIADE, FOSSADELLO DI CAORSO, PIACENZA, FROM 1994 TO PRESENT

▼ **Philippe Starck**
Olly Tango, 1994

DRIADE, FOSSADELLO DI CAORSO, PIACENZA

"Lord Yo" is essentially a plastic reworking of a traditional tub chair. Together with "Miss Trip" and "Olly Tango", it marks a new maturity in Starck's work which has given rise to particularly elegant and rational forms.
»Lord Yo« ist der Neuentwurf eines traditionellen Röhrensessels aus Plastik. Wie »Miss Trip« und »Olly Tango« repräsentiert es eine neue Reife in Starcks Schaffen, die zu eleganten und rationalen Formen geführt hat.
« Lord Yo » est essentiellement une réinterprétation en plastique du fauteuil en rotin traditionnel. Avec « Miss Trip » et « Olly Tango », il annonce une nouvelle maturité dans le travail de Starck, qui a donné naissance à des formes particulièrement élégantes et rationnelles.

▲ **Philippe Starck**
Dr. No, 1996

KARTELL, NOVIGLIO, MILAN, FROM 1996 TO
PRESENT

▲ **Philippe Starck**
Prince Aha, 1996

KARTELL, NOVIGLIO, MILAN, FROM 1996 TO
PRESENT

Philippe Starck

Miss Trip, 1996

*Injection-moulded
polypropylene seat
and laminated wood
back on solid beech
legs | Sitzfläche
aus spritzgußgeform-
tem Polypropylen,
Rückenlene aus
laminiertem Holz,
Stuhlbeine aus
Buche | Siège en
polypropylène moulé
par injection, dossier
en bois laminé, pieds
en hêtre massif*

KARTELL, NOVIGLIO,
MILAN, FROM 1996
TO PRESENT

Roger Tallon

Module 400, 1964

Polished aluminium
frame with latex-foam
seating section |
Rahmen aus polier-
tem Gußaluminium,
Sitzschale mit
Polsterung aus
Latexschaumstoff |
Châssis en aluminium
poli, siège en mousse
de latex

ÉDITIONS LACLOCHE,
PARIS, 1966–1975

The "Module 400" series of 17 designs by Tallon included chairs, tables and stools. Each design used a standard pedestal base which occupied a floor area of 40 × 40 cm. The foam packing material provided an inexpensive, yet comfortable form of upholstery.

Die Möbelserie »Module 400« von Tallon bestand aus 17 unterschiedlichen Stuhl-, Tisch- und Hockermodellen. Jeder Entwurf hat als Basis den gleichen Standardsockel mit einer Grundplatte von 40 × 40 cm. Das Polstermaterial ist Schaumstoff aus der Verpackungsindustrie, eine preiswerte Möglichkeit der Polsterung, die dennoch für Sitzkomfort sorgt.

La série « Module 400 » de 17 modèles, créée par Tallon, comprenait des sièges, des tables et des tabourets. Chacun fait appel au même piètement modulaire, qui occupe une surface au sol de 40 x 40 cm. Le recouvrage en mousse est une solution économique et confortable de rembourrage.

Giuseppe Terragni

Sant'Elia, 1936

Chromed tubular steel frame with leather-upholstered seat, back and armrests | Rahmen aus gebogenem Stahlrohr, verchromt Sitzfläche, Rückenlehne und Armlehnen mit Lederpolsterung | Châssis en tube d'acier chromé, siège, dossier et accoudoirs en cuir rembourré

(REISSUED BY ZANOTTA, FROM 1970)

▼ **Giuseppe Terragni**
Lariana, 1935–1936
(REISSUED BY ZANOTTA, FROM 1971)

► Casa del Fascio (later renamed Casa del Popolo), Como, c. 1936

Michael Thonet

Chair, Model No. 14,
1859

*Bent solid and
laminated beech
construction with
woven cane seat |
Rahmen aus gebo-
gener, laminierter
und massiver Buche,
Sitzfläche aus Rohr-
geflecht | Hêtre cintré
massif et contre-
plaqué, siège canné*

GEBRÜDER THONET,
VIENNA, FROM
1859 TO PRESENT

▼ **Michael Thonet**
Boppard chair II,
1840–1842

MICHAEL THONET,
BOPPARD

The result of extensive experimentation during the late
1850s into the bending of solid wood, the No. 14 chair
remains one of the most successful industrial designed
products of all time. The simplified form of the chair
was developed by Thonet as a means of achieving his
goal of mass-production: by 1930, 50 million examples
had been sold worldwide.

*Der Stuhl Nr. 14, das Ergebnis langjähriger Experimente
mit dem Bugholzverfahren während der späten 1850er
Jahre, ist bis heute eines der erfolgreichsten industriellen
Produkte aller Zeiten. Die reduzierte Form hat Thonet*

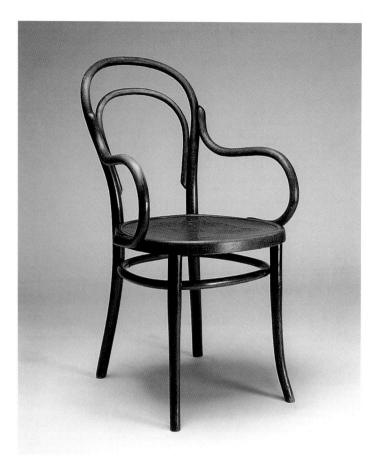

*entwickelt, um seinem Ziel der Massenproduktion näherzu-
kommen. Bis 1930 waren bereits 50 Millionen Exemplare
des Nr. 14 verkauft worden.*

Aboutissement de plusieurs années d'expérimentations
sur le cintrage des bois massifs à la fin des années 1850,
le modèle n° 14 reste l'un des produits industriels les
plus célèbres de tous les temps. Sa forme épurée fut
mise au point par Thonet pour faciliter la production
en grande série. En 1930, 50 millions d'exemplaires en
avaient été vendus dans le monde entier.

Masanori Umeda

Getsuen, 1990

Fabric-covered
polyurethane foam
and Dacron-uphol-
stered steel frame
with carved wood
details and plastic
wheels | Rahmen aus
Stahl mit Details aus
geschnitztem Holz
auf Plastikrollen,
Polsterung aus Poly-
urethanschaumstoff
und Dacron mit
Stoffbezug | Châssis
en acier, rembourrage
en mousse de poly-
uréthane et dacron
recouverts de tissu,
éléments en bois
sculpté, roues en
plastique

EDRA, PERIGNANO,
FROM 1990 TO
PRESENT

▲ **Rocky Semprini &
Mario Cananzi**
Tatlin, 1989

EDRA, PERIGNANO,
FROM 1989 TO
PRESENT

Claiming that, through its affluence, Japan has destroyed its own natural beauty, Umeda uses a variety of floral motifs in order to rediscover the roots of Japanese culture. Also influenced by Memphis, Umeda's designs can be seen as wry Post-Modern commentaries on the friction between the traditional and the contemporary.

Umeda glaubt, daß Japan durch seine Wohlstandsgesellschaft die natürliche Schönheit des Landes zerstört hat und verwendet deshalb eine Vielfalt von Blumenmotiven, um wieder zu den Wurzeln der japanischen Kultur zu gelangen. Beeinflußt auch durch das Memphis-Design, können Umedas Entwürfe als postmodern-ironische Kommentare zu den Gegensätzen zwischen Tradition und Gegenwart verstanden werden.

Masanori
Umeda

Rose, 1990

*Fabric-covered
polyurethane foam
and Dacron-uphol-
stered steel frame
with carved wood
details and chromed
cast-aluminium legs |
Rahmen aus Stahl
mit Details aus
geschnitztem Holz,
Stuhlbeine aus
Gußaluminium,
verchromt, Polsterung
aus Polyurethan-
schaumstoff und
Dacron mit Stoff-
bezug | Châssis en
acier, rembourrage
en mousse de poly-
uréthane et dacron
recouverts de tissu,
éléments en bois
sculpté, pieds en
fonte d'aluminium
chromée*

EDRA, PERIGNANO,
FROM 1990 TO
PRESENT

Prétendant que, par sa richesse, le Japon a détruit sa beauté naturelle,
Umeda se sert de divers motifs floraux pour tenter de redécouvrir les
racines de la culture nippone. Influencées par Memphis, ses créations sont
également un commentaire ironique et postmoderne sur les frictions entre
le traditionnel et le contemporain.

Henry van de Velde

Bloemenwerf, 1895

Walnut frame with leather seat | Rahmen aus Walnußholz, Sitzfläche mit Lederpolster | Châssis en noyer, siège en cuir

SOCIÉTÉ HENRY VAN DE VELDE, IXELLES, FROM 1895

▼ **Henry van de Velde**
Dining room, Bloemenwerf House, Uccle, near Brussels, c. 1896

In 1900, van de Velde moved from Belgium to Germany, where he practised his "Anglicised" version of Art Nouveau. As an important design theorist, as well as a prolific designer, his chairs can be seen as realisations of his desire for functional objects that could exist beyond stylistic convention.

Im Jahr 1900 übersiedelte van de Velde von Belgien nach Deutschland; dort schuf er seine »anglisierten« Jugendstilarbeiten. Als bedeutender Designtheoretiker und als produktiver Praktiker verfolgte er das Ziel, funktionale Objekte zu kreieren, die jenseits aller stilistischen Konventionen Bestand haben sollten: Dafür stehen auch seine Stühle und Sessel.

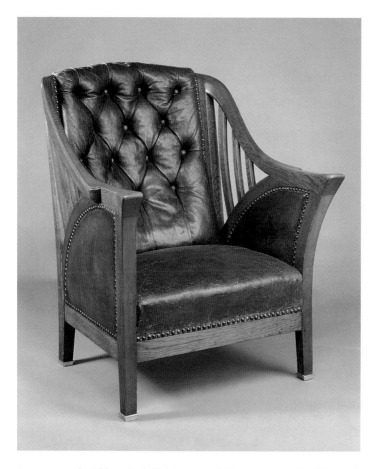

Henry van de Velde

Havana, 1897

Oak frame with buttoned leather-upholstered seat and back and brass sabots | Rahmen aus Eiche, Rückenlehne und Sitzfläche mit durchgeknöpftem Lederpolster, Fuß-manschetten aus Messing | Châssis en chêne, siège et dossier en cuir capitonné et rembourré, sabots en laiton

SOCIÉTÉ HENRY VAN DE VELDE, IXELLES

▼ Henry van de Velde
Bodenhausen arm-chair, 1897–1898
(Batik upholstery by Jan Thorn-Prikker)

SOCIÉTÉ HENRY VAN DE VELDE, IXELLES, 1898–1899

En 1900, van de Velde quitte la Belgique pour l'Allemagne on il crée cette version anglicisée de l'Art nouveau. Important théoricien et créateur prolifique, il réussit à réaliser des sièges illustrant un désir de fonctionnalisme libéré de toute convention stylistique.

Otto Wagner

Armchair for the telegraph office "Die Zeit", 1902

Stained, bent beech frame with woven "Eisengarn" cord seat and upholstered back section, aluminium fittings and sabots | Rahmen aus gebogener Buche, Sitzfläche aus Eisengarngewebe, Rückenlehne gepolstert, Fußmanschetten und Beschläge aus Aluminium | Châssis en hêtre cintré teinté, siège en tressage de corde « Eisengarn », dossier à section rembourrée, sabots et garnitures en aluminium

JACOB & JOSEF KOHN, VIENNA, FROM C. 1902

▼ **Otto Wagner**
Reconstruction of the "Die Zeit" facade

▲ **Otto Wagner**
Stools for the telegraph office "Die Zeit", 1902
JACOB & JOSEF KOHN, VIENNA

Otto Wagner

Armchair for the boardroom of the Austrian Post Office Savings Bank, 1905–1906

Bent solid beech and laminated wood frame with upholstered seat, aluminium fittings | Rahmen aus gebogener, massiver und laminierter Buche, Sitzfläche gepolstert, Fußmanschetten und Beschläge aus Aluminium | Châssis en hêtre massif et bois contre-plaqué, siège rembourré et garnitures en aluminium

JACOB & JOSEF KOHN, VIENNA, FROM C. 1906

▼ Otto Wagner
Stool for the main banking room of the Austrian Post Office Savings Bank, c. 1906

JACOB & JOSEF KOHN, VIENNA

Wagner's chair and stool designs are exceptional for their modernity. The aluminium fittings are not just decorative, but also protect the furniture where it is most sensitive.

Wagners Stuhl- und Hockerentwürfe zeichnen sich durch ihre Modernität aus. Die Beschläge aus Aluminium fungieren nicht nur als Schmuck, sondern schützen die Möbel auch an ihren empfindlichsten Stellen.

Les projets de chaises et de tabourets de Wagner se distinguent par leur modernité. Les ferrures en aluminium ne font pas seulement fonction d'ornementation mais protègent également les meubles aux endroits les plus sensibles.

Hans J. Wegner

Y chair, Model No. 24, 1950

Oak frame with woven paper cord seat | Rahmen aus Eiche, Sitzfläche aus Papierkordelgeflecht | Châssis en chêne, siège en corde de papier tressée

CARL HANSEN & SØN, ODENSE, FROM 1950 TO PRESENT

Wegner has been described as the "chair-maker of chair-makers" and certainly few other designers have consistently produced such high-quality designs. The "Y" chair, sometimes known as the "Wishbone", is Wegner's most commercially successful design. The timeless quality of the "Round" chair led it to be known by its admirers as the "Classic Chair" or simply, "The Chair".

Wegner ist als »Stuhlhersteller par excellence« bezeichnet worden, und ganz sicher haben nur wenige andere Designer immer wieder Entwürfe von so hoher Qualität geliefert. Der »Y«-Stuhl, manchmal auch als »Wishbone« (Brustbein)-Stuhl bezeichnet, war der Verkaufsschlager unter seinen Entwürfen. Die Zeitlosigkeit des »runden« Stuhls führte dazu, daß seine Bewunderer ihn den »Klassischen Stuhl« oder einfach nur »Den Stuhl« nannten.

Hans J. Wegner

Round chair, Model No. JH 501, 1949

Teak frame with woven cane seat | Gestell aus Teak, Sitzfläche aus Rohrgeflecht | Châssis en teck, siège en jonc tressé

JOHANNES HANSEN, SOEBORG, 1949–1992 (REISSUED BY P.P. MØBLER, ALLERØD, FROM 1992)

▼ CBS bought twelve JH 501 chairs for the famous televised presidential debate between John F. Kennedy and Richard M. Nixon in 1961

Wegner a pu être qualifié de « fabricants de sièges par excellence » tant il est certain que peu de designers ont produit avec une telle constance des modèles d'une aussi grande qualité. Le fauteuil « Y », parfois appelé « Wishbone », est celle de ses créations qui a remporté le plus grand succès commercial. La qualité intemporelle du « Fauteuil rond » l'a fait baptiser par ses admirateurs le « Fauteuil classique », ou plus simplement encore « Le Fauteuil ».

Frank Lloyd Wright

Swivel armchair for the offices of the Larkin Company Administration Building, 1904

Painted steel frame with leather-upholstered seat on swivelling steel base terminating on castors | Rahmen aus Stahl, lackiert, drehbar, Sitzfläche gepolstert, auf Rollen | Châssis en acier peint, siège en cuir rembourré sur piètement pivotant en acier, roulettes

VON DORN IRON WORKS COMPANY, CLEVELAND, OHIO

▼ Frank Lloyd Wright
Director's office, Larkin Company Administration Building, Buffalo, New York, c. 1905

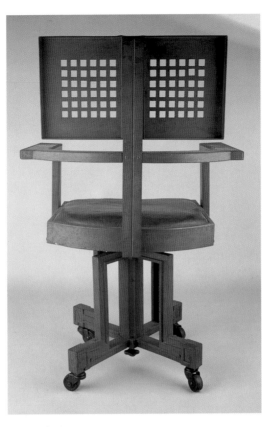

Wright's integrated design for the Larkin Company Building revolutionised the concept of the workplace environment. Echoing the geometry of the building, the office chair was both visually and functionally unified with its surroundings.

Wright hat diesen Bürostuhl auf seinen Gesamtentwurf des Bürogebäudes für die Larkin Company abgestimmt und damit die Vorstellungen vom Arbeitsplatz revolutioniert. In Übereinstimmung mit der Geometrie des Gebäudes war der Bürostuhl sowohl optisch als auch funktionell in seine Umgebung eingebunden.

Le design intégré de Wright pour l'immeuble de la Larkin Compagny révolutionna la conception de l'environnement du lieu de travail. Faisant écho à la géométrie de l'immeuble, ce fauteuil de bureau était à la fois visuellement et fonctionnellement en harmonie avec son environnement.

Frank Lloyd Wright

Peacock chair for the Imperial Hotel, Tokyo, c. 1921–1922

Oak frame with seat and back upholstered in oil cloth | Rahmen aus Eiche, Sitzfläche und Rückenlehne gepolstert | Châssis en chêne, siège et dossier en toile cirée rembourrée

◄Frank Lloyd Wright
Reclining armchair for the Francis W. Little House, Peoria, Illinois, 1903

◄◄Frank Lloyd Wright
Chair for Midway Gardens, Chicago, Illinois, 1914

(REISSUED BY CASSINA)

Sori Yanagi

Butterfly, 1956

*Moulded plywood
with brass stretcher |
Geformtes Schicht-
holz, Spannvorrich-
tung aus Messing |
Contre-plaqué moulé,
tendeur en laiton*

TENDO MOKKO CO.,
TOYKO, FROM
C. 1956

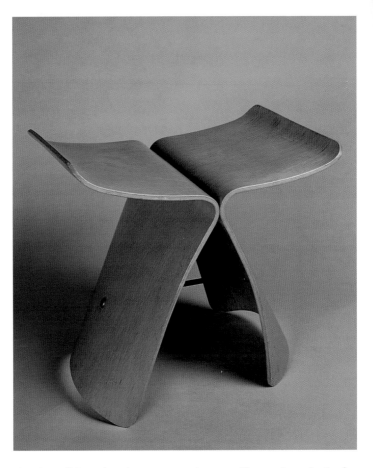

The "Butterfly" stool can be seen as an elegant and harmonic synthesis of Eastern and Western cultures. Highly favoured in America during the 1950s, it was easy to dismantle and transport.

Der »Butterfly«-Hocker stellt eine elegante und harmonische Synthese der östlichen und westlichen Kultur dar. Der leicht zu zerlegende und zu transportierende Hocker war während der 50er Jahre in den Vereinigten Staaten sehr beliebt.

Le tabouret « Butterfly » est une élégante et harmonieuse synthèse entre les cultures de l'Orient et de l'Occident. Très apprécié aux États-Unis dans les années 50, il était facile à démonter et à transporter.

**Marco Zanuso
& Richard
Sapper**

*Stacking child's
chair, Model No.
4999/5, 1961–1964*

*Injection-moulded
polyethylene ribbed
seat section with
separate injection-
moulded polyethylene
legs on rubber feet |
Gerippte Sitzschale
mit separaten Stuhl-
beinen aus spritzguß-
geformtem Polyethy-
len, Stuhlbeine mit
Gummikappen |
Siège à côtes en
polyéthylène moulé
par injection, pieds en
polyéthylène moulés
séparément, patins
en caoutchouc*

KARTELL, NOVIGLIO,
MILAN, FROM 1964
TO PRESENT

The patents expired for polyethylene in the mid-1960s, thereby lowering the
material's cost. Zanuso and Sapper were the first to explore the potential of
this thermoplastic in seat furniture with their injection-moulded stacking
child's chair.

*Der patentrechtliche Schutz für Polyethylen erlosch Mitte der 6oer Jahre, und die
Kosten für dieses Material sanken. Zanuso und Sapper waren mit dem Entwurf
ihres spritzgußgeformten stapelbaren Kinderstuhls die ersten, die die Möglichkeiten dieses Thermokunststoffs für Sitzmöbel nutzten.*

Les brevets d'exploitation du polyéthylène étant tombés dans le domaine
public au milieu des années 60, le prix de ce matériau baissa. Zanuso et
Sapper furent les premiers à mettre à profit le potentiel de ce thermo-
plastique dans la création de sièges, en produisant cette chaise pour enfants, empilable et moulée par injection.

Biographies
Biographien

Hugo Alvar Henrik Aalto (1898–1976)
FINLAND
Born in Kuortane, Finland, Alvar Aalto studied architecture at the Technical University of Helsinki from 1916 to 1921. Initially worked as an exhibition designer and later turned to architecture in 1923 and furniture design in 1925. He became a member of the Congrès Internationaux d'Architecture Moderne in 1928. In 1929 with Otto Korhonen he established an experimental plywood workshop in Turku. In 1935, he founded a furniture design company, Artek, with Harry and Marie Gullichsen and in the same year patented a cantilevered chair support made of wood. Aalto's work was shown in London at the exhibition of Finnish design held at Fortnum and Mason in 1933, at the Paris 1937 Exhibition and the New York 1939 World Fair to great acclaim. In 1957, he was awarded a gold medal by the Royal Institute of British Architects (RIBA).

Alvar Aalto wurde in Kuortane, Finnland, geboren und studierte von 1916 bis 1921 Architektur an der Technischen Universität Helsinki. Zunächst arbeitete er als Ausstellungsgestalter, wendete sich 1923 der Architektur und 1925 dem Möbelentwurf zu. 1928 wurde er Mitglied der Congrès Internationaux d'Architecture Moderne. 1929 richtete er in Turku mit Otto Korhonen eine Experimentierwerkstatt für Schichtholz ein. 1935 gründete er mit Harry und Marie Gullichsen die Designfirma Artek und ließ im gleichen Jahr einen Freischwinger aus Holz patentieren. Aaltos Arbeiten wurden 1933 in London auf der Ausstellung für finnisches Design bei Fortnum und Maason, 1937 auf der Pariser Ausstellung und 1939 auf der New Yorker Weltausstellung gezeigt. 1957 erhielt er die Goldmedaille des Royal Institute of British Architects (RIBA).

Né à Kuortane, en Finlande, Alvar Aalto étudie l'architecture à l'École polytechnique d'Helsinki de 1916 à 1921. À l'origine concepteur d'expositions (1923), il se tourne vers l'architecture et la création de mobilier (1925). Il devient membre des Congrès internationaux d'architecture moderne en 1928. En 1929, avec Otto Korhonen, il crée un atelier expérimental de contre-plaqué à Turku. En 1935, il fonde, avec Harry et Marie Gullichsen, une société de création de mobilier, Artek, et dépose la même année le brevet d'un châssis de chaise en porte à faux et en contre-plaqué. L'œuvre d'Aalto est présentée à Londres lors de l'exposition sur le design finlandais organisée par Fortnum and Mason en 1933, à l'Exposition de Paris de 1937 et à la Foire internationale de New York en 1939, où elle reçoit un accueil remarqué. En 1957, la médaille d'or du Royal Institute of British Architects (RIBA) lui est décernée.

Alvar Aalto

Eero Aarnio

Franco Albini

Eero Aarnio (*1932) FINLAND
Born in Helsinki, Eero Aarnio studied at the Institute of Industrial Arts, Helsinki, graduating in 1957. He established his own design office in 1962 and has since worked primarily as an interior and industrial designer. In 1968, he was awarded an A.I.D. award for the "Pastille" chair.

Eero Aarnio wurde in Helsinki geboren und studierte bis 1957 an der dortigen Universität Industriedesign. 1962 gründete er sein eigenes Designstudio und hat seither vor allem als Innenarchitekt und Industriedesigner gearbeitet. 1968 erhielt er den A.I.D.-Preis für den Stuhl »Pastille«.

Né à Helsinki, Eero Aarnio étudie à l'Institut d'enseignement technique d'Helsinki dont il est diplômé en 1957. Il ouvre son propre bureau de design en 1962 et depuis, se consacre essentiellement au design industriel et domestique. En 1968, il reçoit un prix de l'A.I.D. pour sa chaise « Pastille ».

Franco Albini (1905–1977) ITALY
Born in Robbiate, Como, Franco Albini studied architecture at the Polytechnic of Milan, graduating in 1929. He was active in Gio Ponti's studio until he met the Rationalist, Edoardo Persco, in 1930. In the same year, he established his own practice and subsequently joined by three partners, Franca Helg, Antonio Piva and his son, Marco Albini, in 1952, 1962 and 1965 respectively. As one of the foremost Rationalist designers, he edited *Casabella* from 1945 to 1946. From 1963 to 1977 he taught architectural composition at the Politecnic of Milan. He received Compasso d'Oro awards in 1955, 1958 and 1964.

Franco Albini wurde in Robbiate, Como, geboren und studierte bis 1929 Architektur am Polytechnikum, Mailand. Er arbeitete in Gio Pontis Atelier, bis er 1930 den Rationalisten Edoardo Persco traf. Im gleichen Jahr gründete er sein eigenes Studio, in das 1952, 1962 und 1965 nacheinander Franca Helg, Antonio Piva und Marco Albini, sein Sohn, als Partner eintraten. Als einer der führenden Designer des Rationalismus gab er von 1945 bis 1946 »Casabella« heraus. Von 1963 bis 1977 unterrichtete er Entwurfslehre am Polytechnikum, Mailand. 1955, 1958 und 1964 wurde er mit dem Compasso d'Oro ausgezeichnet.

Né à Robbiate, près de Côme, Franco Albini étudie l'architecture à l'École polytechnique de Milan. Diplômé en 1929, il travaille dans l'agence de Gio Ponti jusqu'à sa rencontre avec le rationaliste Edoardo Persco, en 1930. La même année, il ouvre sa propre agence où le rejoignent trois associés, Franca Helg, Antonio Piva et son propre fils, Marco

Albini, respectivement en 1952, 1962 et 1965.
L'un des plus éminents designers rationalistes,
il dirige *Casabella* de 1945 à 1946. De 1963 à
1977, il enseigne la composition en architecture à l'École politechnique de Milan. Il reçoit
un Compasso d'Oro en 1955, 1958 et 1964.

Ron Arad (*1951) ISRAEL

Born in Israel, Ron Arad studied at the
Jerusalem Academy of Art, 1971 to 1973. Later,
he studied at the Architectural Association,
London, graduating in 1979. In 1981, he
founded his own architectural design office-
cum-showroom, One Off Ltd., in Covent
Garden. The practice later moved to Chalk
Farm, London. He is primarily known for his
furniture designs; however, in recent years he
has received several important architectural
commissions including the interior for the
Tel Aviv Opera House in 1990.

Ron Arad wurde in Israel geboren und
studierte von 1971 bis 1973 an der Jerusalemer
Akademie der Künste, anschließend bis 1979
bei der Architectural Association, London.
1981 gründete er in Covent Garden, London,
One Off Ltd., sein Architekturbüro mit Aus-
stellungsraum. Die Werkstatt verlegte er später
nach Chalk Farm, London. Er machte sich vor
allem mit seinen Möbelentwürfen einen Namen, erhielt in der letzten Zeit aber auch Aufträge für bedeutende Architekturprojekte, darunter 1990 der Innenausbau des Opernhauses
von Tel Aviv.

Né en Israël, Ron Arad fait ses études
à l'Académie des arts de Jérusalem de 1971 à
1973. Plus tard, il suit les cours de l'Architectural
Association de Londres, dont il sort diplômé
en 1979. En 1981, il crée son propre bureau de
design et sa galerie, One Off Ltd., à Covent
Garden, qu'il transfère par la suite à Chalk
Farm, à Londres. Il est surtout connu pour
ses créations de meubles, mais a cependant
récemment reçu plusieurs importantes commandes architecturales, dont l'aménagement
intérieur de l'opéra de Tel Aviv en 1990.

Mario Bellini (*1935) ITALY

Born in Milan, Mario Bellini studied architecture at the Polytechnic of Milan, graduating in
1959. From 1961 to 1963, he was design director at La Rinascente, the influential chain of department stores. In 1963, he founded an architectural office with Marco Romano and later in
1973 established Studio Bellini, Milan. Since
1963 he has held the position of chief design
consultant for Olivetti and from 1978 has been
a research and design consultant for Renault.
Between 1962 and 1965, he was the professor
of design at the Istituto Superiore del Disegno
Industriale, Venice, and since then has been a

visiting lecturer to many design colleges including the Royal College of Art, London.
He has received numerous awards including
several Compassi d'Oro.

Mario Bellini wurde in Mailand geboren
und studierte Architektur am Polytechnikum,
Mailand, wo er 1959 sein Diplom erwarb. Von
1961 bis 1963 leitete er die Designabteilung
der bekannten Warenhauskette La Rinascente.
1963 gründete er mit Marco Romano ein Architekturbüro, und 1973 eröffnete er das Atelier
Bellini, Mailand. Seit 1963 ist er Designberater
für Olivetti, seit 1978 Berater für Forschung
und Design bei Renault. Von 1962 bis 1965
lehrte er Industriedesign am Istituto Superiore
del Disegno Industriale in Venedig; seit 1963
ist er Gastprofessor zahlreicher Universiäten, u.a.
am Royal College of Art, London. Er erhielt
zahlreiche Preise, darunter mehrfach den
Compasso d'Oro.

Milanais, Mario Bellini étudie l'architecture à l'École polytechnique de Milan dont il
sort diplômé en 1959. De 1961 à 1963, il est directeur du design à La Rinascente, l'influente
chaîne de grands magasins. En 1963, il fonde
un cabinet d'architecture avec Marco Romano
et plus tard, en 1973, le Studio Bellini à Milan.
Depuis 1963, il est le principal consultant en
design d'Olivetti et, depuis 1978, consultant
en recherche et design pour Renault. De 1962
à 1965, il est professeur de design à l'Istituto
Superiore di Disegno Industriale de Venise et
enseigne depuis dans de nombreuses écoles
de design dont le Royal College of Art de
Londres. Il a reçu de multiples distinctions
dont plusieurs Compassi d'Oro.

Harry Bertoia (1915–1978) USA

Born in Udine, Italy, Harry Bertoia emigrated
with his family to America in 1930. In 1936,
he graduated from the Cass Technical High
School, Detroit and from 1937 to 1939 trained
on a scholarship at the Cranbrook Academy of
Arts. He established the metalworking studio
there and as head of that department taught
from 1939 to 1943. Later, he worked with
Charles and Ray Eames at the Evans Products
Company developing techniques for moulding
plywood. After the war, he worked for a short
period at the Eameses' Plyformed Products
Company in Venice, California. His innovative
wire chairs designed for Knoll International in
1951 were so commercially successful that the
royalties from this group of designs allowed
him to concentrate solely on his sculpting
career.

Harry Bertoia wurde in Udine, Italien,
geboren und wanderte 1930 mit seiner Familie
nach Amerika aus. 1936 beendete er sein
Studium an der Cass Technical High School,

Ron Arad

Mario Bellini

Harry Bertoia

Osvaldo Borsani

Marcel Lajos Breuer

Detroit. 1937 bis 1939 erhielt er ein Stipendium der Cranbrook Academy of Arts. Anschließend richtete er dort das Cranbrook-Studio für Metallarbeiten ein, das er von 1939 bis 1943 leitete. Dann arbeitete er mit Charles und Ray Eames bei der Evans Products Company an der Entwicklung von Techniken für die Formung von Schichtholz. Nach dem Krieg war er für kurze Zeit bei der Plyformed Products Company der Eames' in Venice, Kalifornien. Seine innovativen Drahtstühle, die 1951 für Knoll International entstanden, waren ein derart großer finanzieller Erfolg, daß die Tantiemen zum Leben ausreichten und er sich ausschließlich der Bildhauerei widmen konnte.

Né à Udine, en Italie, Harry Bertoia émigre en Amérique avec sa famille en 1930. En 1936, il est diplômé de la Cass Technical High School de Detroit et, de 1937 à 1939, bénéficie d'une bourse à la Cranbrook Academy of Arts. Il y fonde l'atelier de travail des métaux et enseigne de 1939 à 1943, en tant que responsable de ce département. Il collabore ensuite avec les Eames à l'Evans Production Company, mettant au point des techniques de moulage du contre-plaqué. Après la guerre, il travaille brièvement pour la Plyformed Products Company des Eames à Venice, en Californie. Ses chaises innovantes en fil de métal, créées pour Knoll International en 1951, rencontrent un tel succès commercial que leurs royalties lui permettent de se consacrer exclusivement à sa carrière de sculpteur.

Osvaldo Borsani (*1911) ITALY
Son of the craftsman Gaetano Borsani, who won a silver medal at the first Monza Triennale in 1927, Osvaldo and his brother, Fulgenzio, founded Tecno in 1952 – the company had formerly been known as the Arredamento Borsani in Varedo and prior to this, Atelier Varedo. From 1952 to the present day, Osvaldo has been the main designer for Tecno, a firm committed to the research and development of high-quality furniture for the office environment.

Osvaldo Borsanis Vater, Gaetano Borsani, war Handwerker und wurde 1927 bei der ersten Triennale von Monza mit einer Silbermedaille ausgezeichnet. Mit seinem Bruder Fulgenzio gründete Osvaldo 1952 die Firma Tecno – das Unternehmen hatte sich zuvor als Arredmento Borsani in Varedo und noch früher als Atelier Varedo einen Namen gemacht. Seit 1952 ist Osvaldo Chefdesigner für Tecno, ein Unternehmen, das sich auf die Erforschung und Entwicklung qualitativ hochwertiger Büroeinrichtungen spezialisiert hat.

Fils de l'artisan Gaetano Borsani qui avait remporté la médaille d'argent de la première Triennale de Monza en 1927, Osvaldo et son

frère Fulgenzio fondent Tecno en 1952, société initialement connue sous le nom d'Atelier Varedo puis d'Arredamento Borsani de Varedo. Depuis 1952, Osvaldo est le principal designer de Tecno, firme italienne de recherche, développement, fabrication et vente de mobilier de bureau de haute qualité.

Marcel Lajos Breuer (1902–1981)
HUNGARY/GERMANY
Born in Hungary, Marcel Lajos Breuer spent a short time working in a Viennese architectural office before studying at the Bauhaus, Weimar, 1920–1924. After graduating, he became master of the furniture workshop there and continued in that capacity when the Bauhaus moved to Dessau in 1925. He directed his own architectural firm in Berlin from 1928–1931 before leaving Germany when he spent a year in London, working first as an architect in partnership with F. S. Yorke and later as Controller of Design at Isokon. In 1937 he emigrated to the United States of America and was an Associate Professor at the School of Design at Harvard University from 1937 to 1946. Between 1937 and 1941 he shared an architectural practice in Cambridge, Massachusetts with Walter Gropius. From 1946 he headed his own firm, Marcel Breuer & Associates in New York until his retirement in 1976.

Marcel Lajos Breuer wurde in Ungarn geboren und arbeitete kurze Zeit in einem Wiener Architekturbüro, anschließend, von 1920 bis 1924, studierte er am Bauhaus in Weimar. Nach der Gesellenprüfung wurde er Leiter der Möbelwerkstatt des Bauhauses und behielt diese Funktion, als das Bauhaus 1925 nach Dessau verlegt werden mußte. 1928 ging er nach Berlin und eröffnete sein eigenes Architekturstudio. 1935 verließ er Deutschland, lebte zunächst in London, wo er als Partner des Architekten F. R. S. Yorke tätig war und später als Designer für die Firma Isokon arbeitete. 1937 wanderte er in die USA aus; von 1937 bis 1946 war er Associate Professor an der School of Design der Havard University. Von 1937 bis 1941 war er mit Walter Gropius Teilhaber eines Architekturbüros in Cambridge, Massachusetts. Von 1946 an leitete er seine eigene Firma, Marcel Breuer & Associates, New York, bis sich 1976 zur Ruhe setzte.

Hongrois d'origine, Marcel Lajos Breuer travaille quelque temps dans un bureau d'architectes viennois avant de suivre les cours du Bauhaus, à Weimar, de 1920 à 1924. Diplômé, il devient responsable de l'atelier du mobilier et conserve ces fonctions lorsque le Bauhaus va s'installer à Dessau en 1925. Il dirige son propre cabinet d'architecture à Berlin de 1928 à 1931 avant de quitter l'Allemagne. Il séjourne deux ans à Londres (1935–1937), d'abord comme architecte, en association avec F. R. S. Yorke, puis comme contrôleur du design chez Isokon. En 1937, il émigre aux États-Unis et devient professeur à la School of Design de l'université d'Harvard, de 1937 à 1946. De 1937 à 1941, il partage un bureau d'architecte à Cambridge, Massachusetts, avec Walter Gropius. À partir de 1946, il dirige sa propre firme, Marcel Breuer & Associates (New York), jusqu'à sa retraite en 1976.

Carlo Bugatti (1856–1940) ITALY

Born in Milan, Carlo Bugatti studied at the Brera Academy of Fine Arts, Milan. In 1888, he designed his earliest known pieces of furniture for his sister, Luiga, on the occasion of her marriage to the artist Giovanni Segantini. In 1900, he created furniture for the Khedive's palace in Istanbul. In 1902, he exhibited at the International Exhibition of Modern Decorative Art, Turin. In 1904, he sold his firm to De Becchi, Milan and moved to Paris where he continued to design, most notably silverware. His sons, Ettore (an automobile designer) and Rembrandt (a sculptor) were highly successful in their chosen fields.

Carlo Bugatti wurde in Mailand geboren und studierte an der Brera Akademie der bildenden Künste, Mailand. 1888 entwarf er für seine Schwester Luiga anläßlich ihrer Hochzeit mit dem Künstler Giovanni Segantini seine ersten bekannten Möbel. 1900 schuf er Möbel für den Palast des Khediven in Istanbul. 1902 stellte er auf der Internationalen Ausstellung Moderner Dekorativer Kunst in Turin aus. 1904 verkaufte er seine Firma an De Becchi, Mailand, und zog nach Paris, wo er außergewöhnliches Tafelsilber entwarf. Auch seine Söhne waren auf ihrem Gebiet äußerst erfolgreich, Ettore als Autodesigner und Rembrandt als Bildhauer.

Né à Milan, Carlo Bugatti fait ses études à l'Académie des beaux-arts Brera à Milan. En 1888, il conçoit ses premiers meubles pour sa sœur, Luiga, à l'occasion de son mariage avec l'artiste Giovanni Segantini. En 1900, il crée un mobilier pour le palais du khédive à Istanbul. En 1902, il participe à l'Exposition d'art décoratif moderne de Turin. En 1904, il vend son entreprise à De Becchi (Milan) et s'installe à Paris où il continue à créer, en particulier des pièces d'argenterie. Ses fils Ettore (ingénieur en automobile) et Rembrandt (sculpteur) connaissent chacun dans leur domaine un très grand succès.

Achille Castiglioni (*1918) ITALY

Born in Milan, Achille Castiglioni trained at the Polytechnic of Milan. In 1944 he set up his own Como-based design office with his brothers,

Livio, who left the partnership in 1952, and Pier Giacomo. In 1956 he became a founder of the Associazione per il Disegno Industriale. In 1957, the brothers held an exhibition entitled "Forme e Colori nella Casa D'Oggi" at the Olmo Villa, Como, which incorporated their highly influential "ready-made" designs. Since 1969, he has taught industrial design at the Polytechnic of Turin and has exhibited at every Milan Triennale since 1947. He has received seven Compasso d'Oro awards and was highly involved in the founding of the Italian A.D.I. awards.

Achille Castiglioni wurde in Mailand geboren und studierte am Polytechnikum, Mailand. 1944 gründete er zusammen mit seinen Brüdern Livio und Pier Giacomo ein Designbüro; Livio verließ die Firma 1952. 1956 war Achille Gründungsmitglied der Associazione per il Disegno Industriale. 1957 veranstalteten die Brüder in der Villa Olmo in Como eine Ausstellung mit dem Titel »Forme e Colori nella Casa D'Oggi«, auf der sie auch ihre äußerst einflußreichen Ready-made-Designs zeigten. Seit 1969 lehrt Achille Castiglioni Industriedesign am Polytechnikum von Turin und hat seit 1947 auf jeder Mailänder Triennale ausgestellt. Sieben Mal wurde er mit dem Compasso d'Oro ausgezeichnet; außerdem hat er sich um die Stiftung des Designpreises A.D.I. sehr verdient gemacht.

Né à Milan, Achille Castiglioni fait ses études à l'École polytechnique de Milan. En 1944, il ouvre un bureau de design à Côme avec ses frères, Livio – qui quittera l'association en 1952 – et Pier Giacomo. En 1956, il fait partie des fondateurs de l'Associazione per il Disegno Industriale. En 1957, les deux frères organisent une exposition intitulée « Forme e Colori nella Casa D'Oggi » à la Villa Olmo, à Côme, incluant des projets de ready-made qui exercent une grande influence. Depuis 1947, il a exposé à chaque Triennale de Milan et enseigne le design industriel à l'École polytechnique de Turin depuis 1969. Il a reçu plusieurs Compassi d'Oro et s'est beaucoup impliqué dans la création des prix A.D.I. italiens.

Wendell Castle (*1932) USA

Wendell Castle studied sculpture at the University of Kansas and graduated in 1961. The leading exponent of the Craft Revival in the United States of America, Castle founded his own school for craftsmanship in wood, 1980. After brief experimentation with fibreglass in the late 1960s, he went on to create extraordinary illusionistic sculptural furniture through the use of virtuoso "trompe d'œil" carving techniques. In recent years he has concentrated on mainly historically based designs produced in exquisitely worked exotic materials.

Carlo Bugatti

Achille Castiglioni

Joe Colombo

Robin Day

Michele De Lucchi

Wendell Castle studierte Bildhauerei an der Universität von Kansas, wo er 1961 den Abschluß machte. Als führender Vertreter des »Craft Revival« in den USA gründete er 1980 seine eigene Schule für handwerkliche Holzbearbeitung. Ende der 60er Jahre hat er kurze Zeit mit Fiberglas experimentiert, sich dann aber wieder der Herstellung seiner skulpturalen Möbel mit den virtuos gearbeiteten, äußerst wirklichkeitsgetreuen Schnitzereien gewidmet. In den letzten Jahren hat er sich vor allem auf Entwürfe nach historischen Vorbildern konzentriert, die er, meisterhaft gearbeitet, in exotischen Hölzern ausführt.

Wendell Castle étudie la sculpture à l'université du Kansas jusqu'à l'obtention de son diplôme en 1961. Représentant notable du « Craft Revival », Castle crée sa propre école de travail du bois en 1980. Après de brèves expériences avec la fibre de verre à la fin des années 60, il conçoit d'extraordinaires meubles-sculptures faisant appel à des techniques de travail sur bois en trompe-l'œil qui révèlent un talent de virtuose. Ces dernières années, il s'est principalement consacré à des créations faisant référence à l'histoire et réalisées dans des matériaux exotiques travaillés avec raffinement.

Joe Colombo (1930–1971) ITALY
Born in Milan, he initially trained as a painter at the Brera Academy of Fine Arts before studying architecture at the Polytechnic of Milan. From 1951 to 1955, he worked independently as a painter and sculptor. He joined the Nuclear Painting Movement and later became a founding member of the Art Concrete Group. In 1962, he opened his own design office and worked for, among others, Kartell, O-Luce, Comfort and Bayer. In 1970, he co-wrote, with Pierre Paulin and Sori Yanagi New Form Furniture: Japan.

Joe Colombo wurde in Mailand geboren und studierte an der Brera Akademie der bildenden Künste Mailand Malerei, dann am Polytechnikum Mailand Architektur. Von 1951 bis 1955 arbeitete er als freier Maler und Bildhauer. Er schloß sich dem »Nuclear Painting Movement« an, war Gründungsmitglied der »Art Concrete Group«. 1962 eröffnete er sein eigenes Designstudio und arbeitete u. a. für Kartell, O-Luce, Comfort und Bayer. 1970 gab er zusammen mit Pierre Paulin und Sori Yanagi als Koautoren »New Form-Furniture: Japan« heraus.

Né à Milan, Joe Colombo s'intéresse d'abord à la peinture à l'Académie des beaux-arts Brera avant d'étudier l'architecture à l'École polytechnique de Milan. De 1951 à 1955, il travaille seul comme peintre et sculpteur, puis rejoint le « Nuclear Painting Movement »

et devient plus tard membre fondateur de l'«Art Concrete Group». En 1962, il crée son bureau de design et travaille, entre autres, pour Kartell, O-Luce, Comfort et Bayer. En 1970, il écrit avec Pierre Paulin et Sori Yanagi New Form Furniture: Japan.

Robin Day (*1915) GREAT BRITAIN
Born in High Wycombe, Robin Day worked for a local furniture manufacturer before training at the Royal College of Art, London, graduating in 1938. He and his wife, Lucienne (the renowned textile designer) opened their own design office in 1948. In the same year, he won first prize with Clive Latimer for the design of a storage unit at the Museum of Modern Art's "International Competition for Low-Cost Furniture Design". In 1949, he was appointed design director at Hille International and has subsequently worked as a design consultant for the company.

Robin Day wurde in High Wycombe geboren und war dort für einen heimischen Möbelhersteller tätig, bevor er sein Studium am Royal College of Art, London, aufnahm; 1938 erwarb er seinen Abschluß. Mit seiner Frau Lucienne (der bekannten Textildesignerin) eröffnete er 1948 ein Designstudio. Im selben Jahr gewann er mit Clive Latimer den ersten Preis für eine gemeinsam entworfene Regaleinheit beim »International Competition for Low-Cost Furniture Design« des Museum of Modern Art. 1949 wurde er Designdirektor des englischen Möbelherstellers Hille International, für den er später als Designberater tätig war.

Né à High Wycombe, Robin Day travaille pour un fabricant local de meubles avant d'étudier au Royal College of Art, à Londres (diplômé en 1938). Avec sa femme Lucienne (créatrice textile renommée), ils ouvrent leur propre studio de design en 1948. La même année, il remporte avec Clive Latimer le premier prix du « International Competition for Low-Cost Furniture Design » du Museum of Modern Art. En 1949, il est nommé directeur du design chez Hille International et travaille régulièrement pour cette société.

Michele De Lucchi (*1951) ITALY
Born in Ferrara, Michele De Lucchi studied in Padua and later at the University of Florence, graduating in 1975 – he subsequently taught there. He designed furniture for Studio Alchimia and in the 1980s for Memphis. He was responsible for the introduction of geometric motifs on the plastic laminates used by Memphis. In 1979, he became a consultant to Olivetti, Ivrea, Italy. He now primarily concentrates on product design.

Biographies | Biographien

Michele De Lucchi wurde in Ferrara geboren und studierte in Padua, später an der Universität von Florenz. Nach seinem Abschluß im Jahr 1975 hatte er dort einen Lehrauftrag. Er entwarf zunächst Möbel für Alchimia und in den 80er Jahren für Memphis. Auf ihn geht die Einführung von geometrischen Motiven auf Kunststofflaminat zurück, die Memphis produzierte. 1979 wurde er Berater für Olivetti, Ivrea, Italien. Heute ist er vor allem als Produktdesigner tätig.

Né à Ferrare, Michele De Lucchi fait ses études à Padoue puis à l'université de Florence (diplôme en 1975) où il enseignera plus tard. Il travaille pour Studio Alchimia et, dans les années 80, pour Memphis. Il est à l'origine de l'introduction de motifs géométriques sur les plastiques lamifiés du groupe. En 1979, il est nommé consultant auprès d'Olivetti, à Ivrea. Actuellement, il se consacre essentiellement à ses activités de designer.

Gionatan De Pas, Donato D'Urbino & Paolo Lomazzi (*1932, *1935, *1936) ITALY
De Pas, D'Urbino and Lomazzi trained at the Polytechnic of Milan, before founding a design practice in Milan in 1966. They received considerable recognition in the 1960s and 1970s for their "Blow" chair and later "Joe" chair. In the 1970s they concentrated their efforts on furniture designs that were flexible, interchangeable and adaptable. They have designed furniture for, among others, Driade, BBB Bonacina, Palina, Zanotta and Poltronova, as well as lighting for Stilnovo.

De Pas, D'Urbino and Lomazzi studierten am Polytechnikum, Mailand, anschließend, 1966, gründeten sie ihr Designstudio in Mailand. In den 60er und 70er Jahren verschafften ihnen die Sessel »Blow« und »Joe« große Anerkennung. In den 70er Jahren konzentrierten sie ihre Entwürfen auf vielseitig einsetzbare, austauschbare und anpassungsfähige Möbel, die sie u. a. für Driade, BBB Bonacina, Palina, Zanotta und Poltronova geschaffen haben. Leuchten entstanden für Stilnovo.

Tous trois étudient à l'École polytechnique de Milan avant de fonder leur agence de design à Milan, en 1966. Ils connaissent un succès considérable avec le fauteuil « Blow » puis le « Joe ». Dans les années 70, ils se concentrent sur la création de meubles souples, interchangeables, adaptables. Ils ont dessiné des meubles pour, entre autres, Driade, BBB Bonacina, Palina, Zanotta et Poltronova, ainsi que des luminaires pour Stilnovo.

Erich Dieckmann (1896–1944) GERMANY
From 1921 to 1925, he studied at the Staatliches Bauhaus, Weimar, and is often regarded as the most important Bauhaus-trained furniture designer after Breuer. Remaining in Weimar, when the Bauhaus moved to Dessau, he was master of the joinery workshop at the Bauhochschule Weimar from 1925 to 1930. From 1931 to 1933, he taught at the Kunstgewerbeschule Burg Giebichenstein, Halle.

Erich Dieckmann studierte von 1921 bis 1925 am Staatlichen Bauhaus, Weimar, und wird neben Marcel Breuer als bedeutendster Möbeldesigner des Bauhauses betrachtet. Er blieb in Weimar, als das Bauhaus nach Dessau umziehen mußte, und leitete die Tischlerwerkstatt der Bauhochschule Weimar von 1925 bis 1930. Von 1931 bis 1933 lehrte er an der Kunstgewerbeschule Burg Giebichenstein, Halle.

De Pas, D'Urbino, & Lomazzi

Erich Dieckmann étudie au Staatliches Bauhaus de Weimar de 1921 à 1925. Il est souvent considéré comme le plus important créateur de meubles formé au Bauhaus, après Breuer. Il reste à Weimar lorsque le Bauhaus s'installe à Dessau et dirige l'atelier de menuiserie du Bauhochschule de Weimar, de 1925 à 1930. De 1931 à 1933, il enseigne à la Kunstgewerbeschule Burg Giebichenstein, à Halle.

Erich Dieckmann

Charles Eames (1907–1978) USA
Born in St. Louis, he initially studied architecture at the university there. In 1936, he received a fellowship at the Cranbrook Academy of Arts, Michigan, where he later taught. His colleagues there included Harry Bertoia, Eero Saarinen and Ray Kaiser, whom he married in 1941. During the Second World War, the Eameses were commissioned by the US Navy to design and produce plywood splints and litters. For this project they developed a new method of bending plywood over three geometric planes into complex curves. From 1939 to 1940 he worked in the architectural office of Eliel Saarinen. In 1940, Eames designed, in collaboration with Eero Saarinen, the winning entry for the Museum of Modern Art's "Organic Design in Home Furnishings" competition. In 1946, Eames was given MoMA's first one-man show titled "New Furniture by Charles Eames". Later in 1948, Eames won second prize at the museum's "International Competition for Low-Cost Furniture Design" for his innovative proposal of a series of mass-producible moulded fibreglass chairs. In collaboration with his wife, Ray, Eames worked closely with the manufacturer Herman Miller, creating highly innovative furniture throughout the 1950s and 1960s. Later, the Eameses concentrated on film-making, toymaking, photography and exhibition design – their patrons for such projects included the US Government and IBM.

Charles Eames

Ray Eames

Charles Eames wurde in St. Louis geboren und studierte Architektur zunächst an der dortigen Washington University. 1936 erhielt er ein Stipendium an der Cranbrook Academy of Arts, Michigan, wo er später auch unterrichtete. Zu seinen Kollegen dort gehörten Harry Bertoia, Eero Saarinen und Ray Kaiser, die er 1941 heiratete. Während des Zweiten Weltkriegs erhielten die Eames' von der US Navy den Auftrag, Beinschienen und Krankentragen aus Schichtholz zu entwerfen und zu produzieren. Für dieses Projekt entwickelten sie eine neue Methode, mit der sich Schichtholz in dreidimensionale Formen biegen ließ. Von 1939 bis 1940 arbeitete er im Architekturbüro von Eliel Saarinen. 1940 entwarf Eames, in Zusammenarbeit mit Eero Saarinen, den preisgekrönten Beitrag zum Wettbewerb »Organic Design in Home Furnishings«, den das Museum of Modern Art ausgeschrieben hatte. 1946 zeigte das MoMA unter dem Titel »New Furniture of Charles Eames« seine erste Einzelausstellung. 1948 gewann Eames mit einer Serie von Stühlen aus geformtem Fiberglas, die zur Massenproduktion geeignet waren, den zweiten Preis des »International Competition for Low-Cost Furniture Design«, den das Museum of Modern Art, New York, ausgeschrieben hatte. Mit seiner Frau Ray arbeitete Eames in den 50er und 60er Jahren eng mit der Firma Herman Miller zusammen, es entstanden äußerst innovative Möbel. Anschließend befaßten sich die Eames' mit der Produktion von Filmen und von Spielzeug, mit Photographie und mit Ausstellungsdesign – für diese Projekte fanden sie Förderung u. a. von der US-Regierung und von IBM.

Né à Saint-Louis, Charles Eames commence par étudier l'architecture à la Washington University de Saint-Louis. En 1936, il reçoit une bourse pour la Cranbrook Academy of Arts, Michigan, où il enseigne plus tard. Parmi ses collègues figurent Harry Bertoia, Eero Saarinen et Ray Kaiser qu'il épouse en 1941. Pendant la seconde guerre mondiale, les Eames reçoivent une commande de l'US Navy pour la conception et la production de civières et de gouttières en contre-plaqué. À l'occasion de ce projet, ils mettent au point une nouvelle méthode pour obtenir des cintrages complexes de contre-plaqué. De 1939 à 1940, il travaille dans l'agence d'architecture d'Eliel Saarinen. En 1940, Eames remporte, en collaboration avec Eero Saarinen, le concours du Museum of Modern Art, New York »Organic Design in Home Furnishings«. En 1946, il est l'objet de la première rétrospective personnelle consacrée à un designer par le MoMA: « New

Furniture by Charles Eames». Plus tard, en 1948, il remporte le second prix du concours « Competition for Low-Cost Furniture Design» organisé par le musée, pour le projet novateur de chaises en fibre de verre moulée pouvant être produites en série. En collaboration avec sa femme Ray, Eames travaille en liaison étroite avec le fabricant Herman Miller, créant tout au long des années 50 des meubles hautement innovateurs et rationnels. Plus tard, le couple se concentre sur la réalisation de films, la fabrication de jouets, la photographie et la conception d'expositions pour des clients comme le gouvernement américain ou la firme IBM.

Ray Eames (1912–1989) USA
Born Bernice Alexandra Kaiser (later in 1954 legally changed to Ray Bernice Alexandra Kaiser) in Sacramento, California. In 1933, she graduated from the May Friend Bennett School in Millbrook, New York, and began studying painting at Hans Hofmann's recently opened school. She continued to paint under Hofmann's direction until 1939. In 1937 her work was exhibited in the first American Abstract Artists' group show staged at the Riverside Museum, New York. In 1940, she commenced weaving classes at Cranbrook Academy of Arts, Michigan under the instruction of Marianne Strengel (at this time Charles Eames was the head of the Industrial Design Department at Cranbrook). A year later, after Charles Eames obtained a divorce from his first wife (née Catherine Dewey Woermann), the couple were married in Chicago. Later the same year, they moved to California and began experimenting with moulding techniques for plywood.

Ray Eames, als Bernice Alexandra Kaiser (1954 gesetzlich geändert zu Ray Bernice Alexandra Kaiser) in Sacramento, Kalifornien, geboren, erwarb ihren Abschluß 1933 an der May Friend Bennett School in Millbrook, New York. Von 1933 bis 1939 studierte sie Malerei an Hans Hofmanns gerade eröffneter School of Art. 1937 wurden ihre Arbeiten auf der ersten Ausstellung der Gruppe »American Abstract Artists« gezeigt, veranstaltet vom Riverside Museum, New York. 1940 schrieb sie sich in die Webkurse der Cranbrook Academy of Arts, Michigan, ein, die von Marianne Strengel veranstaltet wurden. Zu dieser Zeit leitete Charles Eames die Abteilung Industrial Design von Cranbrook. Ein Jahr später, nachdem Charles Eames sich von seiner ersten Frau Catherine Dewey Woermann hatte scheiden lassen, haben Charles und Ray in Chicago geheiratet. Im gleichen Jahr zogen sie nach Kalifornien und begannen mit ihren Experimenten zur Verformung von Schichtholz.

Née Bernice Alexandra Kaiser (modifié officiellement en 1954 en Ray Bernice Alexandra Kaiser) à Sacramento, Californie. En 1933, elle reçoit le diplôme de la May Friend Bennett School de Millbrook, New York, et commence à étudier la peinture dans une école récemment ouverte par Hans Hofmann. Elle continue à peindre sous la direction de celui-ci jusqu'en 1939 et, en 1937, son travail est présenté lors de la première exposition collective des «American Abstract Artists», au Riverside Museum, à New York. En 1940, elle commence à suivre un cours de tissage à la Cranbrook Academy of Arts (Michigan) sous la direction de Marianne Strengel (à cette époque, Charles Eames dirigeait le département de design industriel de Cranbrook). Un an plus tard, après que Charles Eames eut divorcé de sa première femme, le couple se marie à Chicago. Au cours de la même année, ils s'installent en Californie et commencent leurs recherches sur les procédés de moulage du contre-plaqué.

Antonio Gaudí y Cornet (1852–1926) SPAIN
Born in Reus, the son of a metalworker, Antonio Gaudí studied architecture at the Escola Superior d'Arquitectura, Barcelona. His Catalan version of the Art Nouveau style was expressed in his numerous architectural commissions, including Casa Vicens (1878–1885), Palau Güell (1885–1889), Casa Calvet (1889–1900) and Casa Battló (1904–1906) – all are examples of total design integration. His masterwork, the cathedral of La Sagrada Familia, designed between 1883 and 1926, remains unfinished.

Antonio Gaudí wurde in Reus als Sohn eines Metallarbeiters geboren, und er studierte Architektur an der Escola Superior d'Arquitectura in Barcelona. Seine katalanische Version des Jugendstils kam in zahllosen Architekturaufträgen zum Ausdruck, darunter Casa Vicens (1878–1885), Palau Güell (1885–1889), Casa Calvet (1889–1900) und Casa Battló (1904–1906) – allesamt Beispiele für Gesamtkunstwerke. Sein Meisterwerk, die unvollendet gebliebene Kathedrale La Sagrada Familia, entstand zwischen 1883 und 1926.

Né à Reus, fils d'un métallurgiste, Antonio Gaudí étudie l'architecture à la Escola Superior d'Arquitectura de Barcelone. Sa version catalane de l'Art nouveau s'exprime dans de nombreuses commandes d'architecture dont la Casa Vicens (1878–1885), le Palau Güell (1885–1889), la Casa Calvet (1889–1900) et la Casa Battló (1904–1906), exemples d'un travail de création totalement intégré. Son chef-d'œuvre, l'église de La Sagrada Familia, conçue de 1883 à 1926, est resté inachevé.

Frank O. Gehry (*1929) USA
Born in Toronto, Canada, he studied architecture at the University of Southern California, Los Angeles, graduating in 1954. From 1956 to 1957, he pursued post-graduate studies at Harvard University, Cambridge, Massachusetts. In 1962, he established his own architectural office in Los Angeles. He has received many prestigious architectural commissions, including the Vitra Design Museum, Weil am Rhein, Germany.

Frank O. Gehry wurde in Toronto, Kanada, geboren und studierte bis 1954 Architektur an der University of Southern California, Los Angeles. Von 1956 bis 1957 setzte er sein Studium an der Harvard University, Cambridge, Massachusetts, fort. 1962 gründete er sein eigenes Architekturbüro in Los Angeles. Er hat viele bedeutende Architekturaufträge bekommen, darunter das Vitra Design Museum in Weil am Rhein.

Né au Canada, Frank O. Gehry étudie l'architecture à la University of Southern California, Los Angeles, dont il est diplômé en 1954. De 1956 à 1957, il poursuit ses études à Harvard et, en 1962, ouvre son propre cabinet d'architecte à Los Angeles. Il a reçu de nombreuses commandes prestigieuses, dont le Vitra Design Museum de Weil am Rhein, en Allemagne.

Edward William Godwin (1833–1886)
GREAT BRITAIN
Born in Bristol, he trained with the Bristol-based architect and civil engineer, William Armstrong. In 1854, Godwin set up his own architectural office in Bristol. From 1857 to 1859, he lived in Ireland while working with his brother, an engineer. Inspired by the 1862 International Exhibition of Industry and Art, he turned to interior designing. In 1865, he moved to London and a year later worked with William Burges and designed wallpaper for Jeffery & Co. William Watt's Art Furniture Company initially produced his furniture designs and subsequently his designs were manufactured by Gillow, Collingson & Wood, and Green & King. From 1874 to 1878, he collaborated with James Abbott McNeill Whistler and in 1876 he designed houses for Bedford Park. In 1884, he decorated Oscar Wilde's house in Tite Street, London.

Edward William Godwin wurde in Bristol geboren. Seine Ausbildung erhielt er bei William Armstrong, einem in Bristol ansässigen Architekten und Ingenieur. 1854 eröffnete Godwin in Bristol ein eigenes Architekturbüro. Von 1857 bis 1859 arbeitete er zusammen mit seinem Bruder, einem Ingenieur, in Irland. Angeregt durch die International Exhibition of Industry

Antonio Gaudí y Cornet

Frank O. Gehry

Eileen Gray

and Art von 1862, wandte er sich der Innenarchitektur zu. 1865 zog er nach London und ein Jahr später tat er sich mit William Burges zusammen und entwarf Tapeten für Jeffery & Co. Zunächst produzierte William Watts Art Furniture Company seine Möbelentwürfe, später übernahmen Gillow, Collingson & Wood sowie Green & King seine Entwürfe. Von 1874 bis 1878 arbeitete er mit James Abbott McNeill Whistler zusammen. 1876 entwarf er Häuser in Bedford Park. 1884 stattete er Oscar Wildes Haus in der Londoner Tite Street aus.

Né à Bristol, Edward William Godwin se forme dans cette ville auprès de l'architecte et ingénieur William Armstrong. En 1854, il ouvre son agence d'architecture à Bristol. De 1857 à 1859, il vit en Irlande et travaille en compagnie de son frère, qui est ingénieur. Inspiré par l'International Exhibition of Industry and Art de 1862, il se tourne vers la décoration. En 1865, il s'installe à Londres et, un an plus tard, collabore avec William Burges et dessine des papiers peints pour Jeffery & Co. L'Art Furniture Company de William Watt, puis Gillow, Collingson & Wood et Green & King réalisent ses projets de meubles. De 1874 à 1878, il collabore avec James Abbott McNeill Whistler et, en 1876, dessine des maisons pour Bedford Park. En 1884, il décore la maison d'Oscar Wilde, dans la Tite Street, à Londres.

Eileen Gray (1878–1976) IRELAND/FRANCE
Born in Ireland and from an affluent and artistic family background, Eileen Gray studied at the Slade School of Art (1898). In 1902, she moved to France and studied drawing at the Académies Colarossi and Julian. Later, she trained in the art of lacquer with the Japanese craftsman, Sugawara. She spent much of the First World War in London and only returned to Paris in 1918. Prior to 1919, she had worked solely as a furniture designer, but in that year, she began to work as an interior designer. In 1922, she opened the Galerie Jean Désert as a showcase for her own work. In the same year she also came into contact with the De Stijl movement. In 1923, J. J. P. Oud and Walter Gropius reviewed her interior – a Monte Carlo boudoir – at the Salon des Artistes-Décorateurs very favourably. From 1926 onwards, she worked as an architect and exhibited several architectural projects in Le Corbusier's "Pavillon des Temps Nouveaux" at the 1937 Paris Exhibition.

Eileen Gray wurde in Irland geboren. Sie entstammte einer wohlhabenden Künstlerfamilie und begann 1898 ihr Studium an der Slade School of Fine Arts. 1902 ging sie nach Frankreich und studierte Malerei an der Académie Colarossi und der Académie Julian. Später

ließ sie sich von dem japanischen Kunsthandwerker Sugawara in japanischer Lackkunst unterrichten. Während des Ersten Weltkriegs war sie fast durchgehend in London und kehrte erst 1918 nach Paris zurück. Bis 1919 arbeitete sie ausschließlich als Möbeldesignerin, danach auch als Innenarchitektin. 1922 eröffnete sie die Galerie Jean Désert, wo sie ihre Arbeiten ausstellte. Im gleichen Jahr kam sie mit der De Stijl-Bewegung in Kontakt. 1923 veröffentlichten J. J. P. Oud und Walter Gropius eine begeisterte Kritik ihres »Monte Carlo«-Zimmers, das sie auf dem Salon des Artistes Décorateurs ausgestellt hatte. Von 1926 arbeitete sie als Architektin und stellte 1937 während der Pariser Weltausstellung mehrere Architekturmodelle in Le Corbusiers »Pavillon des Temps Nouveaux« aus.

Née en Irlande dans une famille d'artistes aisée, Eileen Gray fait ses études à la Slade School of Fine Arts (1898). En 1902, elle s'installe à Paris et suit des cours de dessin dans les académies Colarossi et Julian. Plus tard, elle se forme à l'art de la laque avec le spécialiste japonais Sugawara. Elle passe la plus grande partie de la première guerre mondiale à Londres et ne revient à Paris qu'en 1918. Ne s'étant jusque-là intéressée qu'à des projets de meubles, elle commence à s'orienter vers la décoration en 1919. En 1922, elle ouvre la Galerie Jean Désert pour présenter son travail. La même année, elle entre en contact avec le groupe De Stijl. En 1923, J. J. P. Oud et Walter Gropius commentent favorablement sa participation au Salon des artistes décorateurs – un boudoir « Monte-Carlo ». À partir de 1926, elle travaille comme architecte et présente plusieurs projets architecturaux dans le pavillon des « Temps Nouveaux » de Le Corbusier, lors de l'Exposition de Paris de 1937.

Hector Guimard (1867–1942) FRANCE
Born in Lyons, he studied at the École Nationale des Arts Décoratifs, Paris, and the École des Beaux-Arts, Paris. From 1894 to 1897, he designed the Castel Béranger apartment building which displays the influence of the Gothic Revival and the Henri II styles. Guimard was the main exponent of French Art Nouveau and his Castel Béranger can be viewed as a manifesto of this new style, which in France was often referred to as "Style Guimard". From around 1894, he was inspired by English Domestic Revival architecture and the designs of Victor Horta. His best-known designs are his swirling cast-iron entrances for the Paris Metro of 1903. In 1920, he produced his first standardised furniture and a year later designed his first standardised buildings. In 1938, he emigrated to the USA.

Hector Guimard wurde in Lyon geboren und studierte an der Pariser École Nationale des Arts Décoratifs und an der École des Beaux-Arts, ebenfalls in Paris. Von 1894 bis 1897 entwarf er das Wohnhaus Castel Béranger, an dem der Einfluß des Gothic Revival und des Henri II.-Stils deutlich werden. Von etwa 1894 an wird der Einfluß der English Domestic Revival-Architektur und der Arbeiten von Victor Horta deutlich. Seine bekanntesten Entwürfe sind die gußeisernen Eingänge für die Pariser Métro von 1903. 1920 produzierte er seine ersten Serienmöbel, und ein Jahr später entwarf er sein erstes standardisiertes Gebäude. 1938 wanderte er in die USA aus.

Né à Lyon, Hector Guimard étudie à l'École nationale des arts décoratifs, et à l'École des beaux-arts de Paris. De 1894 à 1897, il conçoit l'immeuble d'appartements du Castel Béranger aux influences néogothiques et Henri II. À partir de 1894 environ, il s'inspire du style English Domestic Revival et de Victor Horta. Ses créations les plus célèbres sont ses entrées en fonte pour le métro parisien (1903). En 1920, il réalise ses premiers meubles industrialisés et un an plus tard, ses premiers immeubles standardisés. Il émigre aux États-Unis en 1938.

René Herbst (1891–1983) FRANCE
Born in Paris, René Herbst was one of the leading French designers during the inter-war years. In 1929, he founded, with among others Le Corbusier and Jean Puiforcat, the UAM (Union des Artistes Modernes). The UAM was set up as a reaction to the decorative excesses of the then mainstream Art Deco style. He promoted the ideals of Modernism through publications and exhibits at the annual salons and founded his own company to manufacture his furniture in limited editions. Most of his designs were relatively complicated in construction and costly to produce.

René Herbst wurde in Paris geboren und war einer der führenden französischen Designer der Zwischenkriegsjahre. 1929 gründete er u. a. mit Le Corbusier und Jean Puiforcat die UAM (Union des Artistes Modernes). Diese Vereinigung war eine Reaktion auf die dekorativen Exzesse des Art Déco und sollte die Ideale der Moderne durch Veröffentlichungen und Ausstellungen in den jährlichen Salons fördern. Herbst gründete ein Unternehmen, wo er seine Möbelentwürfe in limitierter Auflage produzierte. Die meisten seiner Entwürfe waren relativ kompliziert konstruiert und in der Herstellung sehr teuer.

Né à Paris, René Herbst est l'un des principaux designers français de l'entre-deux guerres. En 1920, il fonde avec, entre autres, Le Corbusier et Jean Puiforcat, l'Union des artistes modernes (UAM), en réaction contre les excès décoratifs du style Art déco alors triomphant. Il promeut les idéaux du modernisme à travers des publications et des expositions lors de salons annuels, et crée sa propre entreprise pour fabriquer ses meubles en nombre limité. La plupart de ses modèles sont assez complexes à fabriquer et coûteux à produire.

René Herbst

Josef Hoffmann (1870–1956) AUSTRIA
Born in Moravia, Josef Hoffmann initially studied architecture in Munich and later trained under Otto Wagner in Vienna. In 1895, he visited Italy and on his return entered Otto Wagner's practice where he worked until 1899. In 1885, Hoffmann founded the "Siebener Club" which included Joseph Maria Olbrich and Koloman Moser as members. In 1897, he joined the Vienna Secession and in 1898 took part in the first Secession exhibition, designing the "Ver Sacrum" room. In 1899, he was appointed the professor of architecture of the School of Applied Arts, Vienna – a position he held until 1941. His work was strongly influenced by the geometry and attenuation of Charles Rennie Mackintosh's designs. He visited England c. 1902 with Koloman Moser and in 1903, given financial backing by Fritz Wärndorfer, Hoffmann and Moser founded the Wiener Werkstätte. During his career he received several important architectural commissions, including Palais Stoclet, Brussels (1905–1911) and the Purkersdorf Sanatorium (1903–1906). In 1905 he left the Vienna Secession and with Gustav Klimt formed the Kunstschau. He took part in many international exhibitions including the Cologne 1914 Deutsche Werkbund Exhibition, the Paris 1925 Exposition des Arts Décoratifs and the Stockholm 1930 Exhibition.

Josef Hoffmann

Josef Hoffmann wurde in Mähren geboren und studierte Architektur in München, später bei Otto Wagner in Wien. 1895 bereiste er Italien und trat nach seiner Rückkehr in Otto Wagners Büro ein, wo er bis 1899 arbeitete. 1885 gründete Hoffmann den »Siebener Club«, dem auch Joseph Maria Olbrich und Koloman Moser angehörten. 1897 trat er der Wiener Secession bei und entwarf zu deren erster Ausstellung 1898 den »Ver Sacrum«-Raum. 1899 bis 1941 war er Professor für Architektur an der Wiener Kunstgewerbeschule. Seine Arbeiten waren stark von den geometrischen und gelängten Entwürfen Charles Rennie Mackintoshs beeinflußt. 1902 bereiste er mit Koloman Moser England, und 1903 gründeten Hoffmann und Moser mit finanzieller Förderung durch Fritz Wärndorfer die Wiener Werkstätte. Zu den bedeutendsten Architektur-

Arne Jacobsen

Finn Juhl

aufträgen gehören das Sanatorium Purkersdorf (1903–1906) und das Palais Stoclet in Brüssel (1905–1911). 1905 verließ er zusammen mit Gustav Klimt die Wiener Secession und gründete 1912 den Wiener Werkbund, den er bis 1920 leitete. Er beteiligte sich an vielen internationalen Ausstellungen, u. a. auch an der Kölner Werkbundausstellung von 1914, an der Pariser Exposition des Arts Décoratifs von 1925 und an der Stockholmer Ausstellung von 1930.

Né en Moravie, Josef Hoffmann commence par étudier l'architecture à Munich avant de travailler pour Otto Wagner à Vienne. En 1895, il visite l'Italie et à son retour, entre au cabinet de Wagner où il travaille jusqu'en 1899. En 1885, il fonde le « Siebener Club » qui compte parmi ses membres Joseph Maria Olbrich et Koloman Moser, rejoint la Wiener Secession en 1897 et prend part, en 1898, à la première exposition du mouvement, pour laquelle il crée la salle « Ver Sacrum ». En 1899, il est nommé professeur d'architecture à la Wiener Kunstgewerbeschule, poste qu'il conservera jusqu'en 1941. Son œuvre est fortement influencée par la géométrie et l'élongation des formes de Charles Rennie Mackintosh. Il visite l'Angleterre vers 1902 en compagnie de Koloman Moser avec lequel il crée les Wiener Werkstätte, soutenu financièrement par Fritz Wärndorfer. Au cours de sa carrière, il reçoit de nombreuses commandes architecturales importantes dont le palais Stoclet, à Bruxelles (1905–1911) et le Purkersdorf Sanatorium (1903–1906). En 1905, il quitte la Wiener Secession et constitue avec Gustav Klimt le Kunstschau. Il participe à de nombreuses expositions internationales dont la Werkbundausstellung à Cologne, en 1914, l'Exposition des arts décoratifs de Paris en 1925 et l'Exposition de Stockholm de 1930.

Arne Jacobsen (1902–1971) DENMARK
Born in Copenhagen, Arne Jacobsen initially trained as a mason before studying architecture at the Royal Academy of Arts, Copenhagen, graduating in 1927. From 1927 until 1930, he worked in the architectural office of Paul Holsoe. In 1930, he established his own design office, which he headed until his death in 1971, and worked independently as an architect and interior, furniture, textile and ceramics designer. He was the Professor of Architecture at the Royal Academy of Arts, Copenhagen from 1956 onwards. His best known projects are St. Catherine's College, Oxford and the SAS Hotel, Copenhagen.

Arne Jacobsen wurde in Kopenhagen geboren und absolvierte zunächst eine Maurerlehre, studierte dann bis 1927 Architektur an

der Königlichen Kunstakademie in Kopenhagen. Bis 1930 arbeitete er dann im Architekturbüro von Paul Holsoe. 1930 gründete er sein eigenes Büro, das er bis zu seinem Tod 1971 leitete. Er arbeitete als Architekt und Innenarchitekt, Möbel-, Textil- und Keramik-Designer. 1956 wurde er Architekturprofessor an der Königlichen Kunstakademie in Kopenhagen. Seine bekanntesten Projekte sind das St. Catherine's College, Oxford, und das SAS Hotel in Kopenhagen.

Né à Copenhague, Arne Jacobsen reçoit une formation de maçon avant d'étudier l'architecture à l'Académie royale des arts de Copenhague d'où il sort diplômé en 1927. De 1927 à 1930, il travaille pour l'architecte Paul Holsoe. En 1930, il ouvre son propre cabinet qu'il dirige jusqu'à sa mort en 1971. Il est à la fois architecte, décorateur, créateur de mobilier, de textiles et de céramique, et professeur d'architecture à l'Académie royale des arts de Copenhague à partir de 1956. Ses projets les plus connus sont St. Catherine's College à Oxford et l'hôtel SAS à Copenhague.

Finn Juhl (1912–1989) DENMARK
Born in Copenhagen, Finn Juhl studied architecture under Kay Fisker at the Royal Academy of Arts, Copenhagen, graduating in 1934. From 1935 to 1945, he worked as an architect in the office of Vilhelm Lauritzen. In 1945, he established his own design practice specialising in furniture and interior design. From 1954 to 1957, he won five gold medals at the Milan Triennale exhibitions. Tribal art and abstract organic sculpture greatly influenced Juhl's work. His designs were unparalleled in the virtuosity of their execution.

Finn Juhl wurde in Kopenhagen geboren und studierte Architektur bei Kay Fisker an der Königlichen Kunstakademie, Kopenhagen, wo er 1934 seinen Abschluß machte. Von 1935 bis 1945 arbeitete er als Architekt im Büro von Vilhelm Lauritzen. 1945 gründete er sein eigenes Designstudio und spezialisierte sich auf Möbeldesign und Innenarchitektur. Zwischen 1954 und 1957 gewann er auf den Ausstellungen der Mailänder Triennale fünf Goldmedaillen. Juhl wurde von der Kunst der Primitiven und der abstrakt-organischen Bildhauerei beeinflußt. In der Virtuosität ihrer Ausführung sind seine Arbeiten unübertroffen.

Né à Copenhague, Finn Juhl étudie l'architecture avec Kay Fisker à l'Académie royale des arts où il obtient son diplôme en 1934. De 1934 à 1945, il travaille pour l'architecte Wilhelm Lauritzen. En 1945, il ouvre son propre studio, se spécialisant dans l'architecture intérieure et le mobilier. De 1954 à 1957, il remporte cinq médailles d'or à plusieurs

Triennales de Milan. L'art primitif et la sculpture abstraite organique ont beaucoup influencé ses travaux. Dans leur virtuosité, ses créations sont sans équivalent.

Kaare Klint (1888–1954) DENMARK
Born in Fredericksberg, Vartov, Kaare Klint studied painting at the Polytechnic of Fredericksberg, from 1903. He worked as apprentice to his architect father, P. V. Jensen Klint and the Copenhagen architects, Kai Nielsen (1911–1912) and Carl Petersen (1914–1917). From 1917, he worked as an independent furniture designer, setting up his own office in 1920 and working for, among others, Fritz Hansen and Rud Rasmussen. In 1924, he established the furniture department at the Royal Academy of Arts, Copenhagen, where he later became professor of architecture in 1944.

Kaare Klint wurde in Fredericksberg, Vartov, geboren und studierte ab 1903 Malerei an dem Polytechnikum von Fredericksberg. Er arbeitete als Praktikant im Architekturbüro seines Vaters P. V. Jensen Klint und bei den Kopenhagener Architekten Kai Nielsen (1911–1912) und Carl Petersen (1914–1917). Ab 1917 war er als freischaffender Möbeldesigner tätig, gründete 1920 ein eigenes Büro und machte Entwürfe u. a. für Fritz Hansen und Rud Rasmussen. 1924 gründete er die Möbeldesignabteilung an der Königlichen Kunstakademie Kopenhagen, an die er 1944 als Architekturprofessor berufen wurde.

Né à Fredericksberg, Vartov, Kaare Klint étudie à l'École polytechnique de cette ville, à partir de 1903. Il effectue son apprentissage auprès de son père, l'architecte P. V. Jensen Klint et auprès d'architectes de Copenhague, Kai Nielsen (1911–1912) et Carl Petersen (1914–1917). À partir de 1917, il est designer de mobilier indépendant. Klint crée son agence en 1920 et travaille pour, entre autres, Fritz Hansen et Rud Rasmussen. En 1924, il fonde le département de mobilier de l'Académie royale des arts, à Copenhague, institution pour laquelle il enseignera plus tard l'architecture.

Yrjö Kukkapuro (*1933) FINLAND
Born in Yiipuri, Yrjö Kukkapuro studied at the Helsinki Institute of Crafts and Design. In 1959, he established his own design studio in Kauniainen and has designed furniture for, among others, Avarte and Haimi. From 1974 to 1978, he was a professor at the Institute of Technology, Helsinki, and from 1978 to 1980 was the institute's rector. He was awarded the Lunning Prize in 1966.

Yrjö Kukkapuro wurde in Yiipuri geboren und studierte an der Kunstgewerbeschule von Helsinki. 1959 gründete er sein eigenes Designstudio in Kauniainen und entwarf Möbel u. a. für Avarte und Haimi. Von 1974 bis 1978 war er Professor am Technischen Institut, Helsinki, von 1978 bis 1980 war er dort Rektor. 1966 wurde er mit dem Lunning-Preis ausgezeichnet.

Né à Yiipuri, Yrjö Kukkapuro fait ses études à l'Institut des arts appliqués et du design d'Helsinki. En 1959, il crée son propre studio de design à Kauniainen et dessine des meubles pour, entre autres, Avarte et Haimi. De 1974 à 1978, il est professeur à l'Institut de technologie d'Helsinki et de 1978 à 1980, il est le recteur de cet institut. Il reçoit le prix Lunning en 1966.

Shiro Kuramata

Shiro Kuramata (1934–1991) JAPAN
Born in Tokyo, Shiro Kuramata studied architecture and later cabinet-making at the Tokyo Technical High School of Art and the Kuwasawa Institute of Design. He subsequently founded his own design practice in 1965. In the early 1980s, he produced furniture designs for Memphis and in the latter half of the decade, for, among others, Vitra, Cappellini, XO and Kokuyo Co. His reputation was established mainly through interior design work, such as his shop projects for Seibu, Esprit and Issey Miyake. In 1981, he was awarded the Japanese Cultural Design Prize.

Shiro Kuramata wurde in Tokio geboren und studierte Architektur an der Technischen Hochschule in Tokio und danach Möbelbau am Kuwasawa-Institut für Design. 1965 gründete er sein eigenes Designstudio. Zu Beginn der 80er Jahre schuf er Möbeldesigns für Memphis, nach 1985 für Vitra, Cappellini, XO und Kokuyo Co. Einen Namen hat er sich als Innenarchitekt gemacht, vor allem mit seinen Ladenprojekten für Seibu, Esprit und Issey Miyake. 1981 wurde er mit dem japanischen Kulturpreis für Design ausgezeichnet.

Né à Tokyo, Shiro Kuramata étudie l'architecture puis l'ébénisterie à l'École technique supérieure de Tokyo et à l'institut de design Kuwasawa. Il crée ensuite son propre studio de design en 1965. Au début des années 80, il travaille pour Memphis puis pour Vitra, Cappellini, XO et Kokuyo Co. Sa célébrité tient surtout à son travail d'architecte intérieur et en particulier à ses réalisations de magasins pour Seibu, Esprit et Issey Miyake. En 1981, il reçoit le Prix culturel japonais du Design.

Erwine & Estelle Laverne (*1909 & *1915) USA
Erwine and Estelle Laverne studied painting under the direction of Hans Hofmann at the Students' Art League, New York, (as did Ray Eames). Together they founded their own manufacturing and retailing company in 1938,

Le Corbusier

Ross Lovegrove

Laverne Originals. Their moulded perspex furniture was extremely popular with interior designers in the late 1950s due to its spatial qualities and can be seen to predict the direction furniture design would take in the 1960s.

Erwine und Estelle Laverne studierten, wie auch Ray Eames, Malerei bei Hans Hofmann an der Students' Art League, New York. Zusammen gründeten sie 1938 die Produktions- und Vertriebsfirma Laverne Originals. Ihre Möbel aus geformtem Plexiglas waren wegen ihrer räumlichen Qualitäten bei den Innenarchitekten der späten 50er Jahre sehr beliebt; sie nahmen das Möbeldesign der 60er Jahre vorweg.

Erwine et Estelle Laverne étudient la peinture sous la direction de Hans Hofmann à la Student's Art League de New York (comme Ray Eames). Ensemble, ils fondent leur propre société de production et de distribution en 1938, Laverne Originals. Leurs meubles en perspex moulé furent extrêmement appréciés par les décorateurs de la fin des années 50 pour leurs qualités spatiales qui annonçaient la direction qu'allait prendre le design de mobilier dans les années 60.

Le Corbusier (1887–1965)
SWITZERLAND/FRANCE
Charles-Édouard Jeanneret was born in La Chaux-de-Fonds, Switzerland. While training at the School of Applied Arts there, he was urged by his teacher, Charles L'Eplattenier, to study architecture. In 1907, he visited Italy and Vienna and in 1908 went to Paris, where he worked in the architectural practice of Auguste Perret. While he met Wolf Dohrn, the director of the Dresdner Werkstätten, as well as Hermann Muthesius and Peter Behrens; he subsequently worked in the latter's office. From 1912 to 1914, he taught at the La Chaux-de-Fonds art school. In 1917, he moved to Paris and met the painter, Amédée Ozenfant, with whom he invented the post-cubist Purism movement. In 1920, they began to publicize their ideas in the journal *L'Esprit Nouveau* and in 1923 Le Corbusier wrote his book *Towards a New Architecture*. He designed the *L'Esprit Nouveau* pavilion at the 1925 Paris Exposition and exhibited his furniture designs at the 1929 Salon d'Automne. These pieces were subsequently put into production by Thonet. He was an active member of the Congrès Internationaux d'Architecture Moderne and his reputation as a leading architect helped disseminate his design philosophy.

Charles-Édouard Jeanneret wurde in Le Chaux-de-Fonds, Schweiz, geboren. Er begann zunächst eine Lehre als Graveur an der Kunstgewerbeschule von Le Chaux, wurde

dann von seinem Lehrer Charles L'Eplattenier gedrängt, Architektur zu studieren. 1907 bereiste er Italien und Wien und ging 1908 nach Paris, wo er im Büro des Architekten Auguste Perret arbeitete. Während seines Aufenthalts in Deutschland traf er Wolf Dohrn, den Direktor der Dresdner Werkstätten, sowie Hermann Muthesius und Peter Behrens, in dessen Architekturbüro er anschließend arbeitete. Von 1912 bis 1914 lehrte er an der Kunstgewerbeschule von La Chaux-de-Fonds. 1917 zog er nach Paris und traf dort den Maler Amédée Ozenfant, mit dem er die postkubistische Richtung des Purismus entwickelte. 1920 begannen die beiden, ihre Vorstellungen in »L'Esprit Nouveau« zu publizieren; Le Corbusier veröffentlichte 1923 sein Buch »Vers une architecture nouvelle«. Für die Pariser Exposition des Arts Décoratifs von 1925 entwarf er den Pavillon von »L'Esprit Nouveau« und stellte 1929, auf dem Salon d'Automne, seine Möbelentwürfe vor, deren Produktion dann die Firma Thonet übernahm. Er war aktives Mitglied des Congrès Internationaux d'Architecture Moderne, und mit seinem Namen als einem der führenden Architekten seiner Zeit verbreiteten sich auch seine Theorien zu Architektur und Design.

Charles-Édouard Jeanneret, dit Le Corbusier, naît à La Chaux-de-Fonds (Suisse). Élève de l'École des arts appliqués locale, il est poussé par son professeur Charles L'Eplattenier, à apprendre l'architecture. En 1907, il voyage en Italie à Vienne et se rend en 1908 à Paris, où il travaille chez Auguste Perret. C'est à cette époque qu'il rencontre Wolf Dohrn, directeur der Dresdner Werkstätte, ainsi que Hermann Muthesius et Peter Behrens. C'est dans l'atelier de ce dernier qu'il travaillera par la suite. De 1912 à 1924, il enseigne à l'école d'art de La Chaux-de-Fonds. En 1917, il s'installe à Paris et rencontre le peintre Amédée Ozenfant avec lequel il lance un mouvement postcubiste, le purisme. En 1920, ils commencent à publier leurs idées dans la revue *L'Esprit nouveau*. Le Corbusier écrit en 1923 son livre *Vers une nouvelle architecture*. Il conçoit le pavillon de *L'Esprit nouveau* pour l'Exposition de 1925 à Paris et expose ses dessins de mobilier au Salon d'automne de 1929. Ses meubles sont par la suite produits par Thonet. Il est membre actif des Congrès internationaux d'architecture moderne, et sa réputation d'architecte majeur contribue à faire connaître sa philosophie du design.

Ross Lovegrove (*1958) GREAT BRITAIN
Born in Cardiff, Wales, Ross Lovegrove studied design at Manchester Polytechnic before attending the Royal College of Art, London, receiving his MA in 1983. From 1983 to 1984, he

worked for Frogdesign, Altensteig, on projects for, among others, AEG and Apple. From 1984 to 1987, he worked as an in-house designer for Knoll International in Paris. In 1987, established with Julian Brown the Lovegrove-Brown design office – the partnership dissolved in 1990. In 1990, he established his own London-based design practice, Studio X, and has since then designed for, most notably, Knoll, Driade, Connolly, Cappellini, Arteluce and Moroso.

Ross Lovegrove wurde in Cardiff, Wales, geboren und studierte Design am Polytechnikum Manchester, wechselte dann an das Royal College of Art, London, wo er 1983 seinen Abschluß machte. Bis 1984 arbeitete er für Frogdesign, Altensteig, u. a. an Projekten für AEG und Apple. Von 1984 bis 1987 arbeitete er als Hausdesigner für Knoll International in Paris. 1987 gründete er mit Julian Brown das Lovegrove-Brown Designstudio, eine Partnerschaft, die 1990 aufgelöst wurde. 1990 eröffnete er dann Studio X, sein Londoner Designbüro, das Entwürfe für Knoll, Driade, Connolly, Cappellini, Arteluce und Moroso geschaffen hat.

Né à Cardiff, Pays-de-Galles, Ross Lovegrove étudie le design à l'École polytechnique de Manchester avant de suivre les cours du Royal College of Art de Londres, où il passe son diplôme en 1983. De 1983 à 1984, il travaille pour Frogdesign, Altensteig, sur des projets pour Apple et AEG. De 1984 à 1987, il est architecte d'intérieur pour Knoll International à Paris. En 1987, il crée en partenariat avec Julian Brown l'agence de design Lovegrove-Brown, dissoute en 1990. La même année, il fonde sa propre agence londonienne, Studio X, et travaille entre autres pour Driade, Knoll, Connolly, Cappellini, Arteluce et Moroso.

Charles Rennie Mackintosh (1868–1928)
GREAT BRITAIN

Born in Glasgow, in 1884 Charles Rennie Mackintosh entered the practice of local architect, John Hutchison, and in 1889, joined the architectural office of Honeyman & Keppie. A year later, he won the Alexander Thomson Travelling Scholarship which enabled him to visit Italy, France and Belgium in 1901. By 1896, he was designing furniture for Messrs. Guthrie & Wells and exhibiting with H. J. MacNair and Frances & Margaret Macdonald as "The Four". In 1897, he won the competition for the new Glasgow School of Art building. In the same year he was commissioned to decorate Miss Cranston's Buchanan Street Tea Rooms and design furniture for her Argyle Street Tea Rooms. In 1900, he exhibited at the Vienna Secession Exhibition to widespread acclaim. In the same year he married Margaret

Macdonald. In 1903, he received the commission for Hill House, Helensburgh, from the publisher, W. W. Blackie. In 1904, he designed the Willow Street Tea Rooms for Miss Cranston. His last major work, the School of Art Library, received little attention when completed in 1909. In 1916, he moved to London and designed textiles for Foxton's & Sefton's. In 1923, he moved to France, where he painted until his death in 1928.

Charles Rennie Mackintosh wurde in Glasgow geboren. 1884 trat er in das Büro des Glasgower Architekten John Hutchinson ein, wechselte 1889 in das Architekturbüro Honeyman & Keppie. Ein Jahr später gewann er das Alexander Thomson-Reisestipendium, was ihm ermöglichte, 1901 Italien, Frankreich und Belgien zu bereisen. Bis 1896 entwarf er Möbel für Messrs. Guthrie & Wells. Zusammen mit H. J. MacNair und France & Margaret Macdonald, der Gruppe »The Four«, stellte er aus. 1897 gewann er den Wettbewerb für das neue Gebäude der Glasgow School of Arts. Im gleichen Jahr erhielt er den Auftrag, Miss Cranston's Buchanan Street Tea Rooms auszustatten und die Möbel für ihren Argyle Street Tea Room zu entwerfen. In 1900 stellte er mit der Wiener Secession aus und erhielt breiten Beifall. In diesem Jahr heiratete er Margaret Macdonald. 1903 erhielt er vom Verleger W. W. Blackie den Auftrag für das Hill House in Helensburgh. 1904 gestaltete er die Willow Street Tea Rooms für Miss Cranston. Seine letzte bedeutende Arbeit, die Bibliothek der Glasgow School of Arts, fand bei ihrer Vollendung im Jahr 1909 schon geringere Aufmerksamkeit. 1916 zog er nach London und entwarf Textilien für Foxton's & Sefton's. 1923 übersiedelte er nach Frankreich, wo er sich bis zu seinem Tod 1928 der Malerei widmete.

Né à Glasgow, Charles Rennie Mackintosh commence à travailler en 1984 pour un architecte local, John Hutchinson, puis pour Honeyman & Keppie en 1889. Un an plus tard, il gagne une bourse de voyage Alexander Thomson qui lui permet de visiter l'Italie, la France et la Belgique en 1901. En 1896, il dessine des meubles pour Guthrie & Wells et expose avec H. J. MacNair ainsi que France et Margaret Macdonald sous le nom de «The Four» (les quatre). En 1897, il remporte le concours pour la construction de la nouvelle École d'art de Glasgow. La même année on lui confie la décoration du salon de thé de Miss Cranston, dans la Buchanan Street, et la création du mobilier de son salon de thé d'Argyle Street. En 1900, sa participation à l'exposition de la Sécession de Vienne est très applaudie. En 1903, l'éditeur W.W. Blackie le choisit pour construire sa maison, Hill House, à Helens-

Charles Rennie Mackintosh

Vico Magistretti

Alessandro Mendini

burgh. En 1904, il réalise les salons de thé de la Willow Street pour Miss Cranston. Sa dernière œuvre importante, la bibliothèque de l'École d'art de Glasgow, fut à peine remarquée lors de son achèvement en 1909. En 1916, il s'installe à Londres et crée des tissus pour Foxton's & Sefton's. En 1923, il part pour la France où il peindra jusqu'à sa mort en 1928.

Vico Magistretti (*1920) ITALY
Born in Milan, Vico Magistretti studied architecture at the Polytechnic of Milan, graduating in 1945. From 1946, he has worked independently for, among others, Cassina, O-Luce, Artemide, Knoll International and Olivetti. He was a commission member for the 1960 and 1964 Milan Triennales and also for the 1959 and 1960 Compasso d'Oro awards. Since 1980, he has been a visiting lecturer at the Royal College of Art, London. He has received numerous awards throughout his career, including two Grand Prix and a Gold Medal at the 1948 and 1954 Milan Triennales and the Compasso d'Oro in 1967 and 1969.

Vico Magistretti wurde in Mailand geboren und studierte bis 1945 Architektur am Politechnikum von Mailand. 1946 hat er als freier Designer u. a. für Cassina, O-Luce, Artemide, Knoll International und Olivetti gearbeitet. 1960 und 1964 gehörte er zur Jury der Mailänder Triennale und 1959 und 1960 zur Jury des Compasso d'Oro. Seit 1980 ist er am Royal College of Art, London. Er hat zahlreiche Preise gewonnen, darunter zweimal den Grand Prix und die Goldmedaille der Mailänder Triennale von 1948 und 1954 sowie den Compasso d'Oro von 1967 und 1969.

Né à Milan, Vico Magistretti étudie l'architecture à l'École polytechnique de Milan dont il est diplômé en 1945. À partir de 1946, il travaille comme consultant pour, entre autres, Cassina, O-Luce, Artemide, Knoll International et Olivetti. Il est membre du jury des Triennales de Milan en 1960 et 1964, et participe au jury du Compasso d'Oro en 1959 et 1960. Depuis 1980, il est conférencier invité au Royal College of Art, à Londres. Il reçoit de nombreuses distinctions tout au long de sa carrière, dont deux Grands Prix, une médaille d'or aux Triennales de Milan de 1948 et 1954, et le Compasso d'Oro en 1967 et 1969.

Bruno Mathsson (*1907) SWEDEN
Born in Värnamo, Bruno Mathsson was trained in his father Karl's cabinet-making workshop. From 1933, he designed furniture primarily for his father's business. In 1936, he was given a one-man show at the Röhsska Art Museum in Gothenburg, Sweden. A year later, he took part in the Paris 1937 Exhibition "Arts et techniques

appliqués à la vie moderne". He was awarded the Gregor Paulsson Medal in Stockholm, in 1955. From 1945 to 1958, he mainly practised architecture, designing several simple structures in glass, wood and concrete for use as summer-houses and school rooms. From 1958, he designed furniture in collaboration with Piet Hein. He exhibited his furniture designs in Stockholm, Oslo, Dresden and New York in 1963, 1976, 1976 and 1982 respectively.

Bruno Mathsson wurde in Värnamo geboren und absolvierte in der Werkstadt seines Vaters eine Lehre als Kunsttischler. Ab 1933 entwarf er Möbel hauptsächlich für das Geschäft seines Vaters. 1936 hatte er eine Einzelausstellung am Röhsska Kunstmuseum in Göteborg, Schweden. Ein Jahr später nahm er an der Pariser Ausstellung »Arts et techniques appliqués à la vie moderne« teil, 1939 an der New Yorker Weltausstellung. 1955 wurde er in Stockholm mit der Gregor-Paulsson-Medaille ausgezeichnet. Von 1945 bis 1958 arbeitete er hauptsächlich als Architekt und entwarf einfache Bauten aus Glas, Holz und Beton, die als Sommerhäuser oder Schulräume genutzt wurden. 1958 begann er zusammen mit Piet Hein Möbel zu entwerfen. Die Entwürfe wurden 1963 in Stockholm, 1976 in Oslo und Dresden und 1982 in New York ausgestellt.

Né à Värnamo, Bruno Mathsson se forme tout d'abord dans l'atelier de son père, l'ébéniste Karl Mathsson. À partir de 1933, il dessine des meubles, essentiellement pour ce dernier. En 1936, il est l'objet d'une exposition personnelle au Röhsska Konstlöjdmuseet de Göteborg et prend part à l'exposition de Paris « Arts et techniques appliqués à la vie moderne » de 1937. Il reçoit la médaille Gregor Paulsson à Stockholm en 1955. De 1945 à 1958, il pratique surtout l'architecture, créant plusieurs constructions simples à partir de verre, de bois et de béton pour des maisons de vacances et des salles de cours. À partir de 1958, il dessine des meubles en collaboration avec Piet Hein. Ses dessins de meubles ont été exposés à Stockholm (1963), Oslo (1976), Dresde (1976) et New York (1982).

Alessandro Mendini (*1931) ITALY
Born in Milan, Alessandro Mendini worked for Nizzoli Associati until 1970. From 1970 to 1976, he was the editor of *Casabella* and founded the journal, *Modo*. In 1973, he became a founding member of Global Tools, a school of radical architecture and Anti-Design. In the late 1970s he was the primary designer at Studio Alchimia. In 1979, he became editor of *Domus* and in the same year received a Compasso d'Oro award. Since 1983, he has been a design lecturer at the School for Applied Arts, Vienna.

Biographies | Biographien

Alessandro Mendini wurde in Mailand geboren und arbeitete bis 1970 für das Architekturbüro Nizzoli Associati. Von 1970 bis 1976 war er Chefredakteur von »Casabella« und gründete die Zeitschrift »Modo«. 1973 war er Mitbegründer der Gruppe Global Tools, einer Schule für radikale Architektur und Anti-Design. Ende der 70er Jahre galt er als der führende Designer von Studio Alchimia. 1979 wurde er Herausgeber der Zeitschrift »Domus« und erhielt den Compasso d'Oro. Seit 1983 lehrt er Design an der Hochschule für Angewandte Kunst in Wien.

Né à Milan, Alessandro Mendini travaille pour Nizzoli Associati jusqu'en 1970, date à laquelle il devient rédacteur en chef du magazine *Casabella* (jusqu'en 1976), avant de créer le journal *Modo*. En 1973, il est membre fondateur de Global Tools, école d'anti-architecture et d'anti-design. À la fin des années 70, il est le principal designer de Studio Alchimia et, en 1979, devient rédacteur en chef de *Domus*. La même année, il reçoit un Compasso d'Oro. Depuis 1983, il enseigne le design à la l'École des arts appliqués de Vienne.

Ludwig Mies van der Rohe (1886–1969)
GERMANY

Born in Aachen, Ludwig Mies van der Rohe initially trained as a builder and later worked as a draughtsman of stucco ornaments for a local architectural office. In 1905, he moved to Berlin and studied under Bruno Paul, designing his first building in 1907. In 1908, Mies joined Peter Behrens' architectural practice staying there until 1911. In 1919, he became actively involved in the revolutionary "Novembergruppe", promoting Modernism through his architectural proposals. In 1926, he was made vice-president of the Deutscher Werkbund and a year later, organized the Stuttgart Exhibition. He designed the German pavilion for the 1929 Barcelona Exhibition and the Tugendhat house, Brno, Czechoslovakia between 1929 and 1930. In 1931, he exhibited at the Berlin Building Exhibition and signed a contract with Thonet-Mundus allowing them the exclusive marketing rights for fifteen of his chair designs, some of which had been designed in collaboration with Lilly Reich. In 1930, he became the last director of the Bauhaus and was responsible for the school's move from Dessau to Berlin. In 1938, he emigrated to America and took up a teaching post at the Illinois Institute of Technology in Chicago.

Ludwig Mies van der Rohe wurde in Aachen geboren. Nach seiner Ausbildung als Maurer im Betrieb seines Vaters arbeitete er bei einem Aachener Architekten als Zeichner von Stuckornamenten. 1905 zog er nach Berlin und arbeitete bei Bruno Paul. Von 1908 bis 1911 war er Mitarbeiter bei Peter Behrens, wo auch W. Gropius und A. Meyer tätig waren. 1907 entstand sein erstes eigenes Gebäude. 1918 schloß er sich der revolutionären Novembergruppe an, förderte als Leiter ihrer Architektursektion die Bewegung der Moderne. 1926 wurde er Vizepräsident des Deutschen Werkbundes, ein Jahr später organisierte er dessen Stuttgarter Ausstellung. Er entwarf den Deutschen Pavillon für die Weltausstellung von Barcelona im Jahr 1929; zwischen 1929 und 1930 entstand das Haus Tugendhat in Brno. 1931 nahm er an der Berliner Bauausstellung teil und unterzeichnete einen Vertrag mit Thonet-Mundus, der er die Exklusivrechte an fünfzehn seiner Stuhlentwürfe übertrug, von denen einige in Zusammenarbeit mit Lilly Reich entstanden waren. 1930 wurde er zum letzten Direktor des Bauhauses in Dessau berufen und war verantwortlich für den Umzug der Schule nach Berlin. 1938 emigrierte er in die USA und erhielt eine Professur am Illinois Institute of Technology in Chicago.

Ludwig Mies
van der Rohe

Né à Aix-la-Chapelle, Ludwig Mies van der Rohe reçoit initialement une formation de constructeur puis travaille comme dessinateur d'ornements en stuc pour un cabinet local d'architecture. En 1905, il part pour Berlin et étudie sous la direction de Bruno Paul, dessinant sa première maison en 1907. En 1908, il entre chez Peter Behrens où il restera jusqu'en 1911. En 1919, il s'implique de plus en plus dans le groupe révolutionnaire Novembergruppe, promouvant le modernisme à travers ses propositions architecturales. En 1926, il est vice-président du Deutsche Werkbund et, un an plus tard, organise l'Exposition de Stuttgart. Il dessine le pavillon allemand de l'Exposition de Barcelone de 1929 et la maison Tugendhat à Brno, en Tchécoslovaquie (1929–1930). En 1931, il participe à l'Exposition de Berlin sur le bâtiment et signe un contrat avec Thonet-Mundus auxquels il accorde des droits exclusifs sur quinze de ses projets de sièges, dont certains ont été réalisés en collaboration avec Lilly Reich. En 1930, il est le dernier directeur du Bauhaus et responsable du déménagement de l'école de Dessau à Berlin. En 1938, il émigre en Amérique et devient professeur à l'Illinois Institute of Technology, à Chicago.

Carlo Mollino

Carlo Mollino (1905–1973) ITALY
Carlo Mollino was born in Turin, the son of the city's most prominent architect/engineer, Eugenio Mollino. He studied engineering before enrolling at Ceradini's Regia School of Architecture. From 1952 until 1968, he taught a course in the history of architecture

Jasper Morrison

Kolman Moser

at the Faculty of Architecture in Turin. During his career, he worked as an independent architect, furniture designer, interior designer, photographer, fashion designer, writer and designer of racing cars, including the "Osca 1100" – the winner of its class at the Le Mans 24-hour race of 1954.

Carlo Mollino wurde in Turin geboren, als Sohn von Eugenio Mollino, dem bekanntesten Architekten und Ingenieur der Stadt. Zunächst studierte er Ingenieurwesen, wechselte dann an die Architekturschule von Ceradini. Von 1952 bis 1968 lehrte er Architekturgeschichte an der Architekturfakultät von Turin. Während seiner vielseitigen Berufslaufbahn arbeitete er als freier Architekt, Möbeldesigner, Innenarchitekt, Photograph, Modeschöpfer, Schriftsteller und Designer von Rennwagen, darunter der »Osca 1100« – 1954 der Sieger seiner Klasse beim 24-Stunden-Rennen von Le Mans.

Né à Turin, Carlo Mollino est le fils du plus célèbre architecte de la ville, Eugenio Mollino. Il étudie d'abord l'ingénierie avant d'entrer à l'École d'architecture Ceradini. De 1952 à 1968, il est chargé d'un cours sur l'histoire de l'architecture à la faculté d'architecture de Turin. Il est à la fois architecte, dessinateur de mobilier, décorateur, photographe, styliste modéliste, écrivain et dessinateur de voitures de course (son « Osca 1100 » remporta les 24 heures du Mans dans sa catégorie en 1954).

Jasper Morrison (*1959) GREAT BRITAIN
Jasper Morrison studied at Kingston Polytechnic and later the Royal College of Art, London, graduating in 1985. In 1986, he founded his own design practice and has since designed furniture for Vitra, Zeus, SCP and Cappellini. The prototypes for some of his furniture are in the collection of the Vitra Design Museum.

Jasper Morrison studierte am Kingston Polytechnikum und bis 1985 am Royal College of Art, London. 1986 gründete er ein eigenes Designstudio und entwirft seither Möbel für Vitra, Zeus, Ide, SCP und Cappellini. Die Prototypen einiger seiner Entwürfe wurden vom Vitra Design Museum erworben.

Jasper Morrison étudie à l'École polytechnique de Kingston puis au Royal College of Art, à Londres, dont il est diplômé (1985). En 1986, il ouvre son propre bureau et crée depuis des meubles pour Zeus, SCP et Cappellini. Des prototypes de ses meubles sont représentés dans la collection du Vitra Design Museum.

Koloman Moser (1868–1918) AUSTRIA
Born in Vienna, Koloman Moser studied painting at the Academy in 1888 and later attended the School of Applied Arts. In 1897, he became

a founding member of the Vienna Secession and two years later began teaching at the School of Applied Arts. His furniture designs were shown at the 1900 Secession Exhibition and the Paris 1900 Exposition. In 1903, with Josef Hoffmann and Fritz Wärndorfer, Moser founded the Wiener Werkstätte. In 1907 he fell out with Wärndorfer and subsequently left the co-operative. From 1908 until his death, he was mainly active as a painter.

Koloman Moser wurde in Wien geboren und studierte ab 1888 Malerei an der Akademie der bildenden Künste in Wien, danach besuchte er die Wiener Kunstgewerbeschule. 1897 war er Gründungsmitglied der Wiener Secession; zwei Jahre später wurde er als Professor an die Kunstgewerbeschule berufen. Seine Möbelentwürfe wurden 1900 auf der Wiener Secessions-Ausstellung und auf der Pariser Weltausstellung gezeigt. 1903 gründete er mit Josef Hoffmann und Fritz Wärndorfer die Wiener Werkstätte, die er 1907 wieder verließ, nachdem er sich mit Wärndorfer überworfen hatte. Von 1908 bis zu seinem Tod arbeitete er hauptsächlich als Maler.

Né à Vienne, Koloman Moser étudie la peinture à l'Académie des beaux-arts de Vienne en 1888 avant de suivre les cours de l'École des arts appliqués. En 1897, il est membre fondateur de la Wiener Secession et deux ans plus tard, commence à enseigner à l'École des arts appliqués. Ses dessins de meubles sont exposés à la section de la Sécession à l'Exposition de Paris de 1900. En 1903, avec Josef Hoffmann et Fritz Wärndorfer, Moser fonde les Wiener Werkstätte. En 1907, il se brouille avec Wärndorfer et quitte la coopérative. De 1908 à sa mort, il se consacre essentiellement à la peinture.

Olivier Mourgue (*1939) FRANCE
Born in Paris, Olivier Mourgue studied interior design at the École Boulle and furniture-making at the National School of Fine Arts, Paris, graduating in 1960. Additionally, he trained from 1958 to 1961 in Sweden and Finland and worked for Maurice Holland, Nordiska Kompaniet, Stockholm, in 1960. In 1963, he worked as an interior designer for the Agence d'Architecture Intérieure Gautier-Delaye, Paris. In 1966, he established his own studio in Paris. Closing the studio in 1976, he moved to Brittany and became a professor at the School of Fine Arts in Brest.

Olivier Mourgue wurde in Paris geboren und studierte Innenarchitektur an der École Boulle und Möbeldesign an der École Nationale des Beaux-Arts in Paris; 1960 machte er dort seinen Abschluß. Weitere Ausbildung erhielt er zwischen 1958 und 1961 in Schweden und Finnland; 1960 arbeitete er für Maurice Holland, Nordiska Kompaniet, Stockholm. 1963 war er als Innenarchitekt bei der Agence d'Architecture Interieure Gautier-Delaye in Paris tätig. 1966 gründete er sein eigenes Atelier in Paris. 1976 schloß er sein Studio wieder und ging in die Bretagne, wo er eine Professur an der École des Beaux-Arts in Brest übernahm.

Né à Paris, Olivier Mourgue étudie la décoration intérieure à l'École Boulle et l'ébénisterie à l'École nationale des beaux-arts dont il sort diplômé en 1960. De 1958 à 1961, il poursuit sa formation en Suède et en Finlande, et travaille en 1960 auprès de Maurice Holland, de la Nordiska Kompaniet, Stockholm. En 1963, à Paris, il est décorateur pour l'agence d'architecture intérieure Gautier-Delaye, et fonde en 1966 son propre studio qu'il ferme en 1976 pour partir en Bretagne et devenir professeur à l'École des beaux-arts de Brest.

Peter Murdoch (*1940) GREAT BRITAIN
Peter Murdoch trained at the Royal College of Art, London, graduating in 1963. In 1968, he established his own design office in London. He is primarily known for his work in graphics, signage and corporate identity. In 1968, he designed, in collaboration with Lance Wyman, the graphics for the Olympics in Mexico City. He has acted as design consultant to Hille International.

Peter Murdoch studierte am Royal College of Art, London und erwarb dort 1963 seinen Abschluß. 1968 gründete er sein eigenes Designbüro in London. Einen Namen macht er sich vor allem mit seiner Graphik, seinen Signets und seinen Arbeiten auf dem Gebiet der Corporate Identity. 1968 entwarf er in Zusammenarbeit mit Lance Wyman die graphische Gestaltung für die Olympischen Spiele in Mexiko-City. Er ist als Designberater für die Firma Hille International tätig gewesen.

Formé au Royal College of Art de Londres, Peter Murdoch est diplômé en 1963. En 1968, il ouvre son bureau de design à Londres et se fait d'abord connaître pour ses travaux dans les domaines du graphisme, de la signalétique et de l'identité institutionnelle. En 1978, il signe en collaboration avec Lance Wyman l'image graphique des Jeux olympiques de Mexico. Il est intervenu comme consultant pour Hille International.

George Nelson (1908–1986) USA
Born in Connecticut, George Nelson studied architecture at Yale University, graduating 1931. In 1932, while on a fellowship at the American Academy in Rome, he was awarded the Prix de Rome for architecture. As a design theorist and architectural critic, he was extremely influential

during the postwar years – he is credited with the invention of the integrated office system and the concept of the shopping mall. From 1935 to 1944, he was editor of *Architectural Forum*. Between 1936 and 1944, he and William Hanby established and operated an architectural practice in New York. In 1946, he was made design director of Herman Miller and, in this capacity, encouraged Charles and Ray Eames to design furniture for the company. A year later with Gordon Chadwick, he formed the architectural practice, George Nelson Associates, specialising in industrial design. He designed several important furniture products for Herman Miller, including the "Basic Storage Components" (1946), the "Comprehensive Storage System" (1958) and, with Bob Propst, the "Action Office 1" system (1965).

Peter Murdoch

George Nelson wurde in Connecticut geboren und studierte bis 1931 Architektur an der Yale University. 1932 gewann er als Stipendiat der American Academy in Rom den Prix de Rome für Architektur. Von 1935 bis 1944 war er Herausgeber der Zeitschrift »Architectural Forum«. In der Nachkriegszeit hatte er als Designtheoretiker und Architekturkritiker großen Einfluß; außerdem gilt er als der Erfinder von Großraumbüro und Einkaufszentrum. 1936 gründete er mit William Hanby in New York ein Architekturbüro, das die beiden bis 1944 führten. 1946 wurde er Designdirektor bei Herman Miller, und in dieser Funktion ermutigte er Charles und Ray Eames, Möbel für das Unternehmen zu entwerfen. Ein Jahr später gründete er mit Gordon Chadwick das Architekturbüro George Nelson Associates, das sich auf Industriedesign spezialisierte. Er entwarf mehrere richtungsweisende Möbelstücke für Herman Miller, darunter »Basic Storage Components« (1946), »Comprehensive Storage System« (1958) und, mit Bob Propst, »Action Office 1« (1965).

George Nelson

Né dans le Connecticut, George Nelson étudie l'architecture à l'université de Yale (diplôme en 1931). En 1932, alors qu'il bénéficie d'une bourse à l'American Academy in Rome, il reçoit le Prix de Rome d'architecture. Théoricien du design et critique d'architecture, il est extrêmement influent pendant les années d'après-guerre. On lui attribue l'invention du système de bureaux intégrés et le concept de centre commercial. De 1935 à 1944, il est rédacteur en chef d'*Architectural Forum*. Entre 1936 et 1944, avec William Hanby, il ouvre et dirige un cabinet d'architecture à New York. En 1946, il est directeur du design chez Herman Miller et, à ce titre, incite Charles et Ray Eames à créer des meubles pour cette société. Un an plus tard, avec Gordon Chadwick, il fonde le cabinet d'architecture George Nelson Asso-

Isamu Noguchi

Verner Panton

Pierre Paulin

ciates spécialisé dans le design industriel. Il dessine plusieurs meubles importants pour Herman Miller, dont les systèmes de rangement « Basic Storage Components » (1946), le « Comprehensive Storage System » (1958) et, avec Bob Probst, l'« Action Office 1 System » (1965).

Isamu Noguchi (1904–1988) USA
Born in Los Angeles, Isamu Noguchi trained as a cabinetmaker in Japan in 1917. From 1921 to 1922, he studied at Columbia University, New York. Subsequently, he worked as an assistant to the director of the Leonardo da Vinci School, New York. From 1927 to 1929, Noguchi worked as an assistant to the sculptor, Constantin Brancusi in Paris, where he met Alberto Giacometti. From 1932, he lived in New York working mainly as a sculptor. He designed a bakelite radio for Zenith, Chicago in 1937 and most notably several pieces of furniture for Herman Miller and Knoll Associates. In the 1980s, he founded a museum in Long Island to display his sculptures.

Isamu Noguchi wurde in Los Angeles geboren und lernte ab 1917 Möbeltischlerei in Japan. Von 1921 bis 1922 studierte er an der Columbia University, New York. Anschließend arbeitete er als Assistent des Direktors der Leonardo da Vinci School, New York. Von 1927 bis 1929 war er Assistent des Bildhauers Constantin Brancusi in Paris, wo er auch Alberto Giacometti kennenlernte. Seit 1932 lebte er wieder in New York und arbeitete hauptsächlich als Bildhauer, entwarf 1937 aber auch das Bakelit-Gehäuse eines Radios für die Firma Zenith, Chicago, und mehrere höchst bemerkenswerte Möbelstücke für Herman Miller und Knoll Associates. In den 80er Jahren gründete er auf Long Island ein Museum, um seine Skulpturen auszustellen.

Né à Los Angeles, Isamu Noguchi apprend l'ébénisterie au Japon en 1917. De 1921 à 1922, il étudie à la Columbia University, New York. Par la suite, il est assistant du directeur de l'école Leonardo da Vinci, à New York. De 1927 à 1929, il est assistant du sculpteur Constantin Brancusi à Paris, où il rencontre Alberto Giacometti. À partir de 1932, il vit à New York, travaillant essentiellement comme sculpteur, bien qu'il ait réalisé en 1937 un poste de radio en bakélite pour Zenith, à Chicago, et plusieurs meubles pour Herman Miller et Knoll Associates. Dans les années 80, il fonde un musée à Long Island pour ses sculptures.

Verner Panton (1926–1998) DENMARK
Verner Panton trained at the Royal Danish Academy of Fine Arts, Copenhagen, and initially worked in Arne Jacobsen's architectural prac-

tice. He established his own design office in 1955 and is credited with the design of the very first single-form injection moulded plastic chair – the stacking chair "Panton", designed by him in 1960. He was a prolific designer of furniture, textiles and lighting as well as exhibitions. In 1971, he co-designed with Joe Colombo and Olivier Mourgue the "Visiona 2" exhibition for Bayer. He received numerous design awards including two A.I.D. awards in 1963 & 1968. He finally settled in Switzerland.

Verner Panton studierte an der Königlichen Kunstakademie in Kopenhagen und arbeitete dann in Arne Jacobsens Architekturbüro. Sein eigenes Büro gründete er 1955. 1960 entwarf er den Stapelstuhl »Panton«, den ersten Stuhl, der komplett aus spritzgußgeformtem Kunststoff hergestellt wurde. Als produktiver und vielseitiger Designer hat er Möbel, Stoffe und Leuchten entworfen sowie Ausstellungsarchitektur. 1971 hat er zusammen mit Joe Colombo und Olivier Mourgue für Bayer die Ausstellung Visiona 2 gestaltet. Er wurde mit vielen Preisen ausgezeichnet, darunter auch zweimal mit dem A.I.D.-Preis (1963 und 1968). Panton lebte zuletzt in der Schweiz.

Formé à l'Académie royale des beaux-arts de Copenhague, Verner Panton avait fait ses débuts dans l'agence d'Arne Jacobsen. Il ouvrit son propre studio de design en 1955 et on lui attribue la conception du tout premier siège en plastique moulé – la chaise empilable « Panton » – qu'il dessina en 1960. Créateur prolifique, il a intervenu aussi bien dans les domaines du mobilier, des textiles et des luminaires que dans celui des expositions. En 1971, il collabora avec Joe Colombo et Olivier Mourgue à la conception de l'exposition Visiona 2 pour Bayer. Il reçut de nombreuses distinctions dont deux prix de l'A.I.D. en 1963 et 1968. A la fin de sa vie, Panton résidait en Suisse.

Pierre Paulin (*1927) FRANCE
Pierre Paulin studied stone-carving and clay modelling at the École Camondo in Paris. He began designing furniture for Thonet in 1954 and Artifort 1958. From 1967 to 1968, he designed a series of chairs using foam upholstery and polyester seats which were developed by Mobilier National. In 1968, he was commissioned to refurbish the Louvre and the following year was awarded an A.I.D. award for the "Ribbon" chair, Model No. 582. In 1970, he designed seating for Expo '70 in Osaka and in 1971, he redesigned the private apartments of the Élysée Palace. In 1975, he founded ADSA + Partners and the practice was joined by Roger Tallon and Michel Schreiber in

1984. He was commissioned in 1983 to design furniture for the presidential office at the Élysée Palace.

Pierre Paulin erhielt seine Ausbildung als Steinmetz und Bildhauer an der École Camondo. 1954 entwarf er seine ersten Möbel für Thonet. Seit 1958 ist er für die Firma Artifort tätig. Von 1967 bis 1968 schuf er eine Serie von Sitzmöbeln mit Schaumstoffpolsterung und Polyestersitzen, die von Mobilier National hergestellt wurden. 1968 erhielt er den Auftrag, den Louvre neu auszustatten, und im Jahr darauf wurde er für den »Ribbon«-Stuhl Nr. 582 mit dem A.I.D.-Preis ausgezeichnet. 1970 entwarf er Sitzmöbel für die Expo '70 in Osaka; 1971 gestaltete er die Privatwohnung des Präsidenten im Élysée-Palast. 1975 gründete er ADSA + Partners, ein Büro, dem sich 1984 Roger Tallon und Michel Schreiber anschlossen. 1983 erhielt er den Auftrag, Möbel für das Arbeitszimmer des französischen Präsidenten im Élysée-Palast zu entwerfen.

Après des études de sculpture sur pierre et de modelage de glaise à l'École Camondo, à Paris, Pierre Paulin commence à dessiner des meubles pour Thonet en 1954 et pour Artifort en 1958. De 1967 à 1968, il crée une série de chaises rembourrées en mousse avec siège en polyester, qui sont fabriquées par le Mobilier National. En 1968, il reçoit une commande de meubles pour le Louvre et l'année suivante se voit décerner un prix de l'A.I.D. pour le siège « Ribbon », modèle n° 582. En 1970, il crée des sièges pour l'Expo '70 d'Osaka et en 1971, redécore les appartements privés du palais de l'Élysée. En 1975, il fonde ADSA+Partners avant d'être rejoint par Roger Tallon et Michel Schreiber en 1984. Le palais de l'Élysée lui commande en 1983 de nouveaux meubles pour le bureau présidentiel.

Jorge Pensi (*1946) SPAIN

Jorge Pensi was born in Buenos Aires. In 1977, he became a founding member of Grupo Berenguer, Design, Form & Communication, together with Alberto Liévore, Oriol Pibernat and Norberto Chaves. Since 1979, he has worked with Perobell and the SIDI group and contributed to the journal, On Diseño. His furniture is manufactured by Amat s. a., Spain, and Thonet, Germany, while his designs for lighting are produced by B-Lux, Spain.

Jorge Pensi wurde in Buenos Aires geboren. 1977 gehörte er mit Alberto Liévore, Oriol Pibernat und Norberto Chaves zu den Gründern der Grupo Berenguer, Design, Form & Communication. Seit 1979 arbeitet er mit Perobell und der Gruppe SIDI zusammen und schreibt für die Zeitschrift »On Diseño«. Seine Möbel werden von Amat SA in Spanien und von

Thonet in Deutschland hergestellt; seine Leuchten produziert der spanische Hersteller B-Lux. Jorge Pensi est né à Buenos Aires. En 1977, il fonde avec Alberto Liévore, Oriol Pibernat et Norberto Chaves, le Grupo Berenguer, Design, Form & Communication. Depuis 1979, il a travaillé avec Perobell et le groupe SIDI et écrit pour le magazine On Diseño. Ses meubles sont réalisés par AMAT s.a., en Espagne, et par Thonet, en Allemagne; ses luminaires par B-Lux, en Espagne.

Jorge Pensi

Gaetano Pesce (*1939) ITALY/USA

Born in La Spezia, Gaetano Pesce studied architecture at the University of Venice from 1959 to 1965 while also training at the Institute of Industrial Design, Venice, from 1961 to 1965. Since then he has worked as a freelance designer, artist and film-maker. His furniture designs are always highly innovative in either the materials or methods of production they use.

Gaetano Pesce wurde in La Spezia geboren und studierte von 1959 bis 1965 Architektur an der Universität von Venedig, von 1961 bis 1965 dort auch Industriedesign. Seitdem arbeitet er als freiberuflicher Designer, Künstler und Filmemacher. Seine Möbelentwürfe sind stets innovativ, entweder hinsichtlich der Materialien oder der Herstellungsverfahren.

Né à La Spezia, Gaetano Pesce étudie l'architecture à l'université de Venise de 1959 à 1965, tout en suivant les cours de l'Institut de design industriel de Venise, de 1961 à 1965. Depuis, il est designer indépendant, artiste et réalisateur de films. Ses créations de meubles sont toujours novatrices, que ce soit par leurs matériaux ou leurs méthodes de production.

Gaetano Pesce

Giancarlo Piretti (*1940) ITALY

Giancarlo Piretti studied at the Institute of Art, Bologna, before working for Castelli, Italy. He subsequently became the company's director of research and design. In the 1980s he designed, with Emilio Ambasz, the "Dorsal" and the "Vertebra", ergonomically conceived seating systems.

Giancarlo Piretti studierte an der Kunstakademie von Bologna, arbeitete dann für die Firma Castelli, Italien. Nach einiger Zeit übernahm er dort die Stellung des Direktors für Forschung und Design. In den 80er Jahren entwarf er mit Emilio Ambasz die nach ergonomischen Gesichtspunkten konzipierten Sitzmöbel »Dorsal« und »Vertebra«.

Giancarlo Piretti étudie à l'Académie d'art de Bologne avant de travailler pour Castelli, où il devient directeur de la recherche et du design. Dans les années 80, avec Emilio Ambasz, il crée « Dorsal » et « Vertebra », deux lignes de sièges ergonomiques.

Giancarlo Piretti

Warren Platner

Gio Ponti

Jean Prouvé

Warren Platner, (*1919) USA
Born in Baltimore, Warren Platner studied
architecture at Cornell University, Ithaca, New
York, graduating in 1941. From 1945 to 1950,
he worked in the design office of Raymond
Loewy and the architectural practices of I. M.
Pei and Kevin Roche & John Dinkeloo. From
1960 to 1965, he worked for Eero Saarinen &
Associates, Birmingham, Michigan. In 1965, he
established his own firm, Platner Associates,
New Haven, Connecticut, and since then has
worked primarily as an architect.

Warren Platner wurde in Baltimore geboren und studierte bis 1941 Architektur an
der Cornell University, Ithaca, New York. Von
1945 bis 1950 arbeitete er im Designbüro
von Raymond Loewy und in den Architekturbüros von I. M. Pei und Kevin Roche & John
Dinkeloo. Von 1960 bis 1965 war er für Eero
Saarinen & Associates, Birmingham, Michigan,
tätig. 1965 gründete er seine eigene Firma,
Platner Associates in New Haven, Connecticut,
und arbeitet seitdem hauptsächlich als
Architekt.

Né à Baltimore, Warren Platner est diplômé d'architecture de Cornell University, Ithaca,
New York. De 1945 à 1950, il travaille dans
l'agence de design de Raymond Loewy, puis
pour I. M. Pei et Kevin Roche & John Dinkeloo.
De 1960 à 1965, il collabore avec Eero Saarinen
& Associates, Birmingham, Michigan, avant
de créer sa propre agence, Platner Associates,
New Haven, Connecticut, en 1965. Il se consacre depuis essentiellement à l'architecture.

Gio Ponti (1891–1979) ITALY
Gio Ponti studied architecture at the Polytecnic
of Milan, graduating in 1921. He initially became a ceramics designer for Richard Ginori
and also practised architecture. In 1928, he
founded the prestigious design journal Domus
and, from 1925 to 1979, was the director of the
Monza Biennale. From 1936 to 1961, he taught
at the Polytecnic of Milan. During the 1950s, he
collaborated on several furniture designs and
interior schemes with Piero Fornasetti. Until
his death in 1979, he was a regular contributor
to both Domus and Casabella.

Gio Ponti studierte bis 1921 Architektur
am Polytechnikum in Mailand. Zunächst war
er als Keramikdesigner für die Porzellanfirma
Richard Ginori tätig, arbeitete daneben aber
auch als Architekt. 1928 gründete er die renom-
mierte Designzeitschrift »Domus« und war
von 1925 bis 1979 Direktor der Biennale in
Monza. Von 1936 bis 1961 lehrte er am Polytechnikum in Mailand. Während der 50er
Jahre schuf er in Zusammenarbeit mit Piero
Fornasetti mehrere Möbelentwürfe und Inneneinrichtungen. Bis zu seinem Tod 1979 schrieb

er regelmäßig für die Zeitschriften »Domus«
und »Casabella«.

Gio Ponti étudie à l'École polytechnique
de Milan, dont il est diplômé en 1921. Il débute
comme designer de céramiques pour Richard
Ginori tout en travaillant sur des projets
d'architecture. En 1928, il fonde le prestigieux
magazine Domus et de 1925 à 1979, il est directeur de la Biennale de Monza. De 1936 à 1961,
il enseigne à l'École polytechnique de Milan.
Au cours des années 50, il collabore avec Piero
Fornasetti sur plusieurs projets de mobilier et
d'aménagements intérieurs. Jusqu'à sa mort,
en 1979, il collabore régulièrement à Domus et
Casabella.

Jean Prouvé (1901–1984) FRANCE
Jean Prouvé came from a highly artistic background. His grandfather had worked as a ce-
ramicist with Émile Gallé's father, and Prouvé's
father, Victor, collaborated with Émile Gallé
and Louis Majorelle on ceramics and marquetry
designs. From 1917 to 1920, Jean Prouvé
trained as a blacksmith and afterwards attended the École Supérieure de Nancy. In 1923,
he opened his own workshop and a year later
was designing and producing modern steel
chairs. In the late 1920s, he worked for Le
Corbusier and became a founding member
of the Union des Artistes Modernes. In 1931,
he established a manufacturing company, Les
Ateliers Jean Prouvé. After 1950, he abandoned
furniture design in favour of architecture.

Jean Prouvé stammte aus einer Künstlerfamilie, sein Großvater hat als Keramiker mit
Émile Gallés Vater zusammengearbeitet, sein
Vater Victor assistierte Gallé bei Keramik-
entwürfen und Louis Majorelle bei Marketerie-
entwürfen. Von 1917 bis 1920 absolvierte
Jean Prouvé eine Lehre als Schmied und besuchte anschließend die École Supérieure de
Nancy. 1923 gründete er seine eigene Werkstatt; ein Jahr später entwarf und produzierte
er moderne Stühle aus Stahl. In den späten
20er Jahren arbeitete er für Le Corbusier
und war Gründungsmitglied der Union des
Artistes Modernes. 1931 gründete er Les
Ateliers Jean Prouvé, ein Herstellungsunter-
nehmen. Nach 1950 wendete er sich vom
Möbeldesign ab und widmete sich ausschließlich der Architektur.

Jean Prouvé est issu d'une famille d'artistes. Son grand-père avait travaillé comme
céramiste avec le père d'Émile Gallé et son père
Victor, avec Émile Gallé et Louis Majorelle, à
la création de céramiques et de marquetteries.
De 1917 à 1920, Jean Prouvé reçoit une formation de forgeron et suit les cours de l'École supérieure de Nancy. En 1923, il ouvre son propre
atelier et, un an plus tard, dessine et réalise

des sièges modernistes en acier. À la fin des années 20, il travaille pour Le Corbusier et devient membre-fondateur de l'Union des artistes modernes. En 1931, il crée une usine de production, Les Ateliers Jean Prouvé. Après 1950, il abandonne le mobilier pour se consacrer à l'architecture.

Ernest Race (1913–1964) GREAT BRITAIN
Born in Newcastle-upon-Tyne, Ernest Race studied interior design at the Bartlett School of Architecture, London, from 1932 to 1935. Afterwards, he worked as a draughtsman for the progressive lighting company, Troughton & Young. In 1937, he went to Madras, India, to visit his missionary aunt who ran a weaving centre there. When he returned he opened a shop in London to sell his aunt's textiles that had been woven to his designs. In 1945, he founded, with the engineer J. W. Noel Jordan, Ernest Race Ltd., with the intention of mass producing low-cost, high-quality, contemporary furniture. In 1953, Race was made a "Royal Designer for Industry". From 1954 onwards, he worked as a freelance designer.

Ernest Race wurde in Newcastle-upon-Tyne geboren und studierte von 1932 bis 1935 Innenarchitektur an der Bartlett School of Architecture, London. Anschließend arbeitete er als Zeichner für die Firma Troughton & Young, Hersteller moderner Beleuchtungskörper. 1937 ging er nach Madras, Indien, um seine Tante zu besuchen, die dort als Missionarin ein Webzentrum betrieb. Nach seiner Rückkehr eröffnete er ein Geschäft in London, wo er Stoffe verkaufte, die bei seiner Tante nach seinen Entwürfen gewebt worden waren. 1945 gründete er mit dem Ingenieur J. W. Noel Jordan die Firma Ernest Race Ltd., um hochwertige moderne Möbel in preiswerten Großserien zu produzieren. 1953 wurde er zum »Royal Designer for Industry« ernannt. Seit 1954 arbeitete er als freischaffender Designer.

Né à Newcastle-upon-Tyne, Ernest Race étudie l'architecture d'intérieur à la Bartlett School of Architecture, à Londres, de 1932 à 1935. Il est par la suite engagé comme dessinateur par la société de luminaires d'avantgarde Troughton & Young. En 1937, il part pour Madras rendre visite à une tante missionnaire qui y dirige un centre de tissage. De retour à Londres, il ouvre une boutique pour vendre les textiles que sa tante réalise selon ses dessins. En 1945, il fonde, avec l'ingénieur J.W. Noel Jordan, Ernest Race Ltd. avec l'intention de produire en série des meubles contemporains de haute qualité et de prix peu élevé. En 1953, Race est nommé «Royal Designer for Industry». À partir de 1954, il travaille comme designer indépendant.

Richard Riemerschmid (1868–1957) GERMANY
Born in Munich, Richard Riemerschmid studied fine art at the Munich Academy from 1888 to 1890. He exhibited at the 1897 Munich Glaspalast Exhibition and a year later designed furniture for the Munich Vereinigte Werkstätten für Kunst im Handwerk, alongside Bruno Paul and Bernhard Pankok. In 1899, he designed furniture for Hermann Obrist and collaborated with him at the 1900 Paris Exposition. He taught at the Nuremberg School of Art from 1902 to 1905, and in 1904, at the St. Louis Exhibition, exhibited an interior he had designed for the school's rector. His first machine-made furniture was produced in the Dresden workshop of his brother-in-law, Karl Schmidt, and was shown at the 1905 Dresden Deutsche Werkstätten Exhibition. He became a founding member of the Deutsche Werkbund in 1907 and began teaching at the Berlin Kunstgewerbemuseum. Between 1912 and 1924, he was the director of the School for Applied Arts in Munich and from 1926 to 1931, he was the principal of the Industrial School in Cologne.

Ernest Race

Richard Riemerschmid wurde in München geboren und studierte von 1888 bis 1890 bildende Kunst an der Münchner Kunstakademie. 1897 beteiligte er sich an der Ausstellung im Münchner Glaspalast und ein Jahr später entwarf er neben Bruno Paul und Bernhard Pankok Möbel für die Vereinigten Werkstätten für Kunst im Handwerk. 1899 entwarf er Möbel für Hermann Obrist, mit dem er auch auf der Pariser Weltausstellung von 1900 zusammenarbeitete. Von 1902 bis 1905 lehrte er an der Nürnberger Kunstschule und stellte 1904 auf der Weltausstellung von St. Louis ein Interieur aus, das er für den Rektor der Nürnberger Kunstschule entworfen hatte. Die ersten Möbelentwürfe, die er für die Serienproduktion geschaffen hatte, wurden in der Dresdner Werkstatt seines Schwagers Karl Schmidt hergestellt und auf der Dresdner Ausstellung der Deutschen Werkstätten von 1905 gezeigt. 1907 war er unter den Gründungsmitgliedern des Deutschen Werkbundes und begann eine Lehrtätigkeit am Berliner Kunstgewerbemuseum. Von 1912 bis 1924 war er Leiter der Kunstgewerbeschule in München, von 1920 bis 1926 Leiter des Deutschen Werkbundes und von 1926 bis 1931 Direktor der Kölner Werkschule.

Richard Riemerschmid

Né à Munich, Richard Riemerschmid étudie les beaux-arts à l'Académie de sa ville, de 1888 à 1890. Il participe à l'Exposition du Glaspalast de Munich en 1897 et, un an plus tard, avec Bruno Paul et Bernhard Pankok, dessine des meubles pour les Vereinigten Werkstätte für Kunst im Handwerk de Munich. En 1899, il crée des meubles pour Hermann Obrist et collabore avec celui-ci pour l'Exposition de Paris

Gerrit Thomas
Rietveld

Eero Saarinen

de 1900. Il enseigne à l'École d'art de Nuremberg de 1902 à 1905, et en 1904, à l'occasion
de l'Exposition de Saint-Louis, présente l'aménagement de l'appartement du recteur de
l'école. Son premier meuble conçu pour être
fabriqué à la machine est réalisé à Dresde dans
l'atelier de son beau-frère, Karl Schmidt, et sera
présenté à l'Exposition des Deutsche Werkstätten de Dresde en 1905. Il est membre fondateur du Deutscher Werkbund en 1907 et commence à enseigner au Kunstgewerbemuseum
de Berlin. De 1912 à 1924, il dirige les Vereinigte Werkstätten de Munich et de 1926 à 1931,
la Werkschule de Cologne.

Gerrit Thomas Rietveld (1888–1964)
NETHERLANDS
Born in Utrecht, the son of a cabinetmaker,
Gerrit Thomas Rietveld worked in his father's
workshop from the age of eleven. In 1911, he
became an independent cabinetmaker and began studying architectural drawing at classes
given by P. J. Klaarhamer. He designed the
prototype of the "Red Blue" chair 1917–1918
and in 1919 became one of the first members
of the De Stijl movement. His celebrated chair
design was first published in De Stijl magazine
and in 1923 it was included in an exhibition at
the Bauhaus. During the 1920s, his most important architectural commission was the
Schröder House (1924). In 1927, he designed
experimental fibreboard and plywood furniture
which was subsequently manufactured by
Metz & Co, Amsterdam. During the de-
pression, Rietveld designed a range of furniture constructed of packing-crate components
in response to the need for low-cost products.
In 1942 he designed a stamped aluminium
chair and in 1957 produced a series of bent
metal chairs. However, for his final design, the
"Steltman" chair of 1963, he returned to the
use of solid wood elements and geometric
formalism.

Gerrit Thomas Rietveld wurde in Utrecht
als Sohn eines Möbelschreiners geboren und
begann mit elf Jahren, in der Werkstatt seines
Vaters zu arbeiten. 1911 machte er sich als
Kunsttischler selbständig und besuchte
Kurse im Bauzeichnen bei P. J. Klaarhamer.
1917–1918 entstand der Prototyp des »Rot-
Blau«-Stuhls und 1919 gehörte er zu den ersten
Mitgliedern von De Stijl. Sein berühmter Stuhlentwurf wurde zuerst in der Zeitschrift »De
Stijl« veröffentlicht und 1923 auf einer Grup-
penausstellung am Bauhaus gezeigt. Das 1924
vollendete Haus Schröder gehörte zu seinen
bedeutendsten Architekturaufträgen in den
20er Jahren. 1927 experimentierte er mit Entwürfen für Möbel aus Spanplatten und Schichtholz, die dann von Metz & Co, Amsterdam,

hergestellt wurden. Während der Weltwirt-
schaftskrise entwarf er Möbel aus Kistenlatten,
um den Bedarf an preiswerten Möbeln zu
decken. 1942 entwarf er einen Stuhl, der aus
Aluminium gestanzt wurde. 1957 produzierte er
eine Serie von Stühlen aus gebogenem Metall-
rohr. Mit seinem allerletzten Entwurf, dem
»Steltman«-Stuhl von 1963, kehrte er jedoch
zum Massivholz und seinem ursprünglichen
geometrischen Formalismus zurück.

Né à Utrecht, fils d'un ébéniste, Gerrit
Thomas Rietveld travaille dans l'atelier de son
père dès l'âge de onze ans. En 1911, il se met
à son compte, commence à étudier le dessin
d'architecture et suit les cours de P.J. Klaarhamer. Il dessine le prototype du fauteuil « rouge
et bleu » (1917–18) et en 1919 devient l'un des
premiers membres du mouvement De Stijl. Ce
célèbre projet de siège est d'abord publié dans
le magazine De Stijl, et en 1923, est inclus
dans une exposition du Bauhaus. Pendant les
années 20, sa commande d'architecture la plus
importante est la Maison Schröder (1924). En
1927, il dessine un mobilier expérimental en
aggloméré et contre-plaqué qui sera ultérieure-
ment produit par Metz & Co, à Amsterdam.
Pendant la crise économique, pour répondre
à la demande de produits bon marché, il crée
une série de meubles à partir de caisses d'emballage. En 1942, il dessine un siège d'aluminium embouti et, en 1957, des modèles en métal cintré. Pour ses derniers dessins – le siège
Steltman de 1963 – il revient cependant au bois
massif et au formalisme géométrique.

Eero Saarinen (1910–1961) USA
Eero Saarinen was the son of the celebrated
Finnish architect and first President of the
Cranbrook Academy of Art, Eliel Saarinen. Born
in Helsinki, he emigrated with his family to the
United States in 1923. Initially he studied sculpture in Paris (1929– 1930) and later architecture at Yale, graduating in 1934. He received a
scholarship there which enabled him to travel
to Europe (1934–1935). On his return, he took
up a teaching position at the Cranbrook Academy of Art. In 1937, he began a collaboration
with Charles Eames which culminated in a
series of highly progressive and prize-winning
furniture designs for the Museum of Modern
Art's 1940 "Organic Design in Home Furnishings" competition. He later produced several
highly successful furniture designs for Knoll
International. He worked in his father's architectural office until Eliel's death in 1950. His
greatest architectural project was the remarkable TWA terminal at John F. Kennedy Airport,
New York.

Eero Saarinen, der Sohn von Eliel Saarinen,
dem berühmten finnischen Architekten und

Biographies | Biographien

ersten Präsidenten der Cranbrook Academy of Art, wurde in Helsinki geboren und emigrierte mit seiner Familie 1923 in die USA. 1929–1930 studierte er Bildhauerei in Paris und anschließend Architektur an der Yale University. Ein Stipendium ermöglichte ihm 1934–1935 eine Europareise. Nach seiner Rückkehr lehrte er an der Cranbrook Academy of Arts. 1937 begann seine Zusammenarbeit mit Charles Eames, die in einer Serie innovativer und preisgekrönter Möbelentwürfe kulminierte, die beim Wettbewerb »Organic Design in Home Furnishings« des Museum of Modern Art 1940 preisgekrönt wurden. In den folgenden Jahren schuf er für die Firma Knoll International sehr erfolgreiche Möbelentwürfe. Bis zum Tod seines Vaters im Jahr 1950 arbeitete er in dessen Architekturbüro. Sein größtes Architekturprojekt war der TWA-Terminal auf den John F. Kennedy Flughafen in New York.

Eero Saarinen est le fils du célèbre architecte finlandais et premier président de la Cranbrook Academy of Arts, Eliel Saarinen. Né à Helsinki, il émigre avec sa famille aux États-Unis en 1923. Après avoir étudié la sculpture à Paris (1929–1930) il apprend l'architecture à Yale, dont il est diplômé en 1934. Il reçoit une bourse qui lui permet de voyager en Europe (1934–1935). À son retour, il commence à enseigner à la Cranbrook Academy of Arts. En 1937, il entame une collaboration avec Charles Eames qui les conduira à mettre au point ensemble une série de meubles très avant-gardistes, primés plusieurs fois lors du concours « Organic Design in Home Furnishings» du Museum of Modern Art de New York. Il dessinera plus tard plusieurs meubles pour Knoll International qui connaîtront un grand succès. Il travaille dans l'agence de son père jusqu'à la mort de celui-ci en 1950. Son plus grand projet architectural reste le remarquable terminal TWA de l'aéroport Kennedy, à New York.

Karl Friedrich Schinkel (1781–1841) GERMANY
Born in Neuruppin, Karl Friedrich Schinkel studied architecture in 1798 under the master builder, David Gilly. From 1802 to 1803, he received various architectural commissions in Brandenburg and Potsdam in addition to designing furniture and continuing his theoretical studies at the Academy of Architecture, Berlin. From 1803 to 1805, he travelled to Italy and on his return he concentrated on his work as a painter. In 1810, he became a building inspector working secretly for the Technical Buildings Inspectorate in Berlin. He designed and furnished buildings for members of the Prussian royal family and undertook several interior

commissions for various ministries. His most important buildings include the Neue Wache, Berlin, of 1816–1818 and the Berlin Playhouse of 1818–1821. In 1820, he became a member of the Academy of Arts, Berlin.

Karl Friedrich Schinkel wurde in Neuruppin geboren und studierte 1798 Architektur an der neugegründeten Berliner Bauakademie bei dem Baumeister David Gilly. 1802–1803 erhielt er bereits die ersten Bauaufträge in Brandenburg und Potsdam, außerdem entwarf er Möbel und setzte sein Studium fort. Von 1803 bis 1805 bereiste er Italien. Nach seiner Rückkehr konzentrierte er sich auf die Malerei. 1810 wurde er zum Geheimen Oberbaurat der technischen Oberbau-Deputation. Er entwarf einige Gebäude und Inneneinrichtungen für die preußische Königsfamilie und übernahm einige Aufträge für die Inneneinrichtung der Ministerien. Zu den großen Bauaufträgen, die er nach 1815 in Berlin erhielt, gehörten die Neue Wache (1816–1818) und das Schauspielhaus am Gendarmenmarkt (1818–1821). 1820 wurde Schinkel in die Berliner Akademie der Künste berufen.

Né à Neuruppin, Karl Friedrich Schinkel étudie l'architecture en 1798 auprès du maître bâtisseur David Gilly. De 1802 à 1803, il reçoit diverses commandes architecturales à Brandenburg et Potsdam tout en dessinant des meubles et en poursuivant ses études théoriques à l'Académie d'architecture de Berlin. De 1803 à 1805, il voyage en Italie et, à son retour, se concentre sur son œuvre de peintre. En 1810, il devient inspecteur des constructions, travaillant en secret pour l'Inspection technique des bâtiments de Berlin. Il décore et meuble des résidences pour la famille royale de Prusse et reçoit plusieurs commandes pour les aménagements intérieurs de divers ministères. Parmi les plus importantes réalisations, la Neue Wache à Berlin (1816–1818) et le Schauspielhaus de Berlin (1818–1821). En 1820, il est nommé membre de l'Académie des arts de Berlin.

Mart Stam (1899–1986) NETHERLANDS
Born Martinus Adrianus Stam in Purmerend, Mart Stam studied drawing in Amsterdam from 1917 to 1919. He worked as a draughts-man for a Rotterdam architectural practice until 1922, when he moved to Berlin. In 1923, he took part in an exhibition at the Bauhaus and, from 1925 to 1928, published many articles on architecture and design. In 1925, he returned to Amsterdam via Paris and a year later made his first cantilevered chair. His chair designs were shown at the Stuttgart 1928 "Der Stuhl" exhibition. He became a founding member, with Gerrit Rietveld and Hendrik

Karl Friedrich Schinkel

Mart Stam

Philippe Starck

Giuseppe Terragni

Petrus Berlage, of the Congrès Internationaux d'Architecture Moderne in 1927. From 1931 to 1932, he worked in Russia as a town planner and, from 1948 to 1952, taught architecture and design in Dresden and Berlin. He retired in 1966 and moved to Switzerland.

Mart Stam wurde als Martinus Adrianus Stam in Purmerend geboren. Nach einer künstlerischen Ausbildung in Amsterdam (1917–1919) arbeitete er bis 1922 als Zeichner in einem Rotterdamer Architekturbüro und ging anschließend nach Berlin. 1923 nahm er an einer Bauhaus-Ausstellung teil. Zwischen 1925 und 1928 veröffentlichte er zahlreiche Artikel zu Fragen von Architektur und Design. 1925 kehrte er über Paris nach Amsterdam zurück und präsentierte ein Jahr später seinen ersten Freischwinger. Seine Stuhlentwürfe wurden 1928 auf der Stuttgarter Ausstellung »Der Stuhl« gezeigt. 1927 gehörte er mit Gerrit Rietveld und Hendrik Petrus Berlage zu den Gründungsmitgliedern der Congrès Internationaux d'Architecture Moderne. Von 1931 bis 1932 arbeitete er in der Sowjetunion als Stadtplaner. Er lehrte von 1948 bis 1952 Architektur und Design in Dresden und Berlin. 1966 zog er sich aus dem Berufsleben zurück und übersiedelte in die Schweiz.

Né Martinus Adrianus Stam à Purmerend, Mart Stam étudie le dessin à Amsterdam de 1917 à 1919, avant de devenir dessinateur dans un cabinet d'architecture de Rotterdam jusqu'en 1922, date de son départ pour Berlin. En 1923, il participe à une exposition du Bauhaus et de 1925 à 1928, publie de nombreux articles sur l'architecture et le design. Il retourne à Amsterdam en 1925, via Paris, et un an plus tard réalise sa première chaise en porte à faux. Ses dessins de sièges sont présentés à l'exposition de Stuttgart de 1928 « Der Stuhl ». Il est membre fondateur des Congrès internationaux d'architecture moderne en 1927, avec Gerrit Rietveld et Hendrik Petrus Berlage. De 1931 à 1932, il travaille en Russie comme urbaniste et de 1948 à 1952, enseigne l'architecture et le design à Dresde et à Berlin. Il se retire en 1966 et s'installe en Suisse.

Philippe Starck (*1949) FRANCE
Born in Paris, Philippe Starck studied at the École Nissin de Camondo. In 1965, he won the La Vilette furniture competition and in 1968 was commissioned by L. Venturi and later Quasar to design inflatable furniture. He subsequently founded one of the first companies to produce such furniture. In 1969, he was appointed art director of the Pierre Cardin studio where he produced 65 furniture designs. In 1979, he founded his own manufacturing company, Starck Products. He has worked as a

product, furniture and interior designer and, in 1982 was selected to design the refurbishment of the President's private apartments at the Élysée Palace. He has designed furniture for Vitra, Disform, Driade, Baleri and Idée. In 1986, he became a visiting lecturer at the Domus Academy, Milan.

Philippe Starck wurde in Paris geboren und studierte an der École Nissin de Camondo. 1965 gewann er den La Vilette-Möbelwettbewerb und erhielt 1968 von L. Venturi und später von Quasar den Auftrag, aufblasbare Möbel zu entwickeln. Danach gründete er eines der ersten Unternehmen zur Produktion solcher Möbel. 1969 wurde er künstlerischer Leiter des Ateliers Pierre Cardin, wo er 65 Möbelentwürfe produzierte. 1979 gründete er die Firma Starck Products. Er arbeitete als Produkt- und Möbeldesigner und als Innenarchitekt. 1982 bekam er den Auftrag, die Privaträume des französischen Präsidenten im Élysée-Palast zu entwerfen. Möbelentwürfe hat er für Vitra, Disform, Driade, Baleri und Idée geschaffen. 1986 erhielt er eine Gastprofessur an der Domus-Akademie in Mailand.

Né à Paris, Philippe Starck suit les cours de l'École Camondo. Dès 1965, il remporte un concours de mobilier pour La Villette et en 1968, se voit commander des projets de meubles gonflables par L. Venturi puis par Quasar. Il crée sur cette lancée l'une des premières sociétés spécialisées dans ce type de mobilier. En 1969, il est nommé directeur artistique du Studio Pierre Cardin pour lequel il réalise soixante-cinq projets de meubles. En 1979, il fonde sa propre société de fabrication, Starck Products. Il intervient comme designer de produits et de meubles et comme décorateur, et en 1982, participe aux nouveaux aménagements des appartements privés du palais de l'Élysée. Il a créé des meubles pour Vitra, Disform, Driade, Baleri et Idée. En 1986, il est nommé professeur invité à l'Académie Domus, Milan.

Giuseppe Terragni (1904–1943) ITALY
Born in Meda, Giuseppe Terragni studied architecture at the Polytechnic of Milan, graduating in 1926. He was one of the founders of Gruppo Sette and, in 1927, began working in Como. In 1928, he took part in the first exhibition of Rational Architecture in Rome. From 1932 to 1936, he designed the Casa del Fascio, Como, and in 1936 he designed the Asilo Sant'Elia. At the outbreak of War World II, he enlisted the army and, in 1943, was returned to Italy from the Russian front, having suffered a nervous breakdown. Tragically, he died a few days after his return home.

Biographies | Biographien

Giuseppe Terragni wurde in Meda geboren und studierte bis 1926 Architektur am Polytechnikum von Mailand. Er war einer der Mitbegründer der Gruppo Sette. Seine berufliche Laufbahn begann er 1927 in Como. 1928 beteiligte er sich an der ersten Ausstellung für Rationale Architektur in Rom. Zwischen 1932 und 1936 arbeitete er an Entwürfen für die Casa del Fascio, Como; 1936 entwarf er das Asilo Sant'Elia. Bei Kriegsbeginn wurde er eingezogen; 1943 kehrte er wegen eines Nervenzusammenbruchs von der russischen Front nach Italien zurück, wo er einige Tage später starb.

Né à Meda, Giuseppe Terragni obtient le diplôme de l'École polytechnique de Milan en 1926. Fondateur du Gruppo Sette, il commence à travailler à Côme, en 1927 et, en 1928, prend part à la première exposition d'architecture rationnelle à Rome. De 1932 à 1936, il dessine la Casa del Fascio, à Côme et en 1936 l'Asilo Sant'Elia. À la déclaration de guerre, il s'engage dans l'armée et est rapatrié du front russe en 1943, victime d'une profonde dépression. Il meurt quelques jours après son retour.

Michael Thonet (1796–1871) AUSTRIA
Michael Thonet was born in Boppard am Rhein, where he established a workshop in 1819. In 1842, he was granted a patent for his new process for bending wood laminates, and in 1849 set up his own furniture manufacturing factory. He exhibited his furniture and won a bronze medal at the London 1851 exhibition. In the early 1900s, several progressive Viennese architects, including Josef Hoffmann, designed furniture for Thonet. Le Corbusier was among the first to use Thonet chairs in a "modern" architectural setting.

Michael Thonet wurde in Boppard am Rhein geboren, wo er 1819 eine Werkstatt gründete. 1842 ließ er sich sein neues Verfahren zur Biegung von laminiertem Holz patentieren, und 1849 gründete er eine eigene Firma zur Herstellung seiner Möbel. 1851 zeigte er seine Möbel auf der Londoner Weltausstellung und gewann eine Bronze-Medaille. Anfang des 20. Jahrhunderts entwarfen einige der fortschrittlichen Wiener Architekten, darunter Josef Hoffmann, Möbel für Thonet. Le Corbusier war einer der ersten, der Thonet-Möbel in eine »moderne« architektonische Umgebung einbezog.

Né à Boppard, où il crée son premier atelier en 1819, Michael Thonet dépose un brevet de cintrage du bois laminé en 1842 et crée sa propre manufacture de meubles en 1849. Il présente ses meubles et remporte une médaille de bronze à l'Exposition de Londres

de 1851. Au début des années 1900, plusieurs architectes d'avant-garde viennois, dont Josef Hoffmann, dessineront des meubles pour Thonet. Le Corbusier est le premier à utiliser des sièges Thonet dans un intérieur « moderne ».

Henry van de Velde (1863–1957) BELGIUM
Born in Antwerp, Henry van de Velde studied painting at the Antwerp Academy (1881–1884) and later in Paris (1884–1885). In 1886 he joined "Als ik Kan" and helped to found "L'Art Indépendant", both Antwerp-based art societies. In 1892, he gave up painting for design and two years later published, *Déblaiements d'art*, which pleaded for a unification of the arts. In 1907, he became a founder member of the Deutscher Werkbund; however, he left the group in 1914 after a disagreement with Hermann Muthesius over the latter's rigorous adherence to industrial standardization. In 1917, he emigrated to Switzerland and in 1920 moved to Holland. From 1926–1936, he was the Professor of Architecture at the University of Ghent. In 1947, he moved back to Switzerland and lived there until his death.

Michael Thonet

Henry van de Velde

Henry van de Velde wurde in Antwerpen geboren und studierte von 1841 bis 1884 Malerei an der Kunstakademie in Antwerpen und von 1884 bis 1885 in Paris. 1886 wurde er Mitglied der Antwerpener Künstlergruppen »Als ik Kan« und »L'Art Indépendant«. 1892 gab er die Malerei zugunsten des Designs auf. 1894 veröffentlichte er die Schrift »Déblaiements d'art«, mit der er für eine Vereinigung der Künste plädierte. 1907 gehörte er zu den Gründungsmitgliedern des Deutschen Werkbundes, verließ die Gruppe jedoch 1914, nachdem er sich mit Hermann Muthesius wegen dessen kompromißlosem Festhalten an industrieller Standardisierung überworfen hatte. 1917 emigrierte er in die Schweiz und ging 1920 nach Holland. Von 1926 bis 1936 lehrte er Architektur an der Universität von Gent. 1947 ging er zurück in die Schweiz, wo er bis zu seinem Tod lebte.

Né à Anvers, Henry van de Velde y étudie la peinture à l'Académie des arts (1881–1884) puis à Paris (1884–1885). En 1886, il rejoint « Als ik Kan » et aide à la création de « L'Art Indépendant », deux sociétés artistiques basées à Anvers. En 1892, il abandonne la peinture pour le design et deux ans plus tard publie *Déblaiements d'art*, qui plaide pour une unification des arts. Il est membre fondateur du Deutsche Werkbund en 1907, mais quitte le groupe en 1914 en désaccord avec Hermann Muthesius sur l'authenticité de l'adhésion de celui-ci à la standardisation industrielle. Il émigre en Suisse en 1917, puis en Hollande en

Otto Wagner

Hans J. Wegner

Frank Lloyd Wright

1920. De 1926 à 1936, il est professeur d'architecture à l'université de Gand. Il retourne en Suisse en 1947 où il demeure jusqu'à sa mort.

Otto Wagner (1841–1918) AUSTRIA
Born in Vienna, Otto Wagner studied at the Technische Hochschule, Vienna (1857), Bauakademie, Berlin (1860) and the Academy of Fine Arts, Vienna (1861–1863). In 1894, he became the head of and a professor at the Academy of Fine Arts, Vienna, where his pupils included Josef Hoffmann, Adolf Loos and Josef Maria Olbrich. In 1895, abandoning the Art Nouveau style, he published a book titled *Moderne Architektur*, which took a stance against historicism. He had a large architectural and design office which was managed by Olbrich and was a member of the Deutscher Werkbund.

Otto Wagner wurde in Wien geboren und studierte an der Technischen Hochschule, Wien (1857), an der Bauakademie in Berlin (1860–1861) und an der Akademie der bildenden Künste in Wien (1861–1863). 1894 wurde er Oberbaurat der Stadt Wien; im gleichen Jahr auch Leiter der Spezialschule für Architektur an der Akademie der bildenden Künste in Wien, wo er auch eine Professur antrat. Zu seinen Schülern gehörten unter anderen Josef Hoffmann, Adolf Loos und Josef Maria Olbrich. 1895 veröffentlichte er seine Antrittsvorlesung »Moderne Architektur«, mit der er gegen den Historismus Stellung bezog. Er war Eigentümer eines großen Architektur- und Entwurfsbüros, das von Olbrich geleitet wurde. Wagner war Mitglied des Deutschen Werkbunds.

Né à Vienne, Otto Wagner fait ses études à la Technische Hochschule de cette ville (1857), à la Bauakademie de Berlin (1860) et à l'Académie de beaux-arts de Vienne (1861–1863). En 1894, il est professeur à l'Académie des beaux-arts de Vienne, dont il est également directeur, enseignant à des élèves comme Josef Hoffmann, Adolf Loos et Josef Maria Olbrich. En 1895, abandonnant le style Art nouveau, il publie un livre intitulé *Moderne Architektur* qui prend position contre l'historicisme. Membre du Deutscher Werkbund, il anime une importante agence d'architecture et de design, dirigée par Olbrich.

Hans J. Wegner (*1914) DENMARK
Hans J. Wegner trained as a cabinetmaker before attending the Copenhagen School of Arts and Crafts, where he later lectured 1946–1953. From 1938 to 1942, he worked as a furniture designer in Arne Jacobsen and Erik Moller's architectural practice. In 1943, he set up his own office in Gentofte and collaborated with

Børge Mogensen in the design of an apartment shown at the Copenhagen 1946 Cabinet-maker's Exhibition. Throughout his long career, he has designed furniture extensively for Johannes Hansen and Fritz Hansen. The Royal Society of Arts, London, made him an Honorary Royal Designer for Industry in 1959.

Hans J. Wegner absolvierte eine Lehre als Möbeltischler, besuchte dann die Kunstgewerbeschule in Kopenhagen, an der er später, von 1946 bis 1953, selbst lehrte. Von 1938 bis 1942 arbeitete er als Möbeldesigner im Architekturbüro von Arne Jacobsen und Erik Moller. 1943 gründete er ein eigenes Studio in Gentofte. Eine in Zusammenarbeit mit Børge Mogensen entstandene Inneneinrichtung wurde 1946 auf der Ausstellung der Kunsttischler in Kopenhagen gezeigt. Er hat zahlreiche Möbelentwürfe geschaffen, u. a. für Johannes Hansen und Fritz Hansen. Die Royal Society of Arts, London, verlieh ihm 1959 den Titel Honorary Royal Designer for Industry.

Hans J. Wegner est formé à l'ébénisterie avant de suivre les cours de l'École des arts appliqués de Copenhague où il enseigne de 1946 à 1953. De 1938 à 1942, il est dessinateur de meubles dans les agences d'architecture d'Arne Jacobsen et d'Erik Moller. En 1943, il ouvre son propre studio à Gentofte et collabore avec Børge Mogensen à la conception d'un appartement présenté à l'Exposition d'ébénisterie de Copenhague, en 1946. Au cours de sa longue carrière, il crée de nombreux meubles pour Johannes Hansen et Fritz Hansen. La Royal Society of Arts de Londres lui décerne le titre de Honorary Royal Designer for Industry en 1959.

Frank Lloyd Wright (1867–1959) USA
Frank Lloyd Wright trained at the Engineering School of Wisconsin before working in the architectural office of J. L. Silsbee. From 1888 to 1893, he worked as a draughtsman with Louis Sullivan. In 1889, he began his own practice as an architect and by 1900 had designed over fifty houses and their interiors. In 1897, he helped to found the Chicago Arts and Crafts Society. Like Charles Voysey, he believed that the machine could be used for the betterment of society when employed sympathetically. Influenced by Japanese forms, his designs were more sophisticated than those of fellow Arts & Crafts designer, Gustav Stickley. In 1909, he travelled to Europe and on his return, his house, "Taliesin", became an architectural school. In 1955, he designed the "Taliesin" Line of furniture which was intended for the mass-market.

Frank Lloyd Wright studierte Ingenieurwissenschaften an der Engineering School of

Photographic Credits | Fotonachweis | Crédits photographiques

Wisconsin und trat dann in das Architekturbüro von J. L. Silsbee ein. Von 1888 bis 1893
arbeitete er als technischer Zeichner für Louis
Sullivan. 1889 machte er sich als Architekt
selbständig und hatte bis 1900 über fünfzig
Häuser samt Inneneinrichtung entworfen. 1897
war er an der Gründung der Chicago Arts &
Crafts Society beteiligt. Wie Charles Voysey
glaubte er, daß die Maschine zur Verbesserung
der Gesellschaft beitragen könne, wenn man
sie nur entsprechend ihrer Eigenschaften ein-
setzt. Beeinflußt durch die japanische Formen-
welt, waren seine Entwürfe eleganter als die
des Arts & Crafts-Designers Gustav Stickley.
1909 bereiste er Europa und richtete nach seiner Rückkehr in seinem Haus »Taliesin« eine
Architekturschule ein. 1955 entwarf er eine
Möbelkollektion für die Serienfertigung, die
er nach seinem Haus »Taliesin« nannte.

   Frank Lloyd Wright se forme à l'Engineering School of Wisconsin avant de travailler
pour l'agence d'architecture de J. L. Sisbee, puis
de collaborer, comme dessinateur, avec Louis
Sullivan, de 1888 à 1893. En 1889, il se met à
son compte et vers 1900, a déjà conçu plus de
cinquante maisons et leurs intérieurs. En 1897,
il participe à la fondation de la Chicago Arts
and Crafts Society. Comme Charles Voysey, il
croit que la machine peut servir à améliorer la
société si elle est employée avec intelligence.
Influencés par les formes japonaises, ses dessins sont plus sophistiqués que ceux de son
confrère en Arts et Crafts, Gustav Stickley. En
1909, il voyage en Europe et à son retour, sa
maison, « Taliesin », est transformée en école
d'architecture. En 1955, il dessine une ligne
de mobilier « Taliesin », destinée à la grande
consommation.

Sori Yanagi (*1915) JAPAN
Sori Yanagi trained at the Tokyo National University of Fine Arts and Music, graduating in
1940. He was an assistant to Charlotte Perriand
from 1940 to 1942 while she was working in
Japan. In 1951, he won the "Japanese Competition for Industrial Design" and a year later,
founded the Yanagi Industrial Design Institute.
In 1977, he became the director of the Japan
Folk Crafts Museum, Tokyo.

   Sori Yanagi studierte an der Staatlichen
Universität für Bildende Künste und Musik in
Tokio; seinen Abschluß erwarb er 1940. Er
arbeitete von 1940 bis 1942 während ihres
Japanaufenthaltes als Assistent von Charlotte
Perriand. 1951 gewann er die Japanese Competition for Industrial Design. Ein Jahr später
gründete er das Yanagi-Institut für Industriedesign. 1977 wurde er zum Direktor des Japanischen Museums für Volkskunst in Tokio
berufen.

   Formé à l'Université nationale des beaux-
arts et de musique de Tokyo, Sori Yanagi en
obtient le diplôme en 1950. Il est assistant de
Charlotte Perriand de 1940 à 1942, lors du
séjour de celle-ci au Japon. En 1951, il remporte
le concours du design industriel japonais, puis,
un an plus tard, crée le Yanagi Industrial Design Institute. En 1977, il devient directeur du
Musée japonais des arts populaires, à Tokyo.

Marco Zanuso

Marco Zanuso (*1916) ITALY
Born in Milan, Marco Zanuso studied architecture at the Polytechnic, graduating in 1939. In
1945, he established his own design practice
and was a director of *Domus* magazine. From
1947 to 1949, was chief editor of the journal,
Casabella. In 1948, he was commissioned by
the Pirelli company to design seating with
foam rubber upholstery – one example, the
"Lady" chair, was awarded a gold medal at the
1951 Milan Triennale. In 1957, he formed a
design collaboration with Richard Sapper.
From this fruitful partnership was born the
innovative Child's chair of 1961 which was the
first sizable object produced in non-reinforced
plastic.

   Marco Zanuso wurde in Mailand geboren
und studierte bis 1939 Architektur am Polytechnikum von Mailand. 1945 gründete er ein eigenes Designstudio und übernahm die Leitung
der Zeitschrift »Domus«. Von 1947 bis 1949
war er Chefredakteur der Zeitschrift »Casabella«. 1948 erhielt er von der Firma Pirelli den
Auftrag, Sitzmöbel mit Schaumstoffpolsterung
zu entwerfen. Einer dieser Entwürfe, der Sessel
»Lady«, wurde auf der Mailänder Triennale von
1951 mit einer Goldmedaille ausgezeichnet.
1957 tat er sich mit Richard Sapper zu einer
Arbeitsgemeinschaft zusammen. Ein Produkt
dieser fruchtbaren Zusammenarbeit war der
innovative Kinderstuhl von 1961 – das erste
größere Objekt, das aus nicht verstärktem
Kunststoff gefertigt wurde.

   Né à Milan, Marco Zanuso est diplômé
de l'École polytechnique de Milan en 1939. En
1945, il ouvre son agence de design et dirige le
magazine *Domus*. De 1947 à 1949, il est rédacteur en chef du magazine *Casabella*. En 1948, il
reçoit commande de Pirelli pour un siège rembourré de mousse de caoutchouc. Sa chaise
« Lady » obtient une médaille d'or à la Triennale de Milan de 1951. En 1957, il commence
à former équipe avec Richard Sapper. De ce
partenariat naît la chaise pour enfants de 1961,
premier objet d'une certaine taille à être produit en matière plastique non renforcée.

Photographic
Credits
Fotonachweis
Crédits photo-
graphiques

L – left/links/
à gauche
C – centre/Mitte/
centre
R – right/rechts/
à droite
p. – page/Seite/
page

page 18 Main: Gordon Logie, Furniture from machines, London, 1947, p. 92, pl. 114 **18** Archival – L: Artek, Helsinki **18** Archival – R: Artek, Helsinki **19** Main: Barry Friedman, New York **20** Main: Artek, Helsinki **20** Archival – L: Artek, Helsinki **21** Main: Artek, Helsinki **21** Archival: Artek, Helsinki **22** Main: Fiell International Ltd., London (photo: Paul Chave) **23** Main: Museé des Arts Décoratifs, Montreal – Gift of Nanette & Eric Brill (photo: Richard P. Goodbody) **23** Archival: Adelta, Dinslaken **24** Main: Adelta, Dinslaken **25** Main: Arflex, Milan **25** Archival: Sotheby's, London **26** Main: Fiell International Ltd., London (photo: Paul Chave) **26** Archival: Studio Year Book, 1932 **27** Main: Poltronova, Montale **27** Archival: Poltronova, Montale **28** Main: Die Neue Sammlung, Staatliches Museum für angewandte Kunst, Munich **28** Archival: Wilhelm Bofinger KG, Ilsfield **29** Main: Fiell International Ltd., London (photo: Paul Chave) **29** Archival: Fiell International Ltd., London (photo: Paul Chave) **30** Main: Fiell International Ltd., London (photo: Peter Hodsoll) **30** Archival: Knoll International, New York **31** Main: Tecno spa, Milan **31** Archival: Tecno spa, Milan **32** Main: Tecno spa, Milan **32** Archival: Tecno spa, Milan **33** Main: Christie's, Amsterdam **33** Archival: Tecta, Lauenförde **34** Main: Barry Friedman, New York **34** Archival – L: Ulrich Gronert, Kunsthandel, Berlin (photo: Lepkowski) **34** Archival – R: Gustav Adolf Platz, Wohnräume der Gegenwart, Berlin, 1933, p. 317 **35** Main: Designsammlung Ludewig, Berlin (photo: Lepkowski) **36** Main: Christie's Images, London **36** Archival: Herbert Bayer, Das federnde Aluminium-Möbel, Wohnbedarf, Zürich 1934 **37** Main: Fischer Fine Art, Vienna **37** Archival: Herbert Bayer, Das federnde Aluminium-Möbel, Wohnbedarf, Zürich, 1934 **38** Main: Fischer Fine Art, Vienna **39** Main: Die Neue Sammlung, Staatliches Museum für angewandte Kunst, Munich **39** Archival: E. Nelson Exton & Frederic H. Littmann, Modern Furniture, London 1936, p. 38 **40** Main: Haslam & Whiteway, London **41** Main: Sotheby's, London **41** Archival – L: Barry Friedman, New York **41** Archival – R: Barry Friedman, New York **42** Main: Zanotta, Milan **42** Archival – L: George Nelson, Chairs, Whitney Publications, New York, 1953, p. 19 **43** Main: Zanotta, Milan **44** Main: Wendell Castle Inc., Scottsville, New York **44** Archival: Wendell Castle Inc., Scottsville, New York **45** Main: Wendell Castle Inc., Scottsville, New York **46** Main: Herman Miller Inc., Zeeland, Michigan (photo: Merrick, Nick, Hedrich-Blessing) **46** Archival: Herman Miller Inc., Zeeland, Michigan **47** Main: Christie's Images, London **48** Main: Fiell International Ltd., London (Bonhams, London) (photo: James Barlow) **49** Main: Fischer Fine Art, Vienna **49** Archival: Kartell, Noviglio **50** Main: Museé des Arts Décoratifs, Montreal – Liliane & David Stewart Collection (photo: Richard P. Goodbody) **51** Main: Zanotta, Milan **51** Archival: Sotheby's, London **52** Archival – Top L: Hille Ltd., Warrington, Cheshire **52** Archival – Top C: Hille Ltd., Warrington, Cheshire **52** Archival – Top R: Hille Ltd., Warrington, Cheshire **52** Archival – Bottom: Hille Ltd., Warrington, Cheshire **53** Main: Fiell International Ltd., London (photo: Paul Chave) **54** Main: Michele De Lucchi, Milan (photo: Studio Azzuro) **55** Main: Zanotta, Milan **55** Archival: Zanotta, Milan **56** Main: Poltronova, Montale **57** Main: Torsten Bröhan, Düsseldorf (photo: Walter Klein) **57** Archival: Torsten Bröhan, Düsseldorf (photo: Walter Klein) **58** Main: Fiell International Ltd., London (photo: Peter Hodsoll) **58** Archival – L: Fifty/50, New York **58** Archival – R: Lucia Eames dba Eames Office, Venice, California (photo: Charles Eames) **59** Main: Fiell International Ltd., London (photo: Peter Hodsoll) **60** Main: Vitra AG, Basle **61** Main: Fiell International Ltd., London (photo: Paul Chave) **61** Archival: Herman Miller Inc., Zeeland, Michigan **62** Main: Fiell International Ltd., London (photo: Paul Chave) **63** Main: Herman Miller Inc., Zeeland, Michigan **63** Archival: Herman Miller Inc., Zeeland, Michigan **64** Main: Fiell International Ltd., London (photo: Peter Hodsoll) **64** Archival: Herman Miller Inc., Zeeland, Michigan (photo: William Sharpe – Effective Images) **65** Main: Benedikt Taschen Archive, Cologne **65** Archival: Galerie Artifical, Nuremberg **66** Main: Stöhr Import-Export GmbH, Besigheim **66** Archival: Benedikt Taschen Archiv, Cologne **67** Main: Zanotta, Milan **67** Archival: Zanotta, Milan **68** Main: Torsten Bröhan, Düsseldorf **68** Archival: Barry Friedman, New York **69** Main: Vitra AG, Basle **70** Main: Haslam & Whiteway, London **71** Main: Sotheby's, London **71** Archival: Victoria & Albert Museum, London **72** Main: Gufram, Balangero **72** Archival: Poltronova, Montale **73** Main: Musée des Arts Decoratifs, Paris **74** Main: Formes Nouvelle, Paris **74** Archival: Art et Décoration, vol. LVII, 1930, p. 33 **75** Main: Formes Nouvelle, Paris **75** Archival: Art et Décoration, vol. LXI, 1932, p. 102 **76** Main: Georg Kargi, Vienna **76** Archival – L: Deutsche Kunst und Dekoration, XLI, 1917/1918 **76** Archival – R: Barry Friedman, New York **77** Main: Sotheby's, London **78** Main: Torsten Bröhan, Düsseldorf (photo: Walter Klein) **78** Archival – L: Barry Friedman, New York **79** Main: Kunsthandel Thomas Berg, Bonn **79** Archival: Moderne Bauformen, VII., 1908, p. 370 **80** Main: Museé des Arts Décoratifs, Montreal – Gift of Geoffrey N. Bradfield (photo: Richard P. Goodbody) **80** Archival: Fritz Hansen, Allerød **81** Main: Fiell International Ltd., London (photo: Paul Chave) **81** Archival: Fritz Hansen, Allerød **82** Main: Fritz Hansen, Allerød **82** Archival: Fritz Hansen, Allerød **83** Main: Fritz Hansen, Allerød **83** Archival – L: Fritz Hansen, Allerød **83** Archival – R: Treadway Gallery Inc., Cincinnati **84** Main: Kohseki Co. Ltd., Kyoto **85** Main: Kohseki Co. Ltd., Kyoto **85** Archival: Kohseki Co. Ltd., Kyoto

86 Main: Cassina, Milan 87 Main: Rud Rasmussen Snedkerier, Copenhagen (photo: Ole Woldbye) 88 Main: Rud Rasmussen Snedkerier, Copenhagen 89 Main: Fiell International Ltd., London (photo: Paul Chave) 89 Archival: Avarte Oy, Helsinki 90 Main: Vitra AG, Basle 90 Archival: Hiroyuki Hirai, Toyko 91 Main: Keicki Tahara, Tokyo 92 Main: Bonhams, London 92 Archival: Fiell International Ltd., London (photo: Peter Hodsoll) 93 Main: Fiell International Ltd., London (photo: Paul Chave) 93 Archival: Cassina, Milan 94 Main: Cassina, Milan 94 Archival – Art et Décoration, vol. LVII, 1930, p. 41 94 Archival – R: Art et Décoration, vol. LVI, 1929, p. 181 95 Main: Kunsthandel Thomas Berg, Bonn 95 Archival: Charlotte Perriand 96 Main: Studio X, London 96 Archival – L: Studio X, London 96 Archival – C: Studio X, London 96 Archival – R: Studio X, London 97 Main: Ceccotti, Cascina 98 Main: Sotheby's, London 98 Archival: Hunterian Art Gallery, University of Glasgow, Glasgow 99 Main: Sotheby's, London 99 Archival: The Studio, 39, 1907, p. 32 100 Main: Fiell International Ltd., London (photo: Paul Chave) 101 Archival – Top: Barry Friedman, New York 101 Archival – Bottom: Barry Friedman, New York 102 Main: Fiell International Ltd., London (photo: Paul Chave) 103 Main: Alessandro Mendini, Milan 104 Main: Barry Friedman, New York 104 Archival – L: Tecta, Lauenförde 104 Archival – R: Innendekoration, 42, 1931, p. 254 105 Main: Fischer Fine Art, Vienna 105 Archival: Fischer Fine Art, Vienna 106 Main: Christie's, Amsterdam 106 Archival: Gustav Adolf Platz, Wohnräume der Gegenwart, Berlin, 1933, p. 313 107 Main: Christina & Bruno Bischofberger Collection, Zurich 107 Archival: Christie's Images, London 108 Main: Cappellini, Arosio 109 Main: Sotheby's, London 109 Archival: Georg Kargi, Vienna 110 Main: Whitechapel Art Gallery, London 110 Archival: Turner Entertainment Co., 1968 – All Rights Reserved 111 Main: Bonhams, London 112 Main: Zanotta, Milan 112 Archival: Zanotta, Milan 113 Main: Zanotta, Milan 113 Archival: Zanotta, Milan 114 Main: Fiell International Ltd., London (photo: Peter Hodsoll) 114 Archival: Herman Miller Inc., Zeeland, Michigan 115 Main: Fiell International Ltd., London (photo: Peter Hodsoll) 115 Archival: Herman Miller Inc., Zeeland, Michigan 116 Main: Cappellini, Arosio 116 Archival: Cappellini, Arosio 117 Main: Idée, Toyko (photo: Tom Vack) 118 Main: 20th Century, Toronto 119 Main: David Rago Inc., Lambertville, New Jersey 119 Archival: George Nelson, Chairs, Whitney Publications, New York, 1953, p. 142 120 Main: Benedikt Taschen Archiv, Cologne 120 Archival: Verner Panton, Basle 121 Main: Verner Panton, Basle 121 Archival: Fischer Fine Art, Vienna 122 Main: Verner Panton, Basle 124 Main: Fiell International Ltd., London (photo: Paul Chave) 124 Archival: Artifort, Lanaken 125 Main: HNB, London 125 Archival: HNB, London 126 Main: B&B Italia, Novedrate 126 Archivals: B&B Italia, Novedrate 127 Main: B&B Italia, Novedrate 127 Archival: B&B Italia, Novedrate 128 Main: Fiell International Ltd., London (photo: Paul Chave) 129 Main: Knoll International, New York 130 Main: Museé des Arts Décoratifs, Montreal – Liliane & David Stewart Collection (photo: Richard P. Goodbody) 130 Archival: Cassina, Milan 131 Main: Fischer Fine Art, Vienna 131 Archival: Stuhlmuseum Burg Beverungen, Beverungen 132 Main: Fiell International Ltd., London (photo: Paul Chave) 133 Main: Museum of Modern Art, New York (Gift of Liberty & Co.) 134 Main: Barry Friedman, New York 135 Main: Torsten Bröhan, Düsseldorf 136 Main: Barry Friedman, New York 136 Archival – L: Theodore M. Brown, The Work of G. Rietveld, Architect, A. W. Bruna & Zoon, Utrecht, 1958, p. 94 136 Archival – R: Barry Friedman, New York 137 Main: Sotheby's, London 138 Main: Fiell International Ltd., London (photo: Peter Hodsoll) 138 Archival: Knoll International, New York 139 Main: Fiell International Ltd., London (photo: Paul Chave) 139 Archival: Knoll International, New York 140 Main: Haslam & Whiteway, London 140 Archival: Tecta, Lauenförde 141 Main: Stuhlmuseum Burg Beverungen, Beverungen 141 Archival: Innendekoration, 38, 1927, p. 449 142 Main: Driade, Fossadello di Caorso 142 Archival: Driade, Fossadello di Caorso 143 Main: Kartell, Noviglio 143 Archival – L: Kartell, Noviglio 143 Archival – R: Kartell, Noviglio 144 Main: Driade, Fossadello di Caorso (photo: Tom Vack) 144 Archival: Driade, Fossadello di Caorso (photo: Tom Vack) 145 Main: Kartell, Milan (photo: Fabrizio Bergamo) 145 Archival – L: Kartell, Milan (photo: Fabrizio Bergamo) 145 Archival – R: Kartell, Milan (photo: Fabrizio Bergamo) 146 Main: Whitechapel Art Gallery, London 147 Main: Zanotta, Milan 147 Archival – L: Zanotta, Milan 147 Archival – R: Zanotta, Milan 148 Main: Museum Thonet – Gebrüder Thonet GmbH, Frankenberg 148 Archival: Museum Thonet – Gebrüder Thonet GmbH, Frankenberg 149 Main: Fiell International Ltd., London 149 Archival: Museum Thonet – Gebrüder Thonet GmbH, Frankenberg 150 Main: Edra Mazzei, Perignano 150 Archival: Edra Mazzei, Perignano 151 Main: Edra Mazzei, Perignano 152 Main: Christie's Images, London 153 Main: Torsten Bröhan, Düsseldorf 153 Archival: Nordenfjeldske Kunstindustrimuseum, Trondheim 154 Main: Fischer Fine Art, Vienna 154 Archival – L: Historisches Museum der Stadt Wien, Vienna 154 Archival – R: Sotheby's, London 155 Main: Paul Asenbaum, Vienna 155 Archival: Fischer Fine Art, Vienna 156 Main: Carl Hansen, Odense 157 Main: P. P. Møbler, Allerød (photo: Schakenburg & Brahl) 158 Main: Christie's, New York 159 Main: Christie's, New York 159 Archival – L: Cassina, Milan 159 Archival – R: Christie's, New York 160 Main: Artery, New York 161 Main: Kartell, Noviglio

"Buy them all and add some pleasure to your life."

Art Now
Eds. Burkhard Riemschneider,
Uta Grosenick

Atget's Paris
Ed. Hans Christian Adam

Best of Bizarre
Ed. Eric Kroll

Bizarro Postcards
Ed. Jim Heimann

Karl Blossfeldt
Ed. Hans Christian Adam

California, Here I Come
Vintage California Graphics
Ed. Jim Heimann

Chairs
Charlotte & Peter Fiell

Classic Rock Covers
Michael Ochs

Description of Egypt
Ed. Gilles Néret

Design of the 20th Century
Charlotte & Peter Fiell

Dessous
Lingerie as Erotic Weapon
Gilles Néret

Eccentric Style
Ed. Angelika Taschen

Encyclopaedia Anatomica
Museo La Specola
Florence

Erotica 17th–18th Century
From Rembrandt to Fragonard
Gilles Néret

Erotica 19th Century
From Courbet to Gauguin
Gilles Néret

Erotica 20th Century, Vol. I
From Rodin to Picasso
Gilles Néret

Erotica 20th Century, Vol. II
From Dalí to Crumb
Gilles Néret

The Garden at Eichstätt
Basilius Besler

Future Perfect
Vintage Futuristic Graphics
Ed. Jim Heimann

Indian Style
Ed. Angelika Taschen

Kitchen Kitsch
Vintage Food Graphics
Ed. Jim Heimann

London Style
Ed. Angelika Taschen

Male Nudes
David Leddick

Man Ray
Ed. Manfred Heiting

Mexicana
Vintage Mexican Graphics
Ed. Jim Heimann

Native Americans
Edward S. Curtis
Ed. Hans Christian Adam

15th Century Paintings
Rose-Marie and Rainer Hagen

16th Century Painitings
Rose-Marie and Rainer Hagen

Paris-Hollywood.
Serge Jacques
Ed. Gilles Néret

Photo Icons, Vol. I
Hans-Michael Koetzle

Photo Icons, Vol. II
Hans-Michael Koetzle

20th Century Photography
Museum Ludwig Cologne

Pin-Ups
Ed. Burkhard Riemschneider

Giovanni Battista Piranesi
Luigi Ficacci

Redouté's Roses
Pierre-Joseph Redouté

Robots and Spaceships
Ed. Teruhisa Kitahara

Seaside Style
Ed. Angelika Taschen

Eric Stanton
Reunion in Ropes & Other Stories
Ed. Burkhard Riemschneider

Eric Stanton
She Dominates All & Other
Stories
Ed. Burkhard Riemschneider

Tattoos
Ed. Henk Schiffmacher

Edward Weston
Ed. Manfred Heiting

www.taschen.com